Dionysus Writes

Dionysus Writes

The Invention of Theatre
in Ancient Greece

Jennifer Wise

Cornell University Press
Ithaca and London

First published 1998 by Cornell University Press
First printing, Cornell Paperbacks, 2000

Printed in the United States of America

Library of Congress Cataloging-in-Publication Data
Wise, Jennifer.
    Dionysus writes : the invention of theatre in ancient Greece / Jennifer Wise
        p.   cm.
    Includes bibliographical references and index.
    ISBN 0-8014-3459-9 (cloth : alk. paper)
    ISBN 0-8014-8693-9 (pbk. : alk. paper)
    1. Theater—Greece—History.   2. Greek drama—History and criticism—Theory, etc.   3. Written communication—Greece—History.   4. Literacy—Greece—History.   5. Dionysus (Greek deity)   6. Literary form.   I. Title.
PA3201.W57   1998
792'.0938—dc21   97-52393

Cornell University Press strives to use environmentally responsible suppliers and materials to the fullest extent possible in the publishing of its books. Such materials include vegetable-based, low-VOC inks and acid-free papers that are recycled, totally chlorine-free, or partly composed of nonwood fibers. Books that bear the logo of the FSC (Forest Stewardship Council) use paper taken from forests that have been inspected and certified as meeting the highest standards for environmental and social responsibility. For further information, visit our website at www.cornellpress.cornell.edu.

Cloth printing   10   9   8   7   6   5   4   3   2   1
Paperback printing   10   9   8   7   6   5   4   3   2   1

FSC FSC Trademark © 1996 Forest Stewardship Council A.C.
        SW-COC-098

For my parents,
Ben and Sheila Wise,
and for
Nicholas Seiflow

Contents

Acknowledgments

MANY SCHOLARS HAVE GIVEN GENEROUSLY OF THEIR TIME AND ADVICE BY reading this manuscript at various stages of its development. I am glad to have this opportunity to express my thanks to Benjamin Bennett, David Blostein, Ronald Bryden, Derrick de Kerkhove, Mechtilde O'Mara, Domenico Pietropaulo, and Colin Visser. I owe a particular debt of gratitude to David Blostein and Mechtilde O'Mara for their thorough, meticulous, and always entertaining commentary on and correction of the whole, and to Benjamin Bennett, both for clarifying my thinking in Chapter 1 and for encouraging me to turn the manuscript into a book. Gordon Shrimpton read parts of the manuscript very thoughtfully when he had little time to spare, and my thanks go to him, as to Michael Sidnell, whose graduate seminar in Theory of Drama at the University of Toronto inspired me so many years ago to embark on this project in the first place. For wrestling my chaotic bibliography into shape and for rectifying countless other inconsistencies, Amanda Heller deserves a citation for bravery, as does David Everard for his labors in the University of Victoria Library.

Excerpts from *The Complete Greek Tragedies,* ed. David Grene and Richmond Lattimore (Chicago: University of Chicago Press, 1991), are reprinted by permission of the publisher.

J. W.

Introduction:
The Theoretical Problem

> Concepts, just like individuals . . . harbor a
> kind of homesickness for the place of their
> birth.   Kierkegaard

A T LEAST SINCE THE START OF THE TWENTIETH CENTURY, WHEN JANE
Ellen Harrison hypothesized that drama arose in Greece out of "orgiastic religion,"[1] students of theatre and drama have looked to ritual for answers to perennial questions about the origins and essence of the art of the
stage. According to Harrison's ritual hypothesis, it is only by an illusion of
historical forgetfulness that the theatre has come to appear as a storytelling
genre, a genre of myth. On the contrary, or so the argument goes, the myths
of the ancient theatre were religious observances in disguise, and Nietzsche
was right after all: the ancient theatre was at root a Dionysian ritual that the
literary genres of tragedy and comedy have since only obscured.

By her own admission, Harrison was neither a historian of the theatre
nor a theorist of art. Like that of Nietzsche, which it resembles in some
ways, Harrison's theory of drama was not a historical account of the emergence of the genre—although it has often been treated as though it were. As
many scholars have since demonstrated, Harrison and Nietzsche were
equally guilty of distorting the historical evidence.[2] Nietzsche, for his
part, eventually came out from under Wagner's influence, abandoned his
Dionysian polemics, and finally admitted the "heresy" that "the Athenians
went to the theatre *in order to hear beautiful speeches*."[3] Harrison never did
test her hypothesis against the historical evidence for drama's emergence.
Nevertheless, the ritual hypothesis was taken up with gusto and eagerly im-

1. Harrison 1991:568 (orig. pub. 1903).
2. Vickers 1973; Silk and Stern 1981; May 1990; Ackerman 1991; Fowler 1991; Schlesier
1991.
3. Cited by Ober and Strauss 1990:259; my italics.

ported into theatre studies, where it has remained in some quarters to this day.[4]

To her own field, Harrison made an invaluable contribution. By refocusing attention away from the Olympian heights and onto the orgiastic rituals practised in the valleys below, Harrison showed that ancient religion was not a matter of doctrine or rational moral codes, but mainly the observance of concrete rites and symbolic actions based on "fear and deprecation" (Harrison 1991:7).[5] Efforts to unearth similarly ritualistic roots for theatrical practice came up empty-handed however. Lacking any concrete historical evidence, Harrison's followers have even been accused of fabricating proto-theatrical rituals that never existed.[6] In fact, classicists who have since examined the evidence have found the ritual hypothesis for theatre to be "crude and unworkable" and ultimately simply "false."[7] But as Robert Ackerman noted as recently as 1991, the "news" of the discrediting of the ritualists has somehow failed to reach the ears of their followers (189).

For the theory and practice of theatre in our own century, the widespread adoption of the ritual hypothesis has meant the perpetuation of a kind of hermeneutic circle, one that continues to deform our understanding of both the history of the theatre and its destiny as an art form. A good example can be seen in official textbook accounts of drama's emergence in Christian Europe. The ritual hypothesis presupposes that evidence crucial to theatre's appearance must be sought within the sphere of religious activity. As a result, historians studying theatrical activities during this period tend to focus mainly on religious and ritual behavior: liturgical drama, biblical cycles, Christian morality plays. The many theatrical and proto-theatrical activities that went on outside of religious contexts—within the spheres of law, rhetoric, education, and commerce, for example—tend to be ignored in favor of demonstrably ritualistic ones.[8] The bias inherent in this historical

4. Bert O. States introduces a 1985 study of the phenomenology of theatre with bald statements of theatre's "probable" ritual origins (1–2), and a popular college textbook, the *HBJ Anthology of Literature* (Stott et al. 1993), introduces the drama section with a description of Greek theatre's "pre-literate," religious, ritualistic roots (682).

5. See esp. Fowler 1991:79.

6. See Taplin 1978:161, 191 n. 3; Pickard-Cambridge 1962:16. Also Burkert 1966:87–121 and Harrison 1991:568.

7. Kirk 1985:248, 223. See also Kirk 1970. Brian Vickers devotes a useful chapter to the "picturesque and attractive theory" built by the ritualists "on no historical basis" (1973:38). Surveying the "modern scholarship . . . [which has] demolished the flimsy and inconsistent evidence" presented by Harrison et al. (33ff.), Vickers concludes that "this whole complex of false ideas, so widely disseminated, must finally be abandoned . . . because there is no actual evidence for any of its assumptions" (42).

8. There are of course exceptions to this trend; see, for example, Jody Enders's *Rhetoric and the Origins of Medieval Drama* (1992).

method would be bad enough by itself; but what is more dismaying is that the findings from these investigations are then taken, in a kind of self-fulfilling historical analogy, as confirmation for the ritualist scenario in Greece. In fact, plentiful evidence exists for medieval Europe that the rise of theatre had other spurs, namely, the spread of literacy and, with it, the ability to write down the tales of bards and minstrels for the first time. Evidence of this kind exists for Greece as well, but the fixation on ritual origins has long obscured it, especially from nonspecialists, to whom it would not occur to seek alternate historical sources. For according to the premises of the ritual hypothesis, nonreligious behavior—such as the literate activities of minstrels, scholars, and law clerks—would have little bearing on theatre practice anyway.

But it does; and the conviction that such nonreligious behavior bears directly on theatrical activities serves as the central premise of this book. My intention here is to recover, for theatre history and dramatic theory alike, some of the evidence for the emergence of theatre which has been neglected as a result of a century-long enchantment with ritual. For too long, theatre history has been written in accordance with a hypothesis which, if not inappropriate to begin with, has in any case been discredited. Not only has the legacy of ritualism been a cart-before-the-horse approach to theatre history; but also ritualism has bequeathed us a faulty theoretical conception of the nature of theatre art itself, particularly insofar as its place within literature is concerned. A better procedure would be to follow the lead of Friedrich Schlegel,[9] to build a theory of genre on the foundation of history rather than the reverse. For to do so is to discover a startling fact about the theatre in ancient Greece, and one that, besides possessing huge theoretical significance for us today, would otherwise remain invisible. Simply put, the fact is this: theatre emerged as the first text-based art in the Western poetic tradition, as an art form whose central generic features depended on the alphabetical literacy of its first practitioners. Theatre may originally have been a Dionysian art form, for there is no denying the identity of drama's patron deity; but this particular god presided over theatre only because, by the time of theatre's appearance in Greece, Dionysus could read and write.

Historically speaking, drama cannot be traced further back in Greece than the sixth century, perhaps to 600 B.C.E. if we believe Herodotus' story about Arion and his addition of verse-speaking satyrs to his choral lyrics. Had theatre been practised earlier, there would surely be some indication of it, for evidence of various other types of performance art—dance, poetry,

---

9. See Schlegel 1957:20 and 1968:19, 60, 76, 78; Peter Szondi provides a useful discussion in "Friedrich Schlegel's Theory of Poetical Genres" (1986:75–94).

solo and choral singing—has survived from before 600, giving a pretty full picture of the diversity of art forms practised in the Archaic period. But it is not until the sixth century, when alphabetical literacy had been employed in Greece for almost two hundred years, that the first references to theatrical form appear. The historical moment of theatre's appearance thus coincides with Greece's literate revolution, a coincidence that has not escaped the notice of a number of scholars.

One of many thinkers of recent years to draw a causal link between Greece's alphabetical literacy and its cultural and intellectual achievements,[10] Derrick de Kerckhove was perhaps the first to focus directly on theatre. In 1981 he argued that "Greek theatre was one of the developments of the phonetic alphabet" (23). In asserting that "the theatre was to oral epic what writing was to speech" (24), de Kerckhove was, on one level, simply making a historical observation: as Greece shifted from an oral to a literate culture, the stories once narrated in epic performance came to be theatrically performed in the written art of drama (Aristotle *Poetics* 1449b7–9).

That the epic was an oral genre, composed without writing, and that theatre, the genre that replaced it, was a written one, composed by literates, are not in themselves contentious ideas. The orality of the Homeric epics is attested almost universally;[11] and the literacy of the ancient theatre is denied

10. Most important among these for theatre research is Havelock 1963, 1977, 1986; Ong 1982; Segal 1986; and de Kerckhove, who in several journal articles explores the relation between alphabetical literacy and the theatre (1979, 1981, 1982, 1983). Charles Segal (1986) touches on the effect of writing on the mythological material of tragedy, and Walter Ong (1982) and Alfred Burns (1981) mention theatre in passing as one of the products of Athenian literacy. Jesper Svenbro (1990) sees the theatre as itself contributing to the literacy of fifth-century audiences. De Kerckhove has argued that theatre not only reflected but in its first appearance actually advanced the epistemological revolution begun by the alphabet. My approach differs radically insofar as I am interested not in the ancient theatre's effects on audiences, but rather in its sources in literate activities outside the theatre. Segal's approach comes close to my own in places, but his focus is on Greek tragedy exclusively; he does not discuss writing from the point of view of drama as a genre. Ong and Burns only make offhand, isolated suggestions about theatre's dependence on writing, which they do not follow up. And while I have greatly benefited from Svenbro's discussion of the *ABC Show*, I think his conclusions are illogical. De Kerckhove has made an interesting case for the theatre as an agent for the transmission of the alphabet's effects, but I remain unconvinced that, as Svenbro suggests, spectators can improve their reading by watching plays. For additional scholars of Greek literacy who connect their findings with the theatre, see footnote 12.

11. See esp. Lorimer 1948; Lord 1960, 1991; Havelock 1963, 1986; Nilsson 1968; Parry 1971, 1989; Ong 1977, 1982; Nagy 1981, 1986; Foley 1981, 1986, 1990, 1991; Goody 1987; Willcock 1990; Powell 1991; and Thomas 1992:12.

by virtually nobody.[12] But de Kerckhove's theory of tragedy is more radical in its implications. It suggests not just that theatre "happened to be" a literate phenomenon, but that it *owes its existence* to the alphabet.

To acknowledge the literate nature of the ancient theatre is one thing; to suggest that the alphabet was responsible for its invention is another altogether. Does a mere scriptory system have the power to create an art form that would not have existed otherwise? After all, a great deal had happened in Greece between the epic and dramatic periods besides the adoption of the alphabet. For a start, society at large had transformed itself from a heroic aristocracy to a mercantile democracy, and this shift in itself could plausibly account for even major changes in a nation's artistic practices.[13] Furthermore, there is something especially paradoxical in the suggestion that an art of real bodies, real voices, and real presences could have been affected in any substantive way by *writing*, which signifies the absence of all these things.

Whether literacy seems capable of having influenced the invention of theatre will therefore depend in the first place on how we choose to view writing. Now, in traditional linguistics from Aristotle to Saussure, writing is seen as an inert medium for representing speech. In a sort of Platonic hierarchy, writing and speech are viewed as related to each other as shadow to substance, false image to primary living reality. As a mere record of speech, writing of any sort is not imagined, within this purview, to have any effects on actual speech practices (besides occasionally "perverting" and masking them).[14]

This view of writing has, however, been replaced in our time by a more dialectical understanding of the way writing systems affect the languages they record. There is no question that, ontogenetically and phylogenetically, speech precedes writing, and may very well continue happily in its absence. But writing is a technology; and as with any technology, its use by humans sets up a dialectical relationship between itself as artifact and the natural entities it represents. As Don Ihde suggests in his *Philosophy of Technology* (1993), the introduction of such "historic" technologies as writing, the map,

---

12. See Page 1987; Turner 1951, 1971; Davison 1962; Harvey 1966; Woodbury 1976; Ong 1982; Kirk 1985:105; Segal 1986, 1992; Harris 1989:35; Vernant and Vidal-Naquet 1990; Svenbro 1990; and Cole 1992.

13. This is essentially the line of argument pursued by Meier (1990), Vernant and Vidal-Naquet (1990), and Goldhill (1990).

14. See Derrida's discussion in *Of Grammatology* (1976) of the evils attributed to writing systems by Saussure, Lévi-Strauss, and Rousseau; a related discussion appears in Thomas (1992:128), and throughout Steiner (1994).

and the clock marks the beginning of a gradual transformation of available ways of seeing the natural phenomena they measure, encode, or record. Just as the clock not only marks time but also alters our perception of it, so too does writing penetrate and transform linguistic communication even while representing it. First, writing freezes the ordinarily ephemeral flux of spoken language in a form that can be "returned to and repeated" (59). By making language into a fixed artifact, writing both distances verbal meaning from its speakers and makes it available for objective analysis, measuring, and comparison. With the existence of the measured artifact come new standards— of intelligibility, accuracy, evidence, proof, and so on—which derive not from the "natural" course of direct involvement in "immediate environments" (59) but from the artifact. As Ihde observes, these artifactual standards—established, for example, by an exactly clocked "minute"—open up a "dialectic" or "difference" between themselves and naturally perceptible standards. This difference brings with it two related consequences. Either "the sheer repeatability of the standard within the artifact [will] be taken as a kind of ideal which nature [can] only approximate" (59), or the differences established between natural and artifactual will provide a set of abstract values against which phenomena begin to be judged, evaluated, and specially privileged.

A good example of the first of these technological effects can be seen in Platonic philosophy. Without appearing to have recognized what he was doing, Plato latched on to the representational structure of writing and built a whole metaphysics around it. In representing verbal material in a fixed and decontextualized form, writing established new standards of ideality, repeatability, and sameness for words, abstract qualities that spoken language, tied as it is to particular instances of utterance and engagement with unique constellations of perceptual data, never attains. As Eric Havelock argued in *Preface to Plato* (1963), the existence of these new decontextualized standards made it possible for Plato to conceive of, and then privilege, the single, repeatable entities of thought we know as the "forms." [15]

In short, Plato takes writing's fixed artifactual standards of noetic purity and semantic stability as *the* standard with which to judge *all* entities. Natu-

15. For Plato, intellectual entities are "always the same in all respects," whereas "the many" objects available to natural perception, "by showing themselves everywhere in a community with actions, bodies, and one another" (*Republic* 5.476a), "wander about, driven by generation and decay" (6.484b). For abstract, decontextualized contemplation, "an *idea* of the beautiful itself . . . always stays the same" (5.479a); "the lovers of hearing and the lovers of sights," by contrast, are "unable to see and delight in the nature of the fair itself" (5.476a–b). These translations are by Allan Bloom (1968).

rally occurring entities, however, which are always in flux and subject to the shifting dynamics of perception, cannot live up to the standards of fixity and repeatability set by writing. As a result, the whole perceptual world of sights and sounds must be devalued in Platonic philosophy, demoted to the status of mere imitations of transcendental signifieds.[16]

The second of Ihde's technological effects might be well exemplified in the Enlightenment semiotics of G. E. Lessing, who imagines a kind of polar continuum, with the "artificial" signs of written language at one end and the "natural" signs of body language at the other. Value here is given to activities, such as poetry and theatre, which "naturalize" phenomena (i.e., move them along the continuum away from their arbitrariness as manufactured signs and toward the naturalness of the living body).[17]

Now, the idea that the two poles in any sort of nature/culture difference will always stand in a mutually constitutive, interdependent relation is an obvious one to any student of dialectics. But in the case of the relation of writing to speech (or texts to phenomena), the dialectical interpenetration of one by the other has not always been self-evident. According to Jack Goody (1986), writing's effects on thought and cultural practices first became apparent when a historical dialectic, usually applied to questions of economic production, was adopted for use in studies of communication practices. In our century, Harold A. Innis (1951) and Marshall McLuhan (1964) were the ground-breakers in exploring the effects of communication systems on cultural life. The enormous popularity of Jacques Derrida's work has contributed further to the general awareness that writing may have been a significant "absent cause" in our intellectual history. Since the 1960s, innumerable books and articles about the consequences of literacy have appeared, and thus even the most skeptical readers today are not likely to deny that a technology as pervasive as writing has had *some* effect on cultural life. More controversial is the question of what those effects are, and how writing brings them about.

Some theorists have seen writing's causality as direct. For example, Robert Logan, who claims membership in the Toronto school of communication theorists along with Innis, McLuhan, and de Kerckhove, credits the alphabet directly with all of the products of Western civilization: codified law, monotheism, abstract science, deductive logic, individualism, democracy, mass education, and capitalism (1986:18ff.). While the alphabet cer-

---

16. This metaphysics is elaborated most fully in Books 5 and 10 of the *Republic*.
17. Useful analyses of Lessing's semiotics can be found in Wellbery 1984:129, and in Wellek 1981 1:165.

tainly had an important role to play in all of these developments, the idea that literacy, or one variant of it, can by itself "cause" anything directly has been criticized for its idealism and mechanistic determinism.[18] As David Olson cautions, writing alone cannot "simply cause social or cognitive changes" (1985:4). The Ashanti warriors in Africa, for example, used writing not to represent speech or to pursue Aristotelian philosophy, but to decorate their war coats (Goody 1968:264). And in ancient Sparta the alphabet was known, but its use was actively discouraged for most purposes except the sending of military messages.[19] The historian of science G. E. R. Lloyd (1990) has mounted an especially trenchant critique of the idea that a whole society, such as that of the sixth-century Greeks, can in truth be said to possess a single "mentality," literate or otherwise.[20] What Lloyd demonstrates is that it is not directly in the psychology or biology of whole historical groups that technological change manifests itself. Rather, technologies are mediated by the concrete "styles of discourse" practised in particular locales at particular historical moments, and especially by the socially and politically specific "contexts of communication" in which these discursive styles are embedded. Rosalind Thomas, the foremost expert on Greek literacy, agrees: it is necessary to accept that the implications of literacy "are culturally determined" (1992:28) and are not by any means automatic or directly physiological.

But even having shown the uselessness of deterministic models (insofar as they are unable to take due account of "the importance of political factors—both as necessary conditions and as positive stimuli" [134]), Lloyd must finally make a pivotal acknowledgment. And what he is forced to confess for language generally can also be said of the various media available for representing it: that different systems *do* have inherent traits, and these traits will naturally be either more or less conducive to the expression, and therefore the development, of certain ideas (136).

Long before McLuhan and Derrida, Wilhelm von Humboldt made it his business to analyze the inherent traits of different writing systems, and he drew a number of conclusions about the relation between writing and civilization. For its ability to signify sound without the added baggage of an

18. For critiques of technological determinism, see Scribner and Cole 1981; Olson 1988; Olson and Hildyard 1985; Finnegan 1977; Taylor 1988; and Thomas 1992:28ff.

19. Cartledge 1978:25–37; Thomas 1992:136–37.

20. Rosalind Thomas (1989, 1992) has demonstrated this general argument at length by showing that Greek society retained many oral features even during periods when writing was used; that levels of literacy were extremely varied, and in some cases probably nonexistent; and that attitudes toward literacy varied throughout the Greek states depending on other sociopolitical factors such as the extent of democracy.

already constituted, value-laden reality of meanings and things, alphabetic writing struck Humboldt as more conducive than other scripts to certain abstract noetic functions. Although Humboldt's Eurocentrism rings hollow today, his main insight has only gained in authority: "Even though we write as we do because that is the way we speak, it is also the case that we speak as we do because that is the way we write."[21] Since Humboldt's time, writing has indeed been observed to affect the speech practices of its users in many concrete ways. In spoken Japanese, for example, written borrowings from Chinese have led to what Florian Coulmas has called a "creolization by writing." As Coulmas explains, spoken Japanese has been shaped in part by the "massive influx of Chinese loan words" which came into the language through the written register (1989:122–24). The large number of homophones that exist today in the Japanese vocabulary can be traced directly to the borrowed writing system and the process of its adaptation to Japanese phonology (127).

But because writing systems are modes of representation which, along with language, get internalized for use in all types of thinking, writing's effects will inevitably manifest themselves even beyond the domain of speech.[22] Consider the nature of scientific inquiry. Eastern and Western historians of science agree that despite comparably magnificent achievements in antiquity, alphabetical Greek and logographic Chinese investigations did take slightly different forms (Lloyd 1990:11). Whereas the abstract, analytical, isolating operations of alphabetical script are clearly reflected in the nature of Western science, Chinese science manifested itself in ways that reproduce the characteristics of Chinese script: in practical, applied inventions directly connected with concrete activities and carried out under rigid hierarchies (125). If writing systems are capable, albeit in a socially mediated way, of influencing their users' speech practices, habits of thought, and scientific activities, there is no reason to suppose that artistic practices alone will somehow remain immune.

Art forms are, after all, concrete social practices too. In heightening our sensitivity to the material dimension of even ordinary speech practices, students of literacy from Havelock (1963) through Ong (1982), Goody (1987), and Thomas (1992) have added greatly to our understanding of just how vulnerable such practices are to technological change. In particular, the work of these scholars has emphasized that real consequences accrue from

21. Humboldt cited in Christy 1989:344.

22. For valuable discussions of the process whereby representing systems are psychologically "internalized," see Olson 1988:423–25; Vygotsky 1978, 1992; and Luria 1981:27–87.

such subtle technological variables as how cultural material is preserved and how it is transmitted. Depending on what technologies are available, not only the "how" of cultural communication but also the "why" of it can change from one social context to the next. The research on which this book is based suggests, likewise, that the society that records its culture in books, teaches it in schools, and transmits it verbatim will function according to different standards and values—and be apt to indulge in different sorts of behaviors—than the society that uses none of these things and depends instead wholly on the embodied wisdom of elders and bards. And a culture like that of the sixth-century Greeks, which records, criticizes, teaches, and transmits its stories and laws through the written medium, is one that is likely to indulge, specifically, in those behaviors that have since been ranged under the heading of "theatre."

This study of the relationship between literacy and the theatre in ancient Greece is divided into four chapters, each of which explores theatre's dependency on the technology of alphabetical writing from a different point of view. Chapter 1, "The ABCs of Acting," outlines the significance of the use of the alphabet to record stories once confined to the oral register. The second chapter, "The Student Body," details the consequences of learning and teaching such narrative material through the agency of the literate classroom rather than through oral instruction. In Chapter 3, "Courtroom Dramas," I show how the writing down of law effected changes to social behavior in the public sphere which further reinforced the shift toward a theatrical style of storytelling. Chapter 4, "Economies of Inscription," contains a discussion of a number of related literary activities—the inscription of city coinage, letters, wills, and ostraka—which together consolidated the shift away from a contextually embedded model of information exchange and toward the kind of highly mobile, cosmopolitan economy of exchange on which the theatre depended.

Although this inquiry ranges widely among social spheres, from poetic performance to education and legal procedures to political economy, the separate investigations are united by the question of alphabetical literacy and the consequences of its earliest uses in ancient Greece. Each chapter is based on a concrete practice or practices for which the evidence is secure. We know for certain that in the sixth century B.C.E. and earlier, the Greeks used the alphabet (Chapter 1); that they learned to write in schools (Chapter 2); that they had public, written law codes (Chapter 3); that they wrote letters, poetry, citizen lists, and wills, and that they used coins and ballots with written inscriptions on them (Chapter 4). While strictly sequenced, each chapter takes its own view of the ways in which the literate practices of ancient Greece would have shaped the mode of representation we know as theatre.

In tracking the generic shift between epic recitation and theatrical representation, we must however take care to conceive of these genres with as much historical accuracy as possible. Without a precise picture of the characteristics of each genre in its time, we will hardly be able to appreciate the nature of the shift from one to the other. And a false impression of each is more likely than not, for our understanding of the relationship between epic and theatre has been so muddled by ritualistic thinking that its distinctive features are often misconstrued. As John Herington has shown (1985), the shift from epic to dramatic poetry was not the generic revolution it is often supposed to be. For theatre is widely assumed to have *introduced* features that in fact it only *retained* from the genres of predramatic poetry: corporeal performance in person before large audiences, impersonation of narrative figures, costumes, music, dance. In addition to Herington, Charles Segal (1992) and Rosalind Thomas (1992) have reminded us that multi-medial corporeality was a defining characteristic of *all* poetry in Greece—before, during, and after the dramatic age of the fifth century.[23] Theatre did introduce certain new generic features into the performance of poetry in Greece, as we shall see. But none of them is connected with the musical, multimedial corporeality which, in the popular imagination—and thanks in part to Nietzsche—theatre alone embodies.[24] By emphasizing the gradual emergence of dramatic form out of epic and lyric recitation, Herington has almost single-handedly repaired the damage done to theatre studies by the assumptions of ritualism. Unfortunately, Herington does not consider the use of writing in his account of this generic shift, an omission that finally leaves it incomplete. He does show that drama appeared as an incorporating fulfillment of a long tradition of competitive epic and lyric recitation; but because he does not consider the impact of literacy, he cannot explain how or why this happened as it did.

In searching for the stimuli for Greece's shift from epic to dramatic performance, one must therefore isolate sufficient causes, and separate them

23. The Homeric epics give us clear pictures of the singing, dancing, and emotional identification that accompanied predramatic performances. Segal (1992:4–29) provides a complete list of scenes of bardic performance from both the *Iliad* and the *Odyssey* with discussion. The lyric poems of Archilochus evince a similar performance style (see Ayrton 1977).

24. In connecting the "birth of tragedy" to the "spirit of music," Nietzsche has given many students of drama the mistaken impression that music was somehow uniquely typical of drama, that music did not also characterize the predramatic genres of epic and lyric, which it did.

from impulses that, although probably buried irretrievably in human pre-history, produce poetic performance itself. Theatre was not the first genre of poetic performance; it was simply the first genre of poetic performance in Greece which made use of unmediated enactment by a number of nonspe-cialist performers, verbatim memorization, and a dialogic style. This generic profile was new to Greece, and all of the performative innovations that went into it, constituting it as the new art of the theatre as distinct from its epic antecedent, are demonstrably dependent on the use of writing.

The evidence suggests that a knowledge and use of writing enabled the first playwrights to manipulate poetic materials in ways that had been un-available to oral bards. In terms of its creation by an individual *reader* of inherited material; in terms of its public submission and transmission by arbitrary and anonymous signs; in terms of its performance by nonspecialist and "other" actors; and in terms of its democratic and nonconservative function in relation to its audience, the dramatic text no less than theatrical performance represented a radical departure from epic narrative, the main genre of poetry practised in Greece before "tragedy and comedy came to light" (*Poetics* 1449a13).

As for the date when writing was first used for poetic composition in Greece, creating the conditions for this gradual generic shift from epic bard to theatrical actor, the archaeological record is clear: alphabetic writing was used to record verse as early as the eighth century B.C.E. For this reason, the dramatists of the fifth century B.C.E., despite what Walter J. Ong has said,[25] were not so much innovators in their use of writing for poetic composition as they were revolutionary in the degree to which they exploited the poten-tialities of literate modes and, in so doing, made use of writing as "text" rather than as a mere reminder of a spoken performance.

Accordingly, the story I tell of theatre's emergence begins with the writ-ing down of archaic stories—stories that had once been confined to the "winged words" of oral recitation. Barry Powell (1991) may be right that these epic stories were written down as early as the late eighth century B.C.E.; or perhaps the most scrupulous of scholars are right when they em-phasize the lateness of the evidence for these early literary activities, and in-sist that we postpone the date of a literary Homer into the sixth century B.C.E. But the extent of textual criticism that is detectable in the sixth cen-tury—as practised by writers such as Xenophanes, Theagenes, and Stesicho-rus[26]—gives us good cause to say with confidence that a written Homer,

25. Ong 1977:72.
26. In addition to Pfeiffer 1968:5–26, see the discussion of Homer's earliest critics in Richardson 1992:30–39, which supports Powell's case for the earliest possible date for a writ-ten Homer. Similar arguments can be found in Segal 1992.

and literary criticism of the works attributed to him, were components of Greek poetic life during the lifetime of Thespis—that is, before the flowering of dramatic form under Aeschylus in the early fifth century B.C.E. The immediate progenitors of Aeschylus were therefore not the orgiastic congregations of goat sacrificers so dear to ritualists, but individual readers of Homer. If Aeschylus was able, by his own admission, to develop his art of drama by cutting thick slices from the Homeric feast (Athenaeus *Deipnosophists* 8.347e), he was able to do this slicing precisely because history had placed into his hands an appropriate tool: a writing implement. For just as the bard is always represented wielding the instrument of his trade, the lyre,[27] fifth-century representations of the playwright, both on vases and in the theatre itself, depict him clutching the instrument of *his* chosen genre— the book roll.[28]

After outlining the technological conditions under which theatre first emerged—and to which it must, as both an art form and a social practice, be considered indebted—I conclude with some suggestions about what these findings might mean for literary and theatrical theory today.

More than a century ago Gilbert Murray expressed his belief that what "enabled Athens to create the drama" was a peculiar sympathy for both sides in any conflict, a sympathy learned from the epics of Homer. In a Homeric world, both Priam and Achilles, both the Trojans and their enemies, both vanquished and victor are invested with equal humanity and honored with equal esteem. And in this Homeric genius for portraying human conflicts in a two-sided way, Murray saw a generic germ of the dramatic style. He was right to do so. But whether this Homeric attitude toward storytelling would, by itself, have created dramatic form is another matter altogether. As David Olson reminds us, "what the mind can do depends on the *devices* provided by culture," not just on how that culture thinks.[29] It is my view that without the advent of a new technology for poetic composition, epic recitation might well have retained its supremacy as a storytelling form and never have produced the drama at all. For in the absence of writing, nothing more highly "theatrical" would have been possible.

27. *Iliad* 9.188, 18.567–604; *Odyssey* 22.340f.; Segal 1992:4, 25.

28. See esp. the Pronomos Vase as reproduced in Winkler and Zeitlin 1990, plate 1; Aristophanes describes Euripides as a writer (frag. 676b Edmonds 1957) and his plays as available to readers aboard ships (*Frogs* 52–53).

29. Cited by Scinto 1986:164.

CHAPTER I

The ABCs of Acting

> This ABC and grammar of acting are . . . not difficult. Without them, it is impossible to live on the stage. Stanislavski

*I*N AN UNKNOWN YEAR IN THE FIFTH CENTURY B.C.E., POSSIBLY AT THE end of the 430s, when Euripides' *Medea* and Sophocles' *Oedipus Tyrannos* were performed, the Athenian poet Kallias wrote and presented a play about the alphabet. Sometimes translated as the *ABC Show,* and sometimes as the *ABC Tragedy,* the *Grammatike Theoria* of Kallias[1] is provocative even in its title: a "theory" for the Greeks was literally a "looking at" (*theoria*), and what is seen (*theasthai*) by the spectators (*theatai*) of this show is a play about letters, about language made visible in the alphabet. A *theoria* of letters thus finds its natural platform on the stage of the theatre (*theatron*), the place for viewing. The etymological and even the practical connections between theatre and theory in general are numerous and provocative, and have often been remarked on before.[2] The *ABC Show,* in thus "showing" writing to its audiences, confirms theatre's theoretical connections, and provides a most bracing opportunity for analyzing the special kinship between an alphabetical and a theatrical manner of making things visible.

The Chorus of this fifth-century play is made up not of Theban elders or the women of Trachis but of the twenty-four letters of the Ionian alphabet, from Alpha through Omega. The prologue consists of a sung list of all the letters in order ("Say Alpha, beta, gamma, delta, and then The God's epsilon,[3] zeta, eta, theta, iota. . . ."); and when the Chorus splits into pairs,

---

1. Frag. 31 A, B, C, D Edmonds 1957. Both Svenbro (1990:381–82) and Harvey (1966:632 n. 13) provide valuable discussions of this fragment. I am in their debt.

2. See esp. Svenbro 1990:383 and Reinelt and Roach 1992:3–4.

3. Svenbro (1990:381–82) restores the original *ei* of the manuscripts, which Edmonds (1957) alters into "epsilon" in his translation; both explain that *ei* was inscribed on the temple at Delphi and was thus known as Apollo's letter.

what is sung is the combinations of consonants and vowels: "Beta alpha: ba. Beta epsilon: be. Beta eta: bē. Beta iota: bi. . . ." The second half-chorus answers: "Gamma alpha: ga. Gamma epsilon: ge. Gamma eta: gē. . . ." Dialogue in the *ABC Show* includes a conversation between what appears to Jesper Svenbro (1990) to be a teacher and two female pupils:

> You must pronounce *alpha* by itself, my ladies, and secondly *ei* by itself. And you there, you will say the third vowel!
>> Then I will say *eta.*
>> Then *you* will say the fourth one by itself!
>> *Iōta.*
>> The fifth—
>> *O.*
>> The sixth, *U,* say alone.
>> *U.*
>> But the last of seven vowels, ŏ, I will pronounce for you. And then put all seven into verse. When you have pronounced them, say them to yourself.[4]

Unfortunately, little more of this fragment has survived. But properly read, it is a pithy lesson in much more than the alphabet. It is a lesson in theatrical theory, too, and a demonstration of the debt owed by theatre to the alphabet.

Now, the phonetic principle of the Greek alphabet is not normally a subject we would associate with the ancient theatre festivals. And yet Kallias was not alone in choosing it as the subject of a play. Even in the earliest extant dramas of the fifth century, dramas ostensibly devoted to a retelling of the stories of mythology and Homeric epic, a concern with alphabetic literacy is palpable everywhere. Including Kallias' *ABC Show,* at least eighty-one separate references to writing can be found throughout the extant plays and fragments; and at least eleven fifth-century plays have plots that depend on the literacy of the characters and their use of texts.[5] And these numbers appear all the more impressive when we remember that the vast majority of

4. Svenbro's translation is used here in the main (1990:382).

5. *Seven Against Thebes, The Women of Trachis, Antigone, Hippolytos, Iphegenia in Aulis, Iphegenia in Taurus, Frogs, Clouds, Birds, Knights.* We might also include Cratinus' *Wineflask* (frag. 195–96 Edmonds 1957), for Niall Slater thinks that this play may have been about a character "writing a comedy"; but the play survives in too fragmentary a form to say whether the episode that features this activity was an isolated one or typical of the whole work (1996:108–9).

plays written in the period have not survived.[6] In both stage action and narration, dramatic characters are represented reading books, sending and receiving letters, writing wills, interpreting written oracles and laws, studying scholarly texts, and keeping expense account records and records of testimony in court. In the Greek dramas, everyone from Athenian dogs (*Wasps* 959–60) to Olympian gods (*Eumenides* 275, *Frogs* 52–53) is depicted as knowing, and using, their ABCs. In conspicuous contrast to the mythic gods and heroes as depicted in Homeric epic, the dramatic characters of the fifth-century theatre inhabit a world where writing is a more or less everyday fact of life.

Within these eighty-plus references, writing is occasionally integral to the plot; sometimes it is used merely as a metaphor, with characters instructing one another to "inscribe" something on the "tablets" of their minds; and sometimes the alphabet is brought visibly onto the stage. In the remaining bit of the Kallias fragment, one of the female writing students physically acts out the shape of the letters *psi* and *omega,* with an effect that was apparently obscene.[7] In this, too, Kallias was in good company, for Sophocles, Euripides, Aristophanes, and others are also reported to have used this same

---

6. None of my sources has attempted to amass a complete list. I count eighty-one references to reading, writing, books, inscription, letters, and waxed tablets. Organized by author only, my list contains the following: Aeschylus *Eumenides* 273–75; *Prometheus Bound* 788–89, 459–61; *Seven Against Thebes* 647, 660; *Suppliants* 178–79; 991–92, 944–49; *The Libation Bearers* 450; *Aitnai* [?] frag. 530 as cited by Pfeiffer 1968:26; Sophocles *Antigone* 450–55, 499, 707–9; *Philoctetes* 1325; *Triptolemus* frag. 540 Nauck 1964; *The Women of Trachis* 46, 155–63, 680–83, 1167; frag. 742 Nauck; *Amphiaraos* (satyr play) (Athenaeus 10.454f. as cited by Svenbro 1990:383); Euripides *Hecuba* 293, *Hippolytus* 452ff., 857–65, 880, 953–54; *Iphigenia in Aulis* 108–23, 891; *Iphigenia among the Taurians* 584–85, 641–42, 763; *Melanippe* frag. 506 Nauck; *Palamedes* frag. 578 Nauck; *Suppliants* 431–37; *Theseus* frag. 382 Nauck; *Trojan Women* 661; Agathon frag. 4 Nauck; Akhaios *Omphale* frag. 33 Nauck; Theodectes frag. 6 Nauck; Aristophanes *Babylonians* frag. 64 Edmonds 1957; *Banqueters* frag. 217 Edmonds; *Birds* 974–91, 1024, 1036, 1277; *The Broilers* frag. 490, frag. 676b Edmonds; *Clouds* 18–24, 30–31, 759–74; *Ecclesiasusae* 1012–20, 1050; *Frogs* 52–53, 1114, 1407–10; *Gerytades* frag. 157 Edmonds; *Knights* 188–89, 190–92, 1256; *Thesmophoriazusai* 768–84; *Triphales* [?] frag. 623 Edmonds; *Wasps* 959–60; Cratinus *The Laws* frag. 122 [?], frag. 274 Edmonds; *The Thracian Women* frag. 71 Edmonds; *The Wine Flask* frag. 195, frag. 196 Edmonds; Kallias, *Grammatical Play* frag. 31A, B, C, D Edmonds; Hermippus *The Porters* frag. 63 Edmonds; Eupolis *Exempt from Service or the Workmen* frag. 35, *Flatterers* 149–153, *Maricas* frag. 193, unknown work, frag. 304 all Edmonds; Plato *The Poet* frag. 114, *Phaon* frag. 173, *Daedalus* [?] frag. 194 all Edmonds; Philonides, unknown work frag. 7 Edmonds; Aristomenes *Wizards* frag. 8–10 Edmonds; Theopompus frag. 77 Pfeiffer 28 n. 2; Nicophon frag. 19. 4 Pfeiffer 28 n. 2.

7. See Edmonds 1957:181; Svenbro 1990:382.

theatrical device.[8] Sophocles' satyr play *Amphiaraos* includes a scene in which an actor dances out the shapes of letters (Athenaeus *Deipnosophists* 10.454f.); and Akhaios, in a fairly lengthy fragment, has a satyr name all the letters in an inscription for the audience, which together spell D-I-O-N-U-S-O-U ([I belong to] Dionysus; frag. 33).[9] In Euripides' *Theseus* (frag. 382), an illiterate rustic, a herdsman, describes what he sees, but cannot himself read, on the side of a ship: "T-H-E-S-E-U-S." The alphabet was also "staged" by Agathon in his *Telephus* (frag. 4) and by Theodectes (frag. 6), and was ultimately parodied by Aristophanes in the *Thesmophoriazusae* (768–84). Spelling out "Euripides," Mnesilochus exclaims, "What a horrible 'R' !"[10]

Why were the Athenian playwrights so taken with the theatrical and thematic possibilities of the alphabet? To begin with, the alphabet was relatively new. From surviving samples of Archaic writing, specifically from inscribed objects such as cups, vases, and tombstones, scholars have dated the earliest use of alphabetic writing in Greece to the middle of the eighth century, circa 740 B.C.E.[11] This means that writing had been in use in Greece for only two hundred years before Thespis won the first known prize for a drama. Now, two hundred years may sound like a long time to us, used as we are to rapid technological change; but Archaic Greek culture functioned so well on an exclusively oral basis that the acquisition of literacy was a slow, uneven, and in some spheres of life barely perceptible process.[12] Even in the fifth century, when schools were widespread and the functioning of the democratic state and its legal institutions depended on writing, country folk may have remained unlettered (Harvey 1966:620), and even some city folk, like Aristophanes' sausage seller, could read and write little, and that with difficulty (*Knights* 188–89, 636, 1030–89). Alphabetical inscriptions that have survived from the eighth and seventh centuries are rarely more than a few lines long, and often betray writing skills of a very rudimentary nature. Indeed, as William Harris (1989) and Rosalind Thomas (1989, 1992) have argued at length, the advance of literacy in Greece was so gradual until the sixth century, and so spotty even thereafter, that many aspects of Greek life remained primarily oral in practice until well into the fourth century B.C.E.[13]

8. Harvey 1966:604; Cole 1981:149 n. 20; Bowra and Higham 1950:459; and Svenbro 1990:383 provide useful discussions of these fragments.

9. This and following fragments are from Nauck 1964; see Svenbro's discussion (1990:377).

10. See Harvey's discussion (1966:632 n. 13).

11. The evidence is discussed at length by Stroud 1989:103–19; Harris 1989:vii; Jeffrey 1990:21; Powell 1991:144ff.; and Thomas 1992:53ff.

12. See esp. W. Harris 1989:vii–115; Thomas 1989, 1992; Steiner 1994.

13. See also Lentz 1989:6ff.

Nevertheless, given the prevalence of references to literate activities in the dramas of the early fifth century, and given the fact that many of these pass without special comment, one might be inclined to distrust the archaeological record and assume that literacy must have been more fully entrenched in Greek life than surviving artifacts would suggest. And there are indeed good reasons to do so, since much of the evidence for literacy in the Archaic period is certain to have disappeared without a trace for purely physical reasons. Leather, wood, and waxed tablets are among the writing materials used by the Greeks which were not durable enough to survive; and their absence in the archaeological record must surely distort to some extent our impressions of the extent of predramatic literacy.

Luckily, however, there is another source for the commencement of literary activities in Greece. This source is the Homeric epics,[14] long recognized by scholars as a "modern and up to date" picture of life in Homer's historical period.[15] Barry Powell's comprehensive survey of the internal and external evidence for dating these poems puts their composition no later than the end of the eighth century B.C.E. And when we examine these predramatic poems, this storehouse of mythic tales from which the early dramatists drew in creating their plays, we are struck by an inescapable realization: Homer's epic heroes, unlike their dramatic embodiments, were illiterate.

Taken together, the *Iliad* and the *Odyssey* constitute a "vast encyclopedia" (Havelock 1986:79) of life during war and during peace, a comprehensive panorama of life as the epic singers knew it. No sphere of human life escaped portrayal in these songs, from the most heroic to the most homely; everything from the proper method of steering a chariot on the battlefield to the domestic arrangements in Penelope's bedroom is honored with representation. Given the completeness of these poems as what an ancient observer called "a fair mirror of human life,"[16] and given especially their penchant for anachronism,[17] one would expect writing to be represented within them if it was known. But in the tens of thousands of lines of Homeric verse, there are no references to alphabetic writing at all, neither as a thing done nor as the subject of a trope.

14. As Gilbert Murray pointed out, many more epics were attributed to Homer, or considered "Homeric," in the ancient world than have come down to us (1907:8–53). I will be using Homer's name to refer to that body of works which, while exemplified to us mainly through the *Iliad* and the *Odyssey,* also included the many stories connected with Thebes, or the *Thebais,* and others, such as the *Cypria, The Sack of Ilion, Homecomings,* and *Telegoneia.*

15. See Bowra 1969:32; more recently Powell 1991.

16. Alcimadas as cited by Pfeiffer 1968:50.

17. Nilsson 1968:211.

The closest encounter with any kind of inscription occurs in the story of Bellerophontes in Book 6 of the *Iliad* (168–170). The "baleful signs" (*semata lugra*) that Bellerophontes takes with him to Lykia could be described as a kind of writing insofar as they are "inscribed in a folding tablet"; but they are also said to have magical powers "enough to destroy life." As Powell has shown, the "fatal letter" motif was inherited into the epics from the ancient East, where such folding tablets were used from an early date (1991:199). Yet the eighth-century singers of the Greek epics evidently had no idea how writing actually worked: the word *semata* is used again in Book 7 of the *Iliad* when the warriors draw lots, and it becomes clear that it is not writing that is being referred to. Each hero puts a mark on his own lot, but these marks are illegible to everyone but the marker (181–89); they are in fact little more than paw prints. Indeed, neither Bellerophontes' symbols nor the warriors' marks are intended to *represent* anything at all; in one case they *are* their own magical effects, in the other they are meaningless scribbles. Clearly, the bards are not here depicting writing in the ordinary sense, as a device for representing speech. Because of this obvious ignorance of the capabilities of the alphabet, readers of Homer since the eighteenth century have concluded with justification that the composer of the *Iliad* and the *Odyssey* was a strictly oral poet who knew nothing at all about the technology of writing.[18]

The picture we get from the epics of a strictly oral society thus confirms the archaeological evidence, which suggests that the widespread use of writing which we see reflected in the fifth-century dramas was a radically new development, and absolutely unprecedented before the end of the eighth century.

Between the later eighth century and the time of Thespis, surviving written artifacts are few and far between; and although these artifacts show that writing was being used before Thespis' time for a wide range of recording activities—dedications, graffiti, private letters, laws—the sample is too small for us to guess at the numbers of people using it at this time. But while scholars continue to disagree about the exact literacy levels of the Greeks at various historical periods, it is certain that at least *some* ordinary citizens, craftsmen, poets, mercenary soldiers, and philosophers were using writing in the seventh and sixth centuries. It is also a near-certainty that by the end of the sixth, its use had become "virtually universal amongst the

---

18. Robert Wood (1976; orig. pub. 1769 and 1775) must be named as the earliest of these; since then, see Lorimer 1948; Parry 1971:xxvii; Willcock 1990; Powell 1991:200; Thomas 1992:12, 50.

men who made up the political and social elites" (W. Harris 1989:29).[19] From this point forward we can more easily watch the advance of literacy in the images painted on the sides of pots, jugs, and vases, which by the beginning of the fifth century have started depicting inscribed scrolls, many in scenes populated by female Muses and women.[20] Three of these that have survived can be dated to before the birth of Aeschylus; and by Sophocles' time, in the early years of the fifth century, the famous Sphinx was already being depicted in visual art as reading from a book between her paws (Pfeiffer 1968:27)—an image that we should keep in mind when considering this playwright's treatment of Oedipus' cleverness in solving her riddle. And on the Pronomos Vase, which remains the most detailed iconographic representation of theatrical activities from the end of the century, the poet is clearly portrayed as a writer, in possession of two book rolls.[21]

Although the spread of the alphabet may initially have been slow, by Kallias' time (i.e., later fifth century) literacy had become widespread enough among the Athenian citizenry at large for Aristophanes to joke that every member of his audience carried his or her own book into the theatre to check the literary allusions (*Frogs* 1114). Between the end of the eighth and the end of the fifth centuries, then, Greece had undergone something approaching a literate revolution, having been transformed from a place in which alphabetical writing was unknown to one where everyday life was so overrun with books and bookmongers (see especially *Birds*) that cheap editions of philosophy could be picked up from the bookstalls for a drachma (Plato *Apology* 26d), and whole shiploads of texts were being exported abroad (Xenophon *Anabasis* 7.5.14). Indeed, in the market of fifth-century Athens, as Eupolis tells us, one was as likely to find books as onions, garlic, and incense for sale (frag. 304 Edmonds 1957). No wonder, then, that the Athenian playwrights were keen to represent writing and its uses: in the period between Homer and Kallias, Greek culture had been transformed by it.[22]

But it is not primarily as a relatively new subject for poetry that the presence of the alphabet is worthy of note in Kallias' play—and, for that matter, in the dozens of other fifth-century dramas, tragedy and comedy alike, that feature writing as a subject. Rather, whether the early dramatists

19. See also W. Harris 1989:48, 56; also Turner 1951; Davison 1962; Harvey 1966; Pfeiffer 1968; Woodbury 1976; Burns 1981; Cole 1981; Stroud 1989; Thomas 1989, 1992; Robb 1994.

20. Pfeiffer 1968:27; Cole 1981:133.

21. See Winkler and Zeitlin 1990 plate 1.

22. See Robb 1994:4–21, 255 for analysis of this transformation.

were aware of it or not (and the likelihood is that they were not), the use of the alphabet had provided them with both the motive and the means to change the nature of poetic performance itself, to revolutionize it along the same lines that writing had altered their culture at large.

Before 534 B.C.E., when Thespis' first documented performance of a drama took place, there is nothing in Greek verbal art that exhibits the style used by Kallias to tell his story.[23] Kallias is not telling a story using his own voice, as the epic bards or their heirs the rhapsodes did; nor has he cast his speakers in roles that are identical to their own real-life identities, as the choral lyricists did. Rather, Kallias' piece, even in its fragmentary condition, exhibits all the salient generic features that we associate with dramatic form: dialogue, real people standing in for fictional characters, a visible enactment of the story rather than a narrative telling of it, and a tendency both toward colloquial speech and away from formulaic diction. Before Thespis' tragic victory in the sixth century, the Greek verbal arts were dominated by a Homeric storytelling style; and while all predramatic poetry was character-ized by the same spectacular performative elements that we find in tragedy and comedy—music, dance, costume, poetic meter, large festival audi-ences[24]—there is nothing in their single-voiced narrative style to prepare us for the genres of enactment which were to emerge out of them and which, by Kallias' time, were to have practically replaced them. In the *ABC Show*, as in all fifth-century drama, what we find is a type of poetic storytelling that represents visually, as the alphabet does; and like the alphabet, in which let-ters arbitrarily signify the sounds of speech, it is a mode of representation in which one thing is given to stand in arbitrarily for something else—actors for letters of the alphabet, young men for female writing students. And un-like any type of narrative that had been seen before, plays were stories that could be taught to and performed by anybody, and this as easily as Kallias' grammar students are shown learning the alphabet. Kallias' grammatical characters, given written letters to repeat, can tell the story by themselves, free from mediation by the skilled narrator who had dominated all previous genres of storytelling, and whose dependence on oral memory had made his poetic speech into a stylized, homogeneous monologue.

That Kallias' mode of representation was a new one, unknown in Greek

23. There is an ancient tradition that holds that it was in fact not Thespis but the choral lyricist Arion of Methymna who, over half a century earlier, had invented the dra-matic style by adding speaking satyrs to his choral songs (Herodotus 1.23). I will be dis-cussing his contribution in Chapter 2. For Thespis' dates, see Pickard-Cambridge 1968:72.

24. See especially Herington 1985 and Gentili 1988 for the "spectacular" qualities of Archaic poetry.

verbal art before the rise of the alphabet, is clear from antique sources. The Homeric epics, for example, provide detailed descriptions of the various performance arts that were practiced in the prealphabetic period of Greek civilization. And while there are many references to the performance of epic lays and to dance (*Iliad* 18.604–5; 24.720–22; *Odyssey* 4.17–19; 8.248–62, 370–80, 470ff.; 23.143–45), there is nothing that remotely resembles drama. Instead, the poetic arts represented in the *Iliad* and *Odyssey* are confined to the performative genre which these works themselves embody: a single bard sings, to his own lyre accompaniment, of the "acoustic renown" of heroes. Later, in the seventh and sixth centuries, when poets such as Alcman, Archilochus, Sappho, and Alcaeus augmented the Greek poetic repertoire with their lyric songs, the focus shifted somewhat away from the legendary deeds of heroes and toward the poet's personal concerns and feelings; but the performance procedure of these lyric singers remained essentially the same as Homer's had been, for their poems are generally intended for one voice,[25] and stylistically they never break away—in neither metrical structure, Homeric formulas, nor modes of thought—from the bardic tradition that preceded them.[26]

Thus, despite drama's maintenance of the luxuriant combination of song, dance, instrumental accompaniment, costume, and verse that had characterized these earlier poetic genres, its many formal and substantive innovations were profound enough for it to be considered a new art in its time.[27] As John Herington in particular has shown, the tradition of performed poetry has a long and vital history in Greece, one that stretches far back into the Bronze Age and defined Greece very much as a "song culture" until the fourth century, when it was transformed, under the influence of literacy, into what Rosalind Thomas has called a culture of "oratory" (1992).[28] The predramatic genre of epic has the longest documented history: current scholarship dates the composition of the Homeric epics to the end

25. The exception to this rule, and one to which we will be returning, is choral lyric, which was written either for performance by a specific group of celebrants (see, for example, Alcman's Maiden-Songs, where the singers are actually named; Edmonds 1952:51ff.), or for the celebration of a particular ritual event, such as a wedding (see Sappho's Epithalamies in Edmonds 1952:283ff.). The choirs for whom such choral lyrics were written are believed by Murray to have been highly trained professionals (1907:95–97).

26. For detailed discussion of this essential point, see Gentili 1988:16, 19, 20; and Miller 1994:20–95.

27. Aristotle *Poetics* 1449b11, 1449b7, 1449a13; Else 1965b; Gernet 1981:57, 17; Vernant and Vidal-Naquet 1990:23–25, 185.

28. See also Havelock, who was the first to describe this shift toward literate modes and the corresponding decline in the cultural primacy of poetic performance (1963, 1986).

of the eighth century B.C.E., although the earliest strata of these poems date back hundreds of years before that.[29] And lyric song, while closely related, is well attested throughout the seventh and sixth centuries.[30] Nevertheless, the traditional dominance by these two predramatic genres of the musical and poetic life of the Greeks—and especially of their musical competitions—was increasingly threatened by the parallel advances of the alphabet and drama. Although the upstart arts of tragedy and comedy were given official recognition at different times,[31] they shared enough formal and functional features, and differed from their poetic forebears in sufficiently similar ways, for them to be considered together as two faces of the new art of the theatre (*Poetics* 1448b12). A fourth-century B.C.E. writer named tragedy "the most people-pleasing and hypnotizing branch of poetry."[32] Such was its success, and comedy's, that even by the fifth century, "no first-rate poet in any of the traditional nondramatic genres was composing in Greece" (Herington 1985:99). As Aristotle remarks, "When tragedy and comedy came to light, poets were drawn either to one or to the other" (*Poetics* 1449a13). That is, whereas poets had in "ancient" times practised other genres (1448b11), particularly heroic epic and iambic lyric, they had turned almost en masse to tragedy and comedy, since these dramatic arts, while containing all the elements of the earlier forms, improved upon them in a number of ways, becoming "in each case a higher kind of art" and more valuable, especially in their appeal to audiences (1449a13; 1462a1–1462b16). Given the frequency among ancient sources of references to the fact, observed by Aristotle, that in drama, for the first time, the audience could "actually see the persons of the story" (1460a16), Herington speculates quite rightly that the generic novelty of drama in its time must have approximated that of the first cinematic spectacles in our century.

From a strictly chronological perspective, then, it is beyond dispute that the emergence and swift poetic hegemony of drama coincided with the advance of the alphabet in Greece. And yet, how many contemporary theorists of drama would be willing to take this coincidence a step further and entertain the idea that Western theatre, which seems to bear a family resemblance to the performative practices of preliterate societies, might be causally connected with a writing system—and a *particular* writing system at that? Surely there is something counterintuitive in the idea that an art so corpo-

29. Powell 1991:114.
30. Edmonds 1952, vols. 1, 2; Davison 1962:149–50; Nilsson 1968.
31. *Poetics* 1449a3–1449b4; Pickard-Cambridge 1968:72ff.
32. *Minos,* cited by Herington 1985:98.

real in nature, so oral in practice, could owe its central generic outlines to something as bookish as literacy. Nevertheless, the appearance of the alphabet in ancient Greece set in motion a whole host of changes in the nature of verbal life. Although these changes are related and were to some extent simultaneous, they can be analyzed separately, and I shall attempt to do so here. Together, and in the space of two hundred years, these literacy-sponsored changes succeeded in eliminating the conditions under which the monologizing poetry of oral epic was composed, and replacing them with ideal cultural circumstances for the creation of dramatic form.

In the first place, the existence of writing changed the nature of memory, and this by itself was almost sufficient to guarantee that the nature of poetry would change accordingly. In the absence of any written records, memory must remain a very approximate thing. In the absence of a (verbatim) written record, there is, in fact, no way to tell if something *has* been memorized or not. Consequently, in periods and places that lack writing, the very concept of exact repetition has no meaning. As I. M. L. Hunter has noted, "The human accomplishment of lengthy verbatim recall arises as an adaptation to written text and does not arise in cultural settings where text is unknown."[33] As the fieldwork of anthropologists and psychologists of memory has confirmed, societies without writing have a different concept of memory than do literates, and do not memorize things exactly.[34] Even oral bards' seemingly virtuoso feats of memory have been observed in our time to consist, in fact, of often radically dissimilar versions of a given narrative, which, however, are "experienced" by the bards themselves as "exactly the same."[35] As Clanchy (1979:233), Goody and Watt (1968:31–34), and Goody (1986:12) have noticed, members of oral societies *perceive* continuity where change is in fact the norm. Mythic narratives, laws, and customs are believed by those who repeat them orally to have been preserved intact for generations, whereas in fact all have undergone enormous changes without anyone noticing.

The continual shedding, without trace, of memories, history, laws, and customs which no longer have present relevance has been called a "homeostasis of orality" (Ong 1982:46): without written records of the progress

33. Cited in Goody 1987:294.
34. Ruth Finnegan (1977, 1990, 1992) is the one dissenting voice here; but as her examples are very brief Inuit poems, they should not be counted as genuine counterevidence. Thomas (1992:39–51) discusses Finnegan's objections usefully, but alas does not analyze the evidence they are based on. See also W. Harris (1989:31–33) against the common assumption that the memory of illiterates is simply better than that of literates.
35. Nilsson 1968:184–205; Lord 1960:17ff.; Goody 1987:86–88.

and change of actuality, a difference between "remembered" and "forgotten" cannot come into existence.[36] Without writing to control its vagaries, the human memory embellishes, deletes, transposes, and forgets altogether, and does so without any awareness of these changes. Recent findings in neurobiology have confirmed Walter Ong's view: memory is but the "storage of fragmentary but 'relevant' features."[37]

Accordingly, the culture dependent on memory will remain at the mercy of memory in maintaining itself. Unable to rely on books, libraries, and archives to keep track of information pivotal to its sense of identity and material well-being, an oral culture must seek and find its knowledge, truth, skills, history, and wisdom about itself in the living memories and speech of its members. Those members of an oral society whose memories stretch back farthest will necessarily be most valuable to the community at large, as will their ability to remember well and pass on what they know in memorizable form to others.

Oral cultures have thus been described as "conservative," in every sense of the word (Ong 1977:119). Given the ephemerality of the spoken word, and the mortality of the oral community's ultimate authorities, its elders, a number of strategies tend to be used in preliterate societies for performing this culturally essential job of conservation. Central among these is the use of constant repetition—of stories, songs, rituals, genealogies, ancestry lists, formulas, phrases, epithets. Ivan Kalmár has written about contemporary West Africans who still sit together throughout the day reciting ancestry lists from memory (1985:156); in oral cultures, the recital of genealogies constitutes a distinct speech genre (Halpern 1990:301–21). And in ancient Greece throughout its oral period, as in so many unlettered societies throughout the world, it was primarily through the recitation of poetry that culture was conserved. As J. A. Notopoulous pithily describes the situation, "the poet is the incarnate book of oral peoples."[38]

In the predramatic poems of Homer and Hesiod, we find perfect examples of the use of poetry as an aid to cultural memory. The catalogues of ships and gods and rivers and the lengthy genealogical lists surely functioned in their time as more than rhetorical ornamentation: they served the practical function of preserving knowledge and history. The stylistic peculiarities of these poems are also comprehensible only if understood as stemming directly from the limitations of an orally dependent cultural memory.

36. Thomas provides a useful discussion of this "structural amnesia" for ancient Greece (1989 passim; 1992:108–12).

37. Changeux 1988:49; see also Loftus 1979, 1980; Finkel 1988:62.

38. Cited in Havelock 1963:57 n. 21.

Not only in Homer and Hesiod, whose works are dated to the eighth century, but also in the lyrics of the seventh century, we find a poetic style that bears all the distinctive traits of an oral composition-in-performance process.[39] As with other oral poetry around the world—from ancient Sumeria, through the former Yugoslavia and into pre-contact North America—the language of the Homeric epics exhibits a "formulaic" linguistic style.[40] Features common to verbal compositions which, like Homer's, were carried out without the aid of writing include a rigid poetic meter, a ring-like, episodic structure, the use of memorable epithets, stock similes, and other such formulaic expressions which can be plugged in whole, as metrics allow, plenty of repetition, and the joining of phrases with principal conjunctions ("and . . . and . . .").[41] These features are common throughout the world to poetry composed in and for oral recitation, and have been observed in North American aboriginal verse as well (Petrone 1990:19–22).

With this oral-formulaic method, it is possible for a singer of tales to recite poems thousands of lines long without the aid of a fixed copy. Rather than memorizing anything verbatim, the *aoidos* or bard learns a vocabulary of formulas and a technique for manipulating and recombining them within metrical constraints. As C. M. Bowra explains:

> The art and the technique of poetry are passed from generation to generation by a strict training in the needs of oral composition and recitation. The young bard learns from his elders the main outlines of stories, the names and personalities of characters, the rules of metre, the appropriate epithets for things and places and people, and, above all, an enormous mass of formulaic phrases, which are his main mater-

---

39. Many scholars have devoted book-length studies to demonstrating that the Archaic poets, particularly Homer, composed their verses orally, without the aid of writing. These include Lorimer 1948; Lord 1960, 1991; Havelock 1963, 1986; Nilsson 1968; Parry 1971, 1989; Ong 1977, 1982; Nagy 1981, 1986; Foley 1981, 1986, 1990, 1991; Goody 1987; Willcock 1990; Powell 1991. Of the more recent discussions of the orality of Archaic poetry, Parry 1989:198–264, Powell 1991:113–200, and Thomas 1992:50ff. are the most critically minded and thorough. Even Thomas—who has made it her business to carry on Finnegan's (1977) work of problematizing the image of oral poetry as popularized in the early days by Lord (1960)—has concluded that "whether or not Homer knew the art of writing, he would have remained an 'oral' poet by any meaningful sense of the word" (1992:50). The same point has been made about the other predramatic poets, notably by Gentili 1988:19–20, 56.

40. See Lord 1960, 1981, 1990, 1991; Parry 1971, 1989; Hatto 1980; Foley 1981, 1986, 1990, 1991; Bauman 1986; Duggan 1990; and Nagler 1990.

41. For this last feature of oral composition, see Fowler 1987:27. Aristotle calls it "parataxis" (*Rhetoric* 3.9.1409a24).

ial in composition and his abiding resource to meet almost any need. Once a phrase has been formed and tested and proved its worth, it commands respect because it is established and comes from the past. It is expected and even demanded in the appropriate context. (1969:4)

In the absence of a written version of any of their materials, then, the oral singers in effect stitched their poems together during performance, plugging their internalized stock of phrases and formulas into appropriate metrical slots. Unlike modern literary texts, which are generally composed once and then perhaps performed many times thereafter, the epic songs that we attribute to Homer—and which he had inherited from a long chain of bards and immortalized under his own name[42]—were in effect created anew each time they were performed, improvised with the aid of a vocabulary of ready-made blocks of utterance which could be "regularly used under the same metrical conditions to express a given essential idea" (Parry 1989:30).

From the Bronze Age down to the end of Greece's strictly oral period, this formulaic compositional style was alone responsible for preserving the valuable "winged words" not just of poetry but of all culturally significant discourse—which were, through these years and beyond, basically one and the same thing.[43] And it did its job well. The oral style, however, for all its efficiency in preserving important cultural materials in the absence of writing, had a number of specific consequences for storytelling.

First among these was that the mythological characters portrayed in poetry could not be represented as individualized, particularized speakers. Consider the representation of speech in the *Iliad* and *Odyssey.* Homer's heroes are simply not characterized by their speech; or rather, if speech is a guide to personality, their personalities are virtually interchangeable. What distinguishes Agamemnon from Odysseus, or Hektor from Menelaus is not a distinctive word choice or the use of characteristic constructions or

42. The question of how we came to attribute these songs to a virtual unknown named Homer has long plagued classical scholarship and continues to be the subject of controversy. The literature on the subject is vast, and the issue too complex to go into here. Powell's (1991) contribution to the debate supports my own view that Homer's name ended up on these stories because he was the foremost singer of them at the time when they were written down, or perhaps that they were written down in his time precisely because the alphabet was available and he was such a masterly singer of them. These hypotheses gain support from twentieth-century researches into oral poetry, particularly those conducted by Lord (1960), which indicate that the notion of authorship, of poetic property, first came on the scene with literacy and when attempts were made to commit poems to writing.

43. See esp. Jaeger 1960, vol. 1, and Havelock 1963, 1978, on the cultural function of poetry in Greece.

metaphors in what they say. Not only does an oral bard think nothing of giving identical speeches to a variety of unlike characters, but his poetic procedure actively encourages him to do so. As M. M. Willcock (1990:10) has shown, the exact same words are spoken by Agamemnon in one place and by Odysseus in another (*Iliad* 9.122–57, 264–99).[44] Roughly the same soliloquy is spoken on one occasion by Odysseus (11.404–10) and on another by Menelaus (17.91–105),[45] and the selfsame formula is used to express the thought of Agenor (21.553–70), Hektor (22.99–130), and Achilleus (22.378–94).[46] In the *Odyssey,* Penelope and Eumaios deliver themselves of the exact same words as well (17.41–44 and 16.23–24),[47] and the list goes on. What distinguishes characters in epic is primarily the bard's use of descriptive epithets: the brilliant Odysseus, the glorious Hektor, the warlike Menelaus. And Hesiod, who rarely attempts to represent the speech of his figures at all, relies similarly on epithets to characterize them: wide-seeing Zeus, glorious Hermes, golden Aphrodite. This use of formulas to particularize and differentiate characters often fails altogether, however, as we see in Hesiod, when for example two or more unlike figures end up with the same epithet ("trim-ankled" for both Medea and Clymene; and Hera, Aglaia, and Ariadne are all indifferently described as someone's "fertile wife" [*Theogony* 497–529; 907–68]).

Because the representation of speech in epic is controlled by the metrical and formulaic consistency demanded by an oral mode, a fictional character, in the hands of an oral storyteller, can be represented as saying only what the available metrical units in a line will permit, and all speeches are

---

44. This is the thirty-five–line offer of treasure that begins, in Lattimore's translation, with "seven unfired tripods; ten talents' weight of gold; twenty shining cauldrons; and twelve horses, strong, race-competitors who have won prizes in the speed of their feet. That man would not be poor in possessions, to whom were given all these have won me, nor be unpossessed of dearly honoured gold." The two speeches end with "All this I will bring to pass for him, if he changes from his anger," and they are identical except that Odysseus says "he," "Agamemnon," and "you" instead of "me," "I," and "him."

45. It is the internal debate weighing two evils which begins "And [or 'deeply'] troubled, he spoke to his own great-hearted spirit: 'Ah me, what will become of me?' " and ends "Yet still, why does the heart within me debate on these things?" and "Then why does my own heart within me debate this?" There are small differences within the two versions of the speech, but the pattern is the same.

46. All three fighters say, "Yet still, why does the heart within me debate on these things?" and two begin with similar utterances: "Ah me! If I run away before the strength of Achilleus," and "Ah me! If I go now inside the wall and the gateway. . . ."

47. Both speeches begin "You have come, Telemachos, sweet light; (and) I thought I would never see you again, when you had gone in the ship to Pylos," and end "But come now. . . ."

largely determined in advance by the existence of tried-and-true schemes. For this reason, speech as represented by the oral means of the epic is not particularized beyond the point of basic pragmatics: the uttering of a threat, the offering of thanks, the announcement of a wish to die at once.

Furthermore, the homogeneity of speech as represented in epic is but a kind of symptom of the fact that the bard speaks in his own voice for all characters. In Homer and Hesiod a single speaker delivers all utterances, both his own narrative and the sayings of the represented figures. To indicate transitions between the two modes, formulaic phrases are used here as well: "So she spoke," "So he spoke," "Then in answer again spoke brilliant swift-footed Achilleus," "Then in answer again spoke powerful Agamemnon." Thus, both in the sameness of speech style from one represented character to the next, and in the fact that in performance, all speech is literally of a single piece—that is, it belongs to one speaker—epic diction turns all speech diversity into a formulaic monologue. And owing to the demands of an oral composition-in-performance style, it could not possibly have done otherwise.

In addition, the partly improvisatory, partly obedient technique of composition-in-performance was not an easy one to learn or master. Requiring a lifetime of practice or apprenticeship, expertise in the oral style of poetic performance was rare. Although, as Kevin Robb puts it, oral poetry is always "hoarded by the entire community," it nevertheless remains in the hands of specialists: "It is everywhere in oral societies discovered to be the special preserve of tribal singers and reciters" (1994:33). In times before writing, traditional narratives had no existence "outside" of the bards who knew how to tell them, and in consequence they remained the exclusive property of those who knew the technique. As we see from a number of contemporary contexts, oral traditional stories and songs are collective property through time (from one generation to another), but they tend to be the monopolized possession of certain specialized individuals or groups at a given moment. In aboriginal Canadian culture, for example, only "certain initiated elders" have the right to tell some stories (Petrone 1990:11), and to this day families possess particular songs over which they have exclusive control. Either one must be a member of a special society, such as the Medewin of the Ojibwa (11), or have learned the special skills of an *aoidos* from apprenticeship to one who has already mastered and internalized them. The esoteric nature of much oral material is obscured by the communal nature of its reception; but all members of the collective are not equally authorized or able to produce it. Accordingly, in the *Odyssey* (17.382ff.), the bard is described as a specialist, a craftsman; and both through the epithets attached to him and through his traditional blindness, the oral singer is always depicted as one of the Muses' special elect, a rare and divine creature (1.335, 7.62–64). Hesiod, too, describes his special initiation into poetry by the Muses (*Theogony* 20–40), a process of divine selection that was assumed to create all poets. Similarly, in contemporary Africa, the *izibongo* singer believes that his skill is "inspired by God[;] it is a gift" (Whitaker 1996:205–7). Thus we can begin to see that traditional poetry's monologic character was, like the formulaic style itself, tied directly to its orality, its confinement to the world of sound. That is, in an oral context, the monological form of poetry is all but guaranteed by the esoteric nature of the technique needed to remember it: the bard *had* to speak for all his characters, for only he knew how to keep the story going.

At some point between the eighth and the sixth centuries, however, the Homeric poems were written down. This event, despite continued uncertainty as to exactly when it took place, was to have incalculable consequences for the history of the performing arts in Greece. In addition to signing the death warrant of the oral style, so to speak, it was to prove the first significant step toward the invention of theatre.

Lamentably, scholars have yet to reach anything approaching a consensus about when Homer was "alphabeticalized." And yet this is hardly to be wondered at, given the fragmentary and circumstantial nature of the evidence. Eric Havelock believed that the epic stories were written down at some point between 700 and 650 B.C.E. (1963:115); Rudolf Pfeiffer can say with confidence only that a text of these works must have been in existence by the sixth century at the latest (1968:8). In 1987, Robert Fowler wrote that "most [scholars] now accept" that a Homeric text existed at the end of the seventh century (33); more recently, however, Barry Powell has argued that the Homeric poems were written down in the earliest days of Greek literacy, that is, toward the end of the eighth century (1991). Depending on whom one wishes to side with, this means that a fixed, written version of Thespis' narrative inheritance either had been available for generations, or was a relative novelty at the time of the first dramatic performances.

Briefly summarized, the evidence is as follows: during the seventh and sixth centuries, the Greeks' love of poetry and competition manifested itself in "numerous and much frequented" contests in the recitation of Homer and Hesiod.[48] Hesiod (frag. 357) and the Homeric *Hymn to Apollo* tell us of the contests held at the festival of Apollo on Delos; Herodotus in *The His-*

---

48. Gentili 1988:156; Bowra 1969:54; also Powell 1991:216.

tory (5.67) tells of choruses sung at Sicyon; Pausanias (10.7.3) saw a tripod inscribed in commemoration of the musical competitions at the Pythian games in 586; and from Dodona, we have a surviving inscription by a competing rhapsode named Terpiscles, who dedicated a tripod to Zeus in celebration of his victory.[49] The competitive recitation of poetry is also known to have taken place at the Panathenaia, which was believed by the ancients to have been either instituted or expanded by Peisistratos around 566.[50]

The fact that artisans from all over the Greek world were representing "Homeric"[51] episodes on their jugs and pots as early as the seventh century does seem to suggest that epic lays were being recited before large festival audiences at least in the century before Thespis (Myres 1958:15). The seventh century also recommends itself as the date for this phenomenon through the evidence of the poetry being written at the time: Callinus (ca. 660) mentions the *Thebais* as Homer's work; Semonides (ca. 630) quotes a line from the *Iliad* and attributes it to "a man of Chios" (said to be Homer's birthplace); and the poets Alcman, Archilochus, and Stesichorus, all of whom were active in the middle years of the seventh century, clearly knew Homer's poetry well.[52] Given that these poets came from different cities, they would have been exposed to Homer either through festival recitations—to which audiences came from far and wide—or through written copies, which themselves could have circulated far and wide. Powell argues that the Homeridai, a society devoted to the preservation and performance of Homer's works, possessed the first manuscript, or copies of it, that went right back to Homer's time (1991:232). But the earliest concrete evidence that we have for the existence of a written version is the rule, datable to the sixth century, which specifies that the reciters at these contests must deliver the stories in their proper order (Plato *Hipparchus* 228b). As Pfeiffer concludes, this contest regulation strongly suggests that "a traditional text must have been available to which the rhapsodes were compelled to keep" (1968:8). And he is probably right. As we see from both Homer's description of bardic procedure in the *Odyssey* (1.340; 7.97; 8.500), and from Albert Bates Lord's fieldwork with oral poetry in the former Yugoslavia (1960:30), unlettered singers are not naturally inclined to think of their repertoire of

49. Gentili 1988:156; Bowra 1969:54.

50. Dillon and Garland 1994:102.

51. These representations seem to have been based most often on mythic narratives other than the *Iliad* or the *Odyssey*.

52. Murray 1907:8; Fowler 1987:8–37. Fowler provides useful lists of the many quotations and imitations of Homer and Hesiod in the seventh- and sixth-century lyric poets, and analyzes them for the probable extent of their reliance on a fixed text.

stories as a continuous, chronological whole. On the contrary, they select an episode to suit the mood of or fulfill a request from the particular audience they happen to be addressing; and they rarely sing any of these discrete, de-contextualized episodes to the end, for events that take place within the audience in the palace or the café are allowed to interrupt the performance. As Homer sings at the start of the *Odyssey,* "Begin it, goddess, at whatever point you will." Epic lays were thus liable to start and stop in a random, episodic way that is quite alien to literates, who are accustomed to thinking in terms of beginnings, middles, and ends, and in terms of an uninterrupted narrative line from cover to cover.[53] Thus, any rule about chronological continuity where Homer is concerned is a probable sign of the presence of literate thinking. C. M. Bowra agrees: the predramatic reciters of Homeric works "must have learned [them] by heart from written texts" (1969:54).

According to Fowler, the existence of a written Homer in the very early sixth century is proved incontrovertibly by internal textual evidence from sixth-century lyric poetry (1987:33–37). That a written Homer existed in the time of such poets as Ibycus and Solon is also suggested by the sixth-century controversy about textual tampering by the Athenians. There was a belief among the ancients that, as a way of justifying their political claims on places such as Salamis, the tyrants of Athens had inserted into the epics passages that were not authentic.[54] This sort of controversy certainly seems to smack of literate thinking.[55] For, as G. S. Kirk observes, "with the concept of the fixed text comes the concept of the correct text" (1985:110), and such anxieties about the authenticity of an official version are not likely to have emerged unless there was in fact a single version that could be held up as the true one. Clearly, by the sixth century, the Homeric poems were being treated as "canonical," "not susceptible of expurgation or amendment" (Myres 1958:20), which does argue in favor of their reduction to writing by this time. And although the evidence here is getting later and later, Cicero repeats an earlier—and, according to Robb, "fairly reliable" (1994:255)—anecdote which credits Hipparchus' father, Peisistratos (born ca. 605–600) with having collected the "scattered songs" of Homer and with having "arranged in their present order" the Homeric works which had previously been sung only in fragments (Gentili 1988:18).

In light of the lateness of such evidence, some scholars are skeptical that

53. Murray provides a lucid account of how the epics, originally sung in self-contained episodes, came to achieve the literary, unified form in which we read them today (1907:20–22).

54. See Murray 1907:11–12; Myres 1958:31.

55. See, for example, Herodotus *History* 5.67, 7.161.

this so-called Peisistratid recension of the epics actually took place. And yet, as John Myres argues, even if such editing did take place under the sponsorship of the Peisistratid tyrants, it is not likely that this would have been the first time the epics were written down (1958:15–16). Were it not for the existence of a few additional scraps of evidence, we should probably have to say simply that the date of the first inscription of the epics is undecidable.

Foremost among these scraps is the lively literary activity of the Ionian philosophers and rhapsodes of the sixth century. From Plato's (later) portrait of the rhapsode Ion, we know quite a lot about what these reciters did. Like actors, they wore beautiful costumes; and like actors, they performed before large festival audiences. But unlike actors, they performed the older, by this time classic poetry of Homer, Hesiod, Archilochus— in short, the monological poetry of the archaic bard. And that they did so from fixed, written copies of these works, at least in the fifth century, is made quite clear by Xenophon, who describes these rhapsodes as "very precise about the exact words of Homer, although very foolish themselves" (*Memorabilia* 4.2, 10); he also reports that a contemporary of Socrates, Euthydemos of Chios, possessed a complete text of Homer with all verses intact (4.2, 10). Plato's depiction of the rhapsode as a mere second-hand "interpreter" (*Ion* 535a) points up nicely the extent to which poetic performance had changed since the days of the oral bards: because he need know nothing himself but how to memorize a particular text, the rhapsode is no longer the kind of expert craftsman that the oral bard was. And Socrates criticizes him for this reason, saying that he possesses no special art or craft (*techne*).

But it is clear from the *Ion* that the rhapsode did in fact have a specialty—albeit not one with which Plato was likely to be impressed. This specialty was *textual interpretation*. Although Socrates quickly denigrates even this skill, since it is evidently not transferable to the work of other poets, Ion is quite proud of his ability to explain and analyze Homeric texts. Now, the criticism of Homer had become something of a minor industry by this time.[56] In his *History of the Peloponnesian War*, Thucydides remarks on the textual inconsistencies in Homer (1.10), as does Herodotus, who claims, after citing lengthy passages from the *Iliad* and the *Odyssey*, that some of these discrepancies are serious enough to cast doubt on the authorship of works traditionally attributed to Homer (i.e., the *Cypria* and *Epigoni*; *History* 2.116–117, 4.32). By the end of the fifth century, such literary debates about the age, origin, authenticity, meaning, and correctness of words in

56. See Lamberton and Keaney 1992.

Homer and elsewhere were raging among Sophists such as Prodicus, Gorgias, Protagoras, and Hippias; and these critics, who, like rhapsodes, wore purple robes and performed at festivals, were equated wherever they went with books and bookishness.[57]

But when Aristotle, in passing, refers to these hair-splitting literary disputes among the "ancient critics of Homer" (*Metaphysics* 1093a26), there is evidence that by "ancient" he meant sixth-century, and that the practice of literary criticism dates back to Thespis' time at least. Pherecydes, a philosopher active in the middle of the sixth century, is the earliest certain writer of prose who can be credited with what we would today call literary criticism. In his book, which Diogenes Laertius (1.119) says was still in existence in the third century C.E., Pherecydes discussed aspects of the epics etymologically, substituting unusual grammatical variants for the names of Homeric gods as a way of explaining their origins (frags. 42, 44, 49 Kirk, Raven, and Schofield 1987). Even if he had not been specifically credited with having been "the first to bring out a book in prose" (Diogenes Laertius 1.116), there would still be little doubt that Pherecydes was a user of texts, since etymological activities of this type would depend on the evidence of letters.[58] The next important pre-Thespian literary critic was Xenophanes of Colophon (born ca. 570). Xenophanes was perhaps the first great skeptic produced by the literate age, and something of a scientific empiricist, too, judging from his surprisingly advanced studies of fossils and his explanatory theory of cyclical ocean levels (Herodian frag. 37).[59] He seems to have been most famous, though, for his criticism of the epic poems, particularly in their representation of gods, which Xenophanes found implausibly anthropomorphic, and immoral.[60] As Diogenes Laertius tells us, Xenophanes wrote not only against Homer and Hesiod, but also against the opinions of a number of philosophers of his own time as well (9.18).[61] Xenophanes' mocking criticism of Homer was not left unchallenged, however. Accordingly, the last of Homer's sixth-century critics who deserves mention here is Theagenes of Rhegium, a little-known writer and rhapsode who is said to have been among the first to defend Homer's works on allegorical grounds.[62] He ar-

57. See esp. Plato *Theaetetus* 162a, *Protagoras, Gorgias;* Aristophanes *Broilers* frag. 490 Edmonds 1957; see also O'Sullivan 1996:115–27.

58. Kirk, Raven, and Schofield doubt that his book would have been the first prose work to be published; but they speculate that his book, and the book of Anaximander—which they think may have been roughly contemporary with it (ca. 547)—may simply have survived in a more substantial form than earlier works (1987:52).

59. Number 184 in Kirk, Raven, and Schofield 1987.

60. Numbers 166, 167, 168, 169 ibid.

61. Number 161 ibid.

62. Pfeiffer 1968:9; see also Myres 1958:34; Richardson 1992:31.

gued that Homer's gods were intended as symbolic representations of the forces of nature, not as literal deities. Thus it was not only by Ion in the fifth century but also by the contemporaries of Thespis in the sixth that textual criticism of Homer was being practiced.

About the works of Thespis almost nothing is known. But the tradition of textual criticism inaugurated in his time, while probably more familiar to us in its late fifth-century, Sophistical incarnation, is one that was to bear its most distinctive fruits in the works of the early tragedians, Aeschylus, Sophocles, and Euripides. For these dramatic works, with their often radical reinterpretation, revision, and alteration of Homeric myth, represent a kind of sustained textual critique of the poetic repertoire of the time.[63] In order to view Thespis' historic performance of a dramatic work in 534 B.C.E. in its proper light, therefore, it must be borne in mind that he lived in a time when the defining performative materials of Greek culture were no longer exclusively oral, but were subject instead to the scrutiny of readers.

Can we imagine the moment when the epics were written down for the first time? To do so requires that we understand just how well suited the alphabet was for recording Greek poetry. As G. E. Lessing pointed out with respect to the artistic media of painting and poetry, a representing medium is likely to have innate potentialities and characteristic weaknesses; and this is true for representing media such as scriptory systems, too. A nonphonetic type of writing, in the form of Linear A and B, was known in Greece before the alphabet; but the samples of Linear B that have come down to us show that it was not a subtle and sensitive recording device like the alphabet.[64] On the contrary, it was so cumbersome and specialist that, in Pylos for example, all writing seems to have been done by the same thirty or so scribes (Stroud 1989:109). Given its characteristics, it is not surprising to find that Linear B seems to have been used only for recording things like inventories (for metalworking, wool production, agricultural produce, defense, trade in imported luxuries, and so on) (108). Most significantly for our purposes, no poetry has been found in this script. As C. M. Bowra describes it, Linear B was "unusually inefficient, even by the standards of its own time." There is

---

63. See Chapter 2, in which these innovations and alterations are discussed with examples. Segal (1986, 1992) also provides excellent discussions of the critical spirit of early drama in comparison with earlier poetry.

64. A convincing solution to the puzzle of Linear A has still not been proposed. See Chadwick 1990:156.

"no sign that the script was used for anything that might be called literature, and if it was, it would have done its task abominably" (1969:4).[65]

In bold contrast to the uses to which Linear B was put, however, the alphabet was used to record poetry almost instantaneously. In fact, the incredible speed with which it was put to this end is so striking that some scholars have been led to hypothesize that the Greek alphabet "might have been invented as a notation for Greek verse" (Wade-Gery 1952:11–14).[66] This does not seem very likely, really, as the Greeks learned phonetic letters from the mercantile Phoenicians in the course of trade: its earliest use in Greece is therefore liable to have been connected with commerce and property (Jeffrey 1990:7–13). Nevertheless, it must be admitted that no commercial uses for writing are actually attested in the writing samples that have survived from the eighth century. On the contrary, nearly all the earliest artifacts show that writing was first used in Greece to record short snatches of hexameter verse, the language of epic poetry (Powell 1991:221). Among these eighth-century inscriptions, which are only a few lines long, the artifact known as "Nestor's cup" (ca. 740–20) constitutes, as Barry Powell points out, the first known literary allusion in the Western tradition, for it refers directly to a royal drinking vessel as described by Homer. The early use of alphabetic writing for recording Greek poetry, and then the Homeric epics, was not coincidental. Both in the phonetic principle itself and in the way the alphabet is learned, there are many clues to be found which explain why the Greeks only started inscribing their oral poetry after they had developed an alphabet.

We can see the characteristics of the Greek phonetic system most vividly when we contrast it with the systems in use elsewhere in the ancient world. In the Chinese system, for example, then as now, the written unit is the morpheme, and there are tens of thousands of them (guesses have been made at fifty thousand; Taylor 1988:203). Since these legions of signs do not code sound directly, they must simply be memorized. As a result, the Chinese system, like Egyptian hieroglyphics, was practically destined to remain in the hands of a specialist elite. Aided neither by an alphabet to organize words along predictable lines, nor by a thoroughgoing phonetic principle, students of such scripts need to be very learned even to use a dictionary properly. Under such learning conditions, Egyptian script could easily be

65. See also Chadwick 1990 passim for detailed description of the ambiguities and peculiarities of Linear B.

66. See also Pfeiffer 1968:23; Powell 1991 passim.

kept a "sacred language" indefinitely; and Chinese writing, too, was used exclusively for "ritual and magic purposes" for over a thousand years (Hagège 1988:79). The illiteracy rate in China even at the beginning of the twentieth century has been estimated at 80 percent (Taylor 1988:207). In short, logographic scripts tend by nature to remain in the hands of a small elite of the specially initiated, for much study is needed to acquire them.

It should be noted, however, that languages "choose" their own most efficient writing system; there is no such thing as a better or worse type of script. As a monosyllabic language with no inflected endings, a number of separate "tones," and an unusually heavy proportion of homophones, Chinese could not efficiently be represented with an alphabet. By the same token, the Greeks modified the Semitic consonantal alphabet into a fully phonetic system complete with vowels because their language demanded it.[67] As Eric Havelock has stressed, however, the Greeks' (necessary) discovery of the vowel made it possible for them to reduce the ambiguity of syllabic writing systems, and in so doing eliminate the dependence on specialist scribes that inhibited the spread of writing elsewhere. With the invention of vowels, writing became genuinely phonetic, and for the first time even nonspecialists were able to read and write (1963:129 n. 6). Consequently, (alphabetic) writing could be, and was, used in Greece immediately for private purposes and by obviously untrained individuals. Eighth-century inscriptions include the personal messages and graffiti of ordinary people (Jeffrey 1990:63); and as writing became more widespread in the following centuries, "the skill was certainly not confined to aristocrats or a class of specialists" (W. Harris 1989:48).[68] Scribal specialists, who in so many other ancient cultures reserved writing for their own exclusionary purposes, did not do so in ancient Greece.[69]

And they could not have done had they tried, for the phonetic principle guaranteed that even unschooled sausage sellers could learn to read and

---

67. Taylor 1988:203–10; Hagège 1988:76; DeFrancis 1989.

68. The question of exactly, or even roughly, how many people were literate in ancient Greece at any given point in the advance of literacy, although interesting in itself, is irrelevant to the present discussion. Regardless of whether there were thirty or thirty thousand literates in the eighth century B.C.E. in Greece, surviving artifacts dated to that period show distinctly that within the same century that the alphabet was developed, it was already being used to record poetry by unskilled hands. William Harris devotes a book to the sensitive question of how many literates Greece possessed, and what level of literacy was likely to have been attained by them (1989:vii–115); Jeffrey 1990, Stroud 1989, Powell 1991:119–86, and Thomas 1992:56–88 discuss the archaeological evidence from the eighth and seventh centuries which proves that early Greek writers were ordinary amateurs.

69. Goody 1986:17; Thomas 1992:57.

write with minimal study. With the acquisition of a mere twenty-four signs (other alphabets have between twenty and thirty-seven), students of the Greek alphabet can transcribe any and every word in their spoken vocabulary without special study. They may not spell these words "correctly," but the phonetic principle will guarantee the decipherability of their writing by anyone who knows the same twenty-four signs. What is more, it is possible with an alphabet to transcribe words one doesn't even know, such as foreign or archaic words, specialist jargon, or words disguised by dialect—a fact which will prove significant for the development of theatre, as we shall see. This connection between phoneticism and ease in transcribing oral material is further demonstrated by the modern Chinese example, where mass education has not been able to proceed without the adoption of the phonetic pinyin script. The creation in Japan of the phonetic Kana scripts between the eighth and twelfth centuries C.E. has helped guarantee the extremely high literacy rates there (although socioeconomic factors have undoubtedly contributed as well; cf. Taylor 1988:210).[70]

As Powell (1991) has demonstrated at length, use of the alphabet was an absolute precondition for the recording of Homer: the artificiality of epic diction, plus the essential role played in it by lengthened and shortened vowels, all but ensured that the Greeks could not have recorded their hexameter poetry without a phonetic system. But there is more to say about the nature of the alphabet than that it was an appropriate recording device for epic verse. One of the first linguists to emphasize the inherent traits of the alphabet was Wilhelm von Humboldt (1767–1835). Through a comparison of the functioning of foreign, logographic scripts with his own culture's alphabetical writing, Humboldt was able to isolate some of the latter's key defining characteristics, and his observations remain valid today. In his treatises "On Alphabetic Writing and Its Connection with the Structure of Language," and "On the Connection of Writing with Language,"[71] Humboldt notes that alphabetic script is distinguished by its tendency to represent sound separated from meaning (Christy 1989:339). In this tendency Humboldt saw more than a mechanical operation; he saw the alphabet's sound/sense separation as effecting a profound change in the relationship between people and their language. To begin with, the use of the alphabet

70. William Harris argues that the high literacy rate in countries such as contemporary Israel and Japan is not proof that mass literacy is unrelated to the writing system: modern industrialized nations have remedies for the absence of phoneticism (such as the printing press, dictionaries, textbooks, and mass education) which Archaic civilizations certainly lacked (1989:46).

71. Cited by Christy 1989:339ff.

requires the breaking down of the sounds of speech into their smallest units. These sounds, called phonemes, are in turn represented by a minimal number of signs—letters—whose main distinguishing feature is that they have no referential function. What a letter represents is not a meaning but just a sound, or range of sounds, which is meaningless in itself. Whereas, for example, Semitic signs such as *bet, mem, 'ayin, yod,* and *rosh* stood originally for "house," "water," "eye," "hand," and "head," the Greek equivalents after the phonetic revolution—*beta, mu, omicron, iota, rho*—have no meaning at all; they represent only sounds (Naveh 1988:84–89). Alphabetic writing thus represents speech by "hearing it"; alphabetic writing acts as the "ear" of speech. And because what is heard must be aurally atomized into representing letters, the sounds of speech become the "subject" of alphabetic writing, a subject requiring analysis.

Logographic writing, on the contrary, could be said to remain comparatively "deaf" to speech. Characters in Chinese, for example, do have a phonetic portion, but it notes only certain features of the word and not its pronunciation. That is, a sign in Chinese may represent a sound, but may also represent a totally different sound in another context. In Chinese, and in the logographic part of Japanese, there are no characters that have "a fixed phonetic value for all elements of the language" (Hagège 1988:77). Because they are disconnected in this way from the sounds of spoken language, logograms, according to Julia Kristeva, encode speech "without hearing/understanding it: without hearing/understanding its ideal and phonetic autonomy as separate from what it designates." In "dissociat[ing] the spoken chain from what it expresses" and encoding only its sounds, alphabetic writing on the contrary frees language up from its referential, world-ordering functions and reveals it as a subject for abstract, acoustical analysis (Kristeva 1989:93–94). In Humboldt's view this promotes a detached, objective contemplation of language because, with the alphabet, it is possible to think of constituent linguistic forms without simultaneously invoking what Kristeva has called the whole "semantic and cosmic classificatory" system which each logogram encodes. For logograms function by actually constituting the speaker's semantic relation to the world. A logogram makes inextricable "the concept, the sound, and the thing"; a Chinese word, for example, "doesn't lose the thing; it only transfers it to a plane where it becomes ordered with others in a regulated system. In this way *la langue* and 'the real' are one and the same thing" (Kristeva 1989:94).

To visualize the alphabet's "speech-centrism" as clearly as possible, we might try the following somewhat silly but effective experiment. Imagine an itinerant Chinese bard singing a long traditional poem about legendary or historical personages and deeds. If the script available to his listeners is a lo-gography, he need only sing the word *ma* with a less than perfectly distinct tone for them to fail utterly to know whether they should write the charac-ter for "agate," or the character for "weights," or for "ant," "masurium," "mother," "clamp," "sacrifice," "scold," or "question particle" (DeFrancis 1989:103). In everyday speech, such extreme ambiguity would not occur; but in poetic speech, surprising words often appear in unexpected places. This is especially true of traditional oral poetry, which preserves archaic forms and accumulates terms and idioms from widely separated geographic locations. If the logographer/spectator of this epic performance heard an unfamiliar word, say "petard," and he did not know the character for it, he would have no choice but to put together a sequence of characters chosen for their pho-netic value. Such a stringing together of characters whose phonetic associa-tions approximate the sound of an unknown spoken word is obviously cumbersome. But its inefficiency lies mainly in the fact that there would be nothing to prevent the next reader of his manuscript from decoding the signs *semantically* and reading, in place of "petard," "creek him two beans" (*pu ta er dou*).[72] This demonstration is fanciful and actually somewhat un-fair, for "petard" is an English, not a Chinese word. But by contrast to the ease with which the Homeric epics could be written down, the unwieldiness of a nonalphabetical system is significant. Having learned twenty-four let-ters, an ancient recorder of a Homeric performance could write down every single word that he heard, even if he had never heard half of them before.

In light of the logographic system's lack of interest in the sounds of speech, it should not be surprising to discover that Chinese verbal culture has no epic (Hsu 1985:378; Lu Hsun 1959:19). Although Tao-ching Hsu in-vokes a political explanation for this "well-known" anomaly—state suppres-sion during the Chou dynasty (1122–255 B.C.E.)—it is equally likely that this absence of a unified body of popular mythology has its source in the writing system. Or, more accurately, one should say "seeming absence," for the Chi-nese writing system may simply never have recorded an epic. Given the likely number of ancient Chinese literates, and given the sacred/hierarchical nature of their involvements, it is plausible that popular Chinese legends and myths from earlier oral times were never recited to anyone who knew enough characters to write them down. In fact there is a story that palace of-ficials in the Chou dynasty were sent into the streets to collect the people's myths and legends; but as a writer from the Han dynasty (206 B.C.E.–220

72. DeFrancis makes this same point, albeit much more effectively, in *The Chinese Language* (1989 passim); Coulmas discusses similar problems in Japanese (1989:127).

C.E.) reports, this was done more as an attempt at surveillance, to learn how the other half lived: "The ancient kings who wanted to know local customs appointed these officers to report on them" (Hsun 1959:23). Thus, if Chinese myths were at any point written down, it would have been by official state scribes, not by the people who actually told and enjoyed these stories themselves. Without accessible and widespread written records of it, traditional material could simply disappear over time. In Greece, by contrast, as the amateurish quality of early hexameter inscriptions shows unmistakably, the means for recording traditional poetry rested in the hands of its audiences from the very beginning of literacy.

In the failure of a Chinese epic to emerge during this time, we find an important indication that the artistic speech practices of the logographic East were headed along a different developmental track than those in the alphabetical West. Whereas the existence of a body of fixed, repeatable narratives provided the Greeks with both the impetus and the raw material for developing an art of enactment in their literate period, the absence of epic material all but guaranteed that the performative arts of music and dance in China would remain tied to (essentially nonnarrative) ceremonial court rituals during an analogous historical period (sixth century B.C.E.).[73] Even thousands of years later, observers from both East and West are still remarking on the profound dissimilarities between the performing arts of the two cultural worlds.[74]

As Tao-ching Hsu notes, a popular storytelling theatre did not emerge in China when it did in the West. Despite ten centuries in which impersonation and dialogue were known,[75] and despite the magnificent spectacles, elaborate dance forms, brilliant musical invention, and stylized ritual performances that may date back to the second millennium B.C.E.,[76] a theatre of plays did not come into being until the thirteenth century C.E. (Hsu 1985:230–301; Dolby 1976:13–15). Although far ahead of the Greek in many ways in the fifth century B.C.E., Chinese culture had nothing that could be compared with the plot-based theatre of repeatable plays by Aeschylus, Sophocles, and Euripides. Chinese performance arts of the time were dis-

---

73. Although Chinese writing is much older than the alphabet, it was not until the thirteenth century C.E. that anything like repeatable plays emerged; a real storytelling tradition is not marked in China until the Ch'ing dynasty, 1644–1911 of our era (Hsu 1985:301, 230).

74. For example, see Artaud 1958; Barba 1990; and Weijie 1990.

75. The first recorded use of a human mask is circa 380 C.E. (Hsu 1985:208).

76. The last emperor of the Hsia dynasty is said to have had "strange and spectacular shows staged by jesters and dwarfs," although Hsu thinks the source unreliable (1985:202).

tinctly nonlinguistic: they showed a lack of interest in human speech and left no written records of things said. Chinese court jesters, who were perhaps the closest historical analogues to Thespis and Aeschylus, are reported, in historical documents, to have mimicked the speech of certain individuals—the governor of Hsuan-Chou, for example—on particular ceremonial occasions.[77] But in the absence of a really flexible mode of transcribing exactly what their verbal imitation consisted of, such impersonations, as Hsu reports, remained tied to the particular moment of their utterance: they did not outlive their original context or produce repeatable plays, let alone a body of dramatic literature. The repeatable elements of Eastern performance arts thus consisted in the ancient world, and still consist to an extent, of nonlinguistic elements: costumes, gestures, dance steps, melodies, and stylized character types.[78]

The "deafness" of logographic script to speech has its advantages: it enables speakers of related but mutually unintelligible languages to communicate by writing. But the result of this politically unifying potentiality in China was that the written register came to dominate Chinese intellectual life at a remarkably early date. As G. E. R. Lloyd puts it, the "widespread intelligibility" of the written script caused China to be "very much a culture mediated by the written, more than by the spoken, word" (1990:112). The early ascendance of the written register over the spoken in China was particularly acute in the sphere of poetry, and did much to determine the shape of Chinese performance arts. For as Oscar Brockett has noted (1982:102), Chinese verse forms before the time of the T'ang dynasty were determined by the number of characters written in a line. A poetic line thus oriented to writing cannot easily be made to fit the rhythms of music, and hence this poetry will tend to stay disconnected from oral performance. The disconnectedness of Chinese writing from the rhythms and sounds of speech is perceptible in traditional Eastern theatrical forms even today. Spoken elements are recessive in general, and those that are used are in some cases so disconnected from the living speech of audiences that it is not unusual for these words to be gibberish to audiences and performers alike (Hsu 1985:210). As Eugenio Barba says, it is in fact part of the "horizon of expectations" of the Eastern spectator that what she or he sees may be unintelligible in its verbal aspect (1990:33).

In Western theatre, by contrast, one sees a distinct and possibly defining focus on the spoken register. Whether capturing the sounds of a tyrant's

77. See Hsu 1985:212.

78. Thomas provides some interesting evidence for Greece that such performative elements can be preserved without the use of writing across the centuries (1992:122).

bombast or a politician's sophistry; whether ridiculing the jargon of a profession or the pretensions of the bookish; whether mimicking the quaint errors of a foreigner or the woeful effusions of teenaged balladeers; whether charting the oral habits of old speech, young speech, or speech between the sheets—that is, regardless of the particular character of the speech it records—it is certain that the Western theatre has kept both ears open to oral language since the genre first appeared. And the same speech-centrism that defines the alphabet, and that came to define the Western theatre, also defined Greek life in other areas. Even long after the introduction of writing into Greece, that is, into the time of Aristotle, culturally significant social discourse continued to be *spoken* discourse, with agonistic oral debate organizing and carrying out most social, political, and intellectual activities.[79] The equation this leaves us with is that the disconnectedness from speech effected by the Chinese writing system is replicated both within culturally significant discourse generally and within the representational style of Eastern performance art; and the sensitivity to spoken language exemplified by the alphabet similarly manifests itself within Greek discursive style overall as well as in the speech-conscious representations of Greek theatre.

Had alphabetic writing been available to ancient Chinese court jesters, there is obviously no guarantee that a body of epic writings, and then a literary theatre, would necessarily or automatically have materialized. Social and political factors were also at work.[80] But while some of these factors certainly created suitable conditions in Greece for a secular, popular, and poetic use of writing from an early date, and while others certainly discouraged it in the East, the practice of recording traditional oral narrative was itself made available to the Greeks owing to the inherently open-eared, "speaker-friendly" nature of the alphabet.

The sound-sensitivity of alphabet, coupled with the fact that it could be, and was, used for recording poetic performance by any ordinary Greek almost at once, thus enabled poets and performers to preserve their narrative legacy in an unusually copious form. Aeschylus is said to have described his plays as "slices from the great banquets of Homer"; Sophocles' use of Homeric material gained him the appellation *philhomeros* and *Homerikotatos* (Athenaeus *Deipnosophists* 8.347e; 7.277e). Indeed, numerous ancient sources, from Herodotus to Isocrates to Plato to Aristotle, leave little doubt that in their time, the dramatist's art was considered a continuation, through new formal means, of the telling of stories first told in traditional epic recitation (Herington 1985:103–4). As Eric Havelock notes, "The

79. See esp. Lloyd 1990 and Thomas 1992.
80. See Burn 1960:157; Harris 1989:61; and Hsun 1959:19ff. for some of these.

Athenian stage plays, composed closer to the native vernacular, became the Attic supplement to Homer" (1963:48). Aristotle leaves little doubt about the indebtedness of drama to the survival of Homeric epic: Homer provided the model of a "dramatic" "metrical representation of heroic action" for tragedy, and "was the first to mark out the main lines of comedy as well" (*Poetics* 1448b11–12; 1449b7ff.).

The alphabetical conservation of Homer also had the effect of ensuring that, while already ancient in the dramatists' time, these works would stay alive for contemporary audiences. With the alphabet, all kinds of archaic words could be preserved before their use died out and their meanings were lost forever. Because the forms and sounds of poetic words had been preserved in text, rhapsodic performers generations after Homer were given access to their meanings as well. Partly through etymology and partly as a result of having the whole poem before them in fixed form, performers of a written narrative could maintain access through time to the meaning of a word such as "phlegm," as Prodicus did (Pfeiffer 1968:40). In fact, from Aristotle we learn that "glosses" of rare or obsolete words were a common feature of epic texts (*Poetics* 1459a9f.); and Rudolf Pfeiffer considers the possibility that these glosses date back to the sixth century, although the word itself (*glossai*) first appears in the fifth (1968:12). Consequently, the recitation of even very old traditional material never could degenerate into a ceremonial incantation of meaningless sounds, as such material did in the East. What writing itself does for cultures generally, then, alphabetic writing did for Western performers: it enabled them to have access to the "real semantic history" of their performative material (Ong 1982:8). If the recorders of Homer had had instead a pictographic or logogrammatic system at their disposal, they would have been very seriously discouraged by it from even attempting to include the many unconventional or unfamiliar words of the traditional epic vocabulary.[81]

The importance of this relatively easy, nonspecialist access to writing for the development of theatre is also suggested by events centuries later in Europe and England. Despite the alphabet, scribal elites retained control of writing, at least in part by associating writing with Latin, a language not spoken by the vast majority of people.[82] But as soon as writing started being used to record the vernaculars of Europe, the alphabet's "ear" for speech was as quickly exploited for recording poetic performances as it had been in ancient Greece. In fact, among the very first written documents in the vernac-

---

81. See Havelock and Hershbell 1978:5–10; Powell 1991:71–107.
82. See esp. Auerbach 1965.

ular to appear in Europe between the ninth and twelfth centuries were, conspicuously, jongleurs' manuscripts; and once performers with scripts replaced oral bards, actors were soon to follow (Auerbach 1965:280–94). If it is
fair to generalize from the evidence of only two such occurrences of theatre's
emergence in the West, it would seem that this chain of generic shifts—
from (nonliterate) oral bards, through individual jongleurs or rhapsodes
reciting from a written record of an epic performance, to groups of actors
with a common text written explicitly for them—amounts to a kind of rule.

Nevertheless, the mere survival of the Homeric narrative legacy would not
in itself have been enough to stimulate the invention of an art of enactment.
What created the conditions for the generic shift from epic to drama was
that Thespis and his heirs inherited these stories in a form that made them
visible to the eye. As perhaps the first poets ever to have before them complete texts of the epics from start to finish, the early dramatists were in a position to notice things that may never have been seen so clearly before. And
much of what they saw, they changed. Whereas oral audiences had previously had access to Homer's stories only through ephemeral performances of
them, the dramatists could scrutinize these works as critics and readers. And
their use of writing in the composition process gave them the means not
only to reflect their criticisms in their poetry, but also to regard their own
works with an equally critical eye, freed as they were from the demands of
oral compositional techniques.[83]

The first thing to go was the formulaic style itself. The mere existence
of writing meant that embodied memory was no longer needed for cultural
continuity, and the mnemotechnics of oral poetry were rendered obsolete.
Indeed, when we compare the language of oral epic with that of drama, we
find differences that could not be more pronounced. First among these is
the "paradox," noted by Walter Ong, that drama, while the first poetic genre

83. That the dramatists used writing to compose is suggested, of course, by their literacy, for which they provide ample enough proof throughout their plays (see note 6). Many
contemporary scholars are quick to remind us, however, that as late as Aristotle, playwrights were still being called the "makers" of their plays rather than the writers of them
(see, e.g., Page 1987:108). Aristotle, however, was clearly not intending to suggest that the
dramatists did not use writing; he was speaking of the construction, or making, of plots
and poetry generally. The fact remains that in the century before Aristotle, dramatists were
already and explicitly being represented as the *writers* of their plays (Cratinus *Wineflask*
frags. 195 and 196 Edmonds 1957; Aristophanes frag. 676b ibid.). K. J. Dover further tells us
that the dramatists had to submit their plays to the archon months in advance of their performance, which strongly suggests that they wrote them (1972:15).

to be controlled by writing from the start,[84] should also have been the first language genre to "make deliberate use of colloquial speech" (1977:72). In light of what has been said so far, however, it may not be so paradoxical at all. Given the tendency of writing to make obsolete the need for memorable, formulaic expression, and given the capacity of alphabetical script to encode speech-as-spoken, it would stand to reason that it was not in spite of but rather because of drama's literary character that it quickly distinguished itself as the genre of contemporary speech par excellence.

In providing an easy and responsive method for transcribing pronunciation, use of the alphabet opens up to poetic composition the ability to "hear" the speech of individuals. Cut loose by writing from the formulaic and metrical constraints of composition-in-performance, storytellers could begin to exploit this alphabetical potential to the full, and the early dramatists did. The representation of the idiosyncratic speech of individuals could not be pursued in epic speech beyond a very rudimentary degree, and seems to be atypical of non-alphabetical theatres as well. But in the dramas of fifth-century Greece, the accents, nuances, and social values inherent in each character's language are not only emphasized individually, but also brought into an even sharper relief through contact with the speech of other characters. In Bakhtinian terminology, the separate discourses of drama can be said to mutually illuminate and comment on one another.

Consider, for example, the unadorned, mocking verbal blasts of Sophocles' Antigone: "I knew it; of course I did. For it was public" (*Antigone* 492); "I know that I will die—of course I do. . . . I count that as a profit" (504); "Why do you wait, then? Nothing that you say pleases me; God forbid that it should" (545).[85] Her expressions, rhetorically spare and pointed, are characterized by a certain amount of aggressive overstatement and are rooted in intensely felt but often unreasoned emotion: "Oh, oh, no! Shout it out. I will hate you still worse for silence—should you not proclaim it to everyone" (99–101); "If you talk like this I will loathe you. . . . Let me alone and my folly with me, to endure this terror. No suffering of mine will be enough

84. Ong does not himself *prove* that drama was the first genre to use writing from the start, but all evidence does point in that direction. By "from the start," I assume he means that plays were written *before* they were performed, whereas the use of writing for the epic had been after the fact, that is, only for recording a performance. If epic was orally composed, we are left only with lyric as an alternate contender for the title of first literary genre. Less is known about the compositional methods of elegists and iambicists of the seventh and sixth centuries. They may still have been in the habit of composing their songs out loud, perhaps to lyre accompaniment, but there is no certain proof either way.

85. All translations of the tragedies are from Grene and Lattimore 1991.

to make me die ignobly" (109–14). The contrast with, say, the speech of another Sophoclean heroine, Deianira, could not be greater. Whereas an epic bard might have, in his own stereotyping voice, described Heracles' wife as "the gentle Deianira," the "long-suffering Deianira," or the like, Sophocles the playwright portrays the character through the qualities of her speech. Her meekness and lack of self-confidence are conveyed through her characteristic use of qualifications, a kind of continual verbal self-subversion: "Zeus of the contests made the end good—if it has been good" (*The Women of Trachis* 25–26); "For here I have taken on a girl—no, I can think that no longer—a married woman" (536–37); "Well, the move is made, unless you think I am acting rashly. If so I will stop" (586–87). She speaks with the unfocused wordiness of a young girl, with full self-disclosure, as if she were always aware of being answerable to someone else, of having to prove that she has been a good girl: "I do not speak of the manner of their struggles for I do not know. Someone who watched the spectacle unafraid could tell" (21–23); "Something has happened which, if I tell you, my friends, will seem a marvel such as you never thought to hear. . . . I want to tell you this in detail, so you may know the whole story" (672–79); "I neglected none of the instructions that the beast the centaur explained to me. . . . And I did only what I was told to do" (680–81); "And this is what I did" (688); ". . . as you saw" (692). Her many uses of the words "house" and "home," her tags of endearments ("dear friends," "my friends," "dear women," "O kindest of men") and easy resort to clichéd truisms (1–3, 92–93, 548–49) mark her speech with its distinctively sweet, trusting, domestic flavor, and contrast it with the speech of others. Or consider the language of Creon, with its heavy reliance on metaphors and images of control: Antigone is a horse to be broken (*Antigone* 522–23), his citizens growling animals who must be brought under the yoke (324); tongues must be kept under lock and key (200). People are described by him as animals and objects: Ismene is a viper (531), Polynices a meal for birds and dogs (207), Antigone a furrow for Haemon's plow (569). He is every inch the tyrant, and his distrustful, advantage-seeking nature manifests itself in an overwhelming number of profit, monetary, and bribery images (325–34, 343–46, 361, 1094–95, 1096, 1107, 1118, 1127, 1130). This high level of speech particularization, carried out with such consistency throughout a work, is unthinkable without the aid of writing. Oral composition cannot help but flatten out and homogenize the representation of individual figures' speech—and this regardless of the poet's own sensitivity and artistic genius, which in Homer's case were immense.

Individualized speech is manifested equally in tragedy and comedy, and was to remain a distinguishing characteristic of the dramatic genres throughout history. As we saw earlier, the alphabet's special relation to spoken language is evidenced especially in the ease with which it can represent even foreign, incoherent, or otherwise semantically opaque language. Exploiting the abilities of his writing system, Thomas Dekker would carry on the dramatic tradition by representing the sounds of Dutch speech (*The Shoemaker's Holiday*); Shakespeare would do the same for the sounds of French speech (*Henry V*). Earlier in the tradition, we find Aristophanes using the alphabet for inscribing the incoherent jargon of Persians (*Acharnians*),[86] and recording the imaginary dialect of frogs in his comedy of that name. In Euripides' *Orestes,* the alphabet proves its elasticity in transcribing foreign "babble" at length, as translated here into an equivalent mangling of English:

> Greekish sword—kill dead!
> Trojan scared, oh.
> Run, run.
> Jump in slippers, fast, fast,
> clop-clop clamber over roof
> Hole in beams, inside court,
> jump down
> *boom!*
> below.
> Oh, oh,
> Where can run, where go?
> Mebbe foreign ladies know?
> Up, up,
> Soar in air, him shimmer nothing?
> Swim in sea—mebbe? mebbe?—
> Where godbull ocean cradles world
> flowing water with?
> (1368–79)

As a final example of the subtlety and particularity of speech representation that could be attained by a poet who had learned his ABCs, we might look at the sentry's speech to Creon in *Antigone*. David Grene, who translated it, remarked on a number of features which may not be obvious to a reader of the English version: "He speaks with marked clumsiness ... the royal presence makes him think apparently that he should be rather

---

86. See the Athenian Society text (1931 1:106) for an English rendering of this foreign babble.

grand. . . . He uses odd bits of archaism or somewhat stale poetical passages, particularly in catch phrases" (1991:169). Here is the speech:

> My lord, I will never claim my shortness of breath
> is due to hurrying, nor were there wings on my feet.
> I stopped at many a lay-by in my thinking;
> I circled myself till I met myself coming back.
> My soul accosted me with different speeches.
> "Poor fool, yourself, why are you going somewhere
> When once you get there you will pay the piper?"
> "Well, aren't you the darling fellow! Stopping again?
> and suppose Creon hears the news from someone else—
> don't you realize you will smart for that?"
> I turned the whole matter over. I suppose I may say
> "I made haste slowly" and the short road became long . . . (242–53).

This speech—pompous, apologetic, and endlessly digressing—continues in this vein until Creon finally shouts, "For god's sake, tell me and get out of here!" (267).

As even these perfunctory examples should attest, the use of a written alphabet—for breaking up words and putting them back together in new ways, for catching exact rhythms and idiosyncratic constructions, for combining different styles and meters in the same work and maintaining the integrity of each—gave the poet a device for recording speech with vastly more individuality than was formerly possible. Unencumbered by the formulaic, mnemonic demands of oral recitation, the dramatic writer could, with the help of this new technological "ear" of speech, record human discourse with a freedom not to be matched until the invention of the wax cylinder.

This shift from the mnemonically oriented formulaic language of epic to a dramatic language of fixed, individualized vernacular speech did not happen all at once, of course. The grand hexameters of Homeric diction remained widely in use in lyric composition throughout the seventh and sixth centuries. Even between the heroic Aeschylus and the "bookish" Euripides one can see an ongoing movement, with the advance of literacy, away from the language of stereotype and toward a language of idiosyncratic contemporary speech.

In addition to particularizing their characters' speech far beyond anything that an oral bard could have managed, the early dramatists eliminated a number of other features of Homeric diction. Oral epic, composed as it was of blocks of formulaic utterance which were "stitched together" in performance, could be likened to ordinary speech in one respect. In oral discourse, as Wallace Chafe has shown, speakers tend similarly to stitch together "the relatively brief, relatively independent idea units" of their thought with the help of "flow-monitoring devices" such as "you know," "so," "anyway," "so I said," and so on (1985:12). In lengthy oral recitations of modern works such as the African "Bagre" (Goody 1987:79, 168) or the Canadian aboriginal story of "The Girl Who Married the Bear" (Petrone 1990:12), we find evidence for the universality of this method of composition in oral storytelling. By contrast, a composition that has been put together at leisure, in a spatiotemporal context *not* inhabited by a listening audience, has no need of these flow-monitoring devices; and indeed no direct references to "you," to the listener, can be found in any of the tragic texts that have come down to us (Taplin 1977:131).[87]

The elimination of vocatives to the audience is just one of the changes to composition that followed from the dramatists' use of the written medium. Because it both freed language from the demands of memory and arrested its course in visible space, writing also stretched its users' control over it. A writer can manipulate longer units than a speaker can, and indulge in more complex, multidimensional functions. The increased length of the units of language that the poet can master with the help of writing can be seen, first, at the level of the sentence: subordinate and relative clauses barely exist at all in Homer but flourish in the writings of the classic dramatists (Kalmár 1985:157). Increased complexity can also be seen at the level of the story as a whole. In oral composition, stories "are built up largely from self-contained episodes," and themes are abandoned after they have served their purpose in the individual locales (Bowra 1969:50–51). As a result, both the *Iliad* and the *Odyssey* contain what C. M. Bowra describes as "real contradictions" from episode to episode (1969:51). When it becomes possible to see the beginning, middle, and end of a composition simultaneously, however, the concept of an organic, unified structure comes into existence. Aristotle speaks of a poem as an animal whose head, body, and tail the eye takes in at once—a statement that could never have been made of poetry before the use of writing (*Poetics* 1451a). Nor, in an oral milieu, could one speak of a poetic composition as a visible design or "painting," a trope Aristotle also resorts to in describing tragic composition (1450b). But when all elements of a plot are set down on paper, the relationships among them

87. The situation is obviously different in Old Comedy, in which the chorus addresses the audience directly. See, for example, the *parabasis* of Aristophanes' *Frogs,* ll. 674–737.

can become apparent, visible at a glance (Ong 1982:148). In preliterate epic, language is confined to the "winged words" of oral speech; its parts must follow and actually replace one another in time. It is only when put in visible space that they can be co-present and available for comparison. With written texts come poetic questions of thematic and verbal consistency, and of relationships between part and whole.

From the appearance in their texts of an exact, continuous line of Homeric verse,[88] we can be fairly certain that the tragedians had before them a written copy of the epics (Pfeiffer 1968:111). As the first genre to benefit from the preexistence of stories that did not inhere in a particular speaker or in any live performative context, drama was also the first Western verbal art to be composed "as a self-contained, discrete unit, defined by closure" (Ong 1982:148)—that is, to exhibit a unified, non-episodic structure. As Charles Segal has stressed, the "deferred relation" between literate storytelling and audience reception also permits the composition to be worked on, in private, over time, and to be edited, corrected, reorganized, and constructed throughout with the tightness and thematic consistency that we associate with the works of all the fifth-century dramatists (1986:77). Examples of this feature of dramatic form are perhaps not necessary; but if we compare, with Aristotle, the unity of the *Oedipus* with the "several separate actions" that make up the epics, we cannot but be impressed with the extent to which the ability to see the whole plot at a glance enabled the dramatists to unify and concentrate their stories beyond anything that could have been achieved by an extemporizing bard (*Poetics* 1462b9–15).

Not only did relationships between the elements of a story become visible to Homer's literate followers, but also these same elements started to be viewed as possessing relationships that were not confined to their narratological function. As I noted earlier, alphabetical script sunders the palpable connection that exists in speech between word and meaning, between the signifier (the word "tree"), and the signified that it refers to in reality (the class of organic entities with roots, trunk, and leaves). Gerd Baumann (1986) maintains that in an oral culture, words represent the world indexically: to define the meaning of a word, one simply points to the object or state of affairs. Because orally dependent language must always be "sponsored" language (R. Harris 1989:100ff.) that is, sponsored by some speaker, language in a preliterate environment will always be embedded in some concrete context of actual use, engaged in an indexical pointing-to-the-world. But within the

---

88. Pfeiffer 1968 cites *Antigone* 29–30, *Hecuba* 1078, *Suppliants* 800f., and *Ion* 504f.

second-order symbolic system of writing, words begin to refer to other words within the system, to define one another outside of their indicating function. By becoming a static, visible object for sight—a "thing" to look at—language loses the illusion it has in speech of being a transparent referential medium. Writing distances words from their relation with reality and brings their relationships to one another into consciousness.

What results is a new awareness of a systematic dimension of language, of the fact that words define other words arbitrarily in addition to defining the world referentially. In culture generally, this abstracted view of language has been credited with the birth of abstract philosophy and of linguistic studies. But it was also one of the central driving forces at work in the new genre of drama, tragedy especially. In the dramatic rewriting of Greek mythic material, we find a "problematic of the signifier" which is noticeably absent by comparison in the epic versions. When the warriors of epic speech are said to be "god-supported" or "worthy of honor," these words refer unproblematically to the aid of the gods and the battle renown of fighting mortals which constitute the stuff of heroic legend. In the dramas, however, characters use words that are explicitly ambiguous; the same word means one thing to one speaker, something else entirely to another. In tragic speech, words have lost their Homeric transparency of meaning and have become question marks that must be negotiated within the linguistic system itself. Accordingly, the number of words and concepts in drama which are semantically uncertain, intentionally ambiguous, is notably high. In the *Oedipus* alone, there are fifty words whose meanings are made problematic;[89] and although few dramas can lay claim to that statistic, all are marked by an actively questioning attitude to the meaning of words.[90] What *is* honor? A convention of war or a virtue in itself? If a virtue, what kind? What is "love?" What are the different kinds? Does the word "love" contain within it certain inherent contradictions—a love of family bound to conflict with a love for the polis? And what of "polis"? What is its relationship with smaller units? With the nonhuman realm? What is "law?" Is it the opposite of "nature," or do the two words have some other relationship than as simple contraries? Words in drama have been unmoored from a certain and stable relationship with extraverbal reality and have instead become objects in their own right, objects whose limits, powers, and peculiarities as meaning-generating entities can be explored.

89. J. P. Vernant 1978:175 refers to the number collected by Arnold Hug.
90. Vernant analyzes occurrences and types of ambiguity in the *Agamemnon* and *Antigone* (1978:175–76).

This distancing of speech from speakers, which theorists today commonly call alienation, has determined the form and function of drama in a number of ways, some of which we shall explore in Chapter 4. For the moment I will only point out that alienation does not so much introduce new features into language use as it makes old ones apparent and available for conscious reflection. To alienate language through writing is simply to *see* linguistic mechanisms that were invisible previously. Words *do* define one another systematically, and always have; but contextually embedded speech gives them the *illusion* of referring directly to the world of our experience. Like Brecht's decision to let the lighting apparatus of the stage be seen by the audience, writing's alienation of language simply shows what was always there in speech, but which the directness and diaphanousness of spoken language tended to disguise.[91]

Evidence of this new problematic of language spawned by writing can be seen in nearly all fifth-century drama. The conflict in *Antigone* stems directly from mutually incompatible definitions of law and duty. No single and certain referent for *nomos* (law, custom) is attainable; the word has become an abstract problem for analysis.[92] The same can be said of *kratos* (might, power, rule) in the *Suppliants,* of *omma* and *phainesthai* (eye, to make visible, bring to light) in the *Women of Trachis,* of *dike* (justice) throughout the *Oresteia,* and *sophia* (wisdom) in the *Bacchai,* or of the semantic relationship between *eidos* (that which is seen, known) and *agnoia* (want of perception, ignorance) in the *Oedipus.*[93] As Jean-Pierre Vernant and Pierre Vidal-Naquet observe, this linguistic indeterminacy marks a profound shift from the "stable realities" of earlier forms, and defines the particular character of dramatic language (1990:186, 38–64).

The abstract, analytical relationship to mythic material that we find in the dramatic rewritings of it stems from the fact that the eye had begun to take over many of the functions once performed exclusively by the ear. A linguistic record of experience, previously communicated from mouth to ear in the form of myths, elders' maxims, and ritual recitations, could now be made in "visual space" instead: on stone, pottery, animal skin, papyrus, or even, as at Delphi, on the surface of a bean. And as early as the sixth century, as Frances Yates implies, this technique for encoding information in visual space had been internalized, providing a model for representation in "mental" or imaginary space as well. In *The Art of Memory,* Yates points out

---

91. This aspect of writing in its relation to speech is described with uncharacteristic lucidity by Derrida in *Speech and Phenomena* (1973).

92. Vernant adds *dike, philos* and *philia, kerdos, time, orge,* and *deinos* to the list of problematic words in the *Antigone* (1978:495 n. 5).

93. Discussion of some of these terms can be found in Seale 1982:211 n. 3.

that, by Simonides' time in Greece, memory had become associated not with the sounds of words, but with the visualization of fixed images (1966:1ff.). In an oral context, as witnessed by the *Iliad* (3.250–325), events are remembered and described through the order in which people speak; memory has the paratactic structure of oral syntax ("and then . . . and then . . . and then"). By Simonides' time, however, things are being remembered through their physical disposition in space.[94] Rather than being associated with a temporal sound sequence, memory is experienced in terms of simultaneous spatial arrangement—a habit of thought that would, of course, be encouraged by the ability of writing to subordinate clauses, hold related concepts in view simultaneously, and arrange them. As Havelock, Ong, de Kerckhove, and Segal have argued, this shift from sound to sight, from a mental soundscape to a visible landscape or "scene," is modeled on the example set by the existence of visible written records. It is a shift for which the tragic texts and fragments provide direct evidence in their many references to memory as a writing on the mind.[95]

We also find evidence of this "hypervisualized noetic world" (Ong 1982:127) somewhat later in Platonic philosophy. Continually exhorting his interlocutors and readers to imagine visual images of "ideas" which have an eternal (i.e., non–temporally linked) "form," Plato actively reflects this literate shift from temporal "hearing" to spatial, static "viewing." The mode whereby knowledge was received and disseminated had shifted from remembering what one heard to "seeing" the truth. In Plato's intellectual "scenes," such as the Cave of Book 10 of *Republic,* no less than in the fifth-century practices of theatregoing and reading itself, we see evidence of a move to visualization. And by Aristotle's time, memory is directly equated with the order of letters in the alphabet (*On Memory and Reminiscence* 452b16–25).[96] Theatre's emergence at a time when this shift from sound to sight was under way cannot be a mere coincidence. Nor is it likely to be coincidental that the most elaborate of the memory systems that developed out of Simonides' technique were to take the form of "Memory Theatres."[97]

94. Instead of recollecting the events at a banquet by saying which guests spoke in what order, as Homer would have done, Simonides reconstructs the event by saying where everyone was located in the room (Yates 1966:1).

95. Pfeiffer provides a useful list of the relevant passages in plays and fragments (1968:26 and notes).

96. See Yates 1966:35.

97. In de Kerckhove's view, Simonides "may have been the first Greek thinker to conceptualize the interiorization of visible space" and imagine memory as "a container, a mental box to store and classify representations and abstractions" (1981:32). See the Memory Theatres of Giulio Camillo and Robert Fludd as reproduced and discussed by Yates 1966:129–72, 320–67.

This heightened emphasis on the visual manifested itself in Thespis' time in a preference for *seeing* a story rather than simply *hearing* it narrated by a bard. This generic shift, between the aurality of epic and the visibility of the new theatrical forms, is given unmistakable expression by one of Euripides' characters in *Iphigenia among the Taurians:*

> I have heard marvelous tales from story-tellers,
> But nothing to compare
> With this event which my own eyes have seen.
> (900–903)

In preliterate storytelling, it was in the acoustic chain of sung or spoken incidents that a plot inhered. Despite the musical, instrumental, performative *mode* of epic recitation, a performing bard's stories were verbally given, temporally arranged, and taken in by the ears. With the advent of theatrical form, a story came to be something that one sees. These words from *Iphigenia among the Taurians* are spoken immediately after a discussion about the nature of writing, and are delivered to a group of characters who are themselves lettered. But the passage is also "addressed" to Euripides' theatrical audience. In juxtaposing the hearing of tales from storytellers with the seeing of an event with one's own eyes, Euripides is undoubtedly making a metatheatrical statement about the virtues of his chosen genre. That storytelling had, by Euripides' time, come to be associated with sight rather than sound is also reflected in Aristotle's later writings on poetics. Indicative of a notable departure from oral compositional methods, Aristotle advises the aspiring playwright to "keep the scene before his eyes" while writing (*Poetics* 1455a14ff.). As Aristotle explains, physical impossibilities and visual contradictions are "not noticed" in epic because "we do not actually see the persons of the story" (1460a15–17). The dramatist, on the contrary, must concern himself with moving speakers around visibly before the audience's eyes; he cannot simply dispense with a character once he finishes speaking, as the epic singers did.[98]

This shift from oral hearing to literate seeing has been studied for medieval Europe as well. Through his work on the period between 1066 and 1307, M. T. Clanchy (1979) has found that the spread of literacy in Europe had consequences for communication practices which were strikingly analogous to those that took place in Greece between the turn of the millennium and the classic age of Athens. Whereas preliterate Europeans would custom-

---

98. See Bowra 1969:50 on the "real contradictions" that are possible and inevitable in oral compositional methods.

arily have remembered a dying man's last will and testament by having "heard" it themselves at his bedside, they began to remember having "seen" a seal placed on a document, and to consider this as evidence for the genuineness of the will (203). The technological effect of writing on wills, knowledge, stories, and other information is thus to make them all, for the first time, objects for the eye rather than for the ear exclusively.[99] And once the possibility existed of making what was formerly only "heard" actually "visible," the Greeks were liable to have jumped at the chance: from the Archaic into the classical period, Greek usage records a highly valued distinction between hearing and sight. What was "heard [from another]" had the value of mere "hearsay"; what one saw with one's "own eyes" was more worthy of trust.[100] For this reason, it comes as no surprise to learn that drama was the most "people-pleasing" genre of poetry in antiquity; for in the words of one member of the ancient theatre audience, drama meant that Homer's stories could at last be not "merely heard, but also seen" (Herington 1985:103–4).[101]

In addition to making things visible, the evidence of letters will also tend to reveal the difference between myth and history, and to bring the category of fiction into existence for the first time. Especially from the Platonic texts, it is clear that the Homeric poems had customarily been expected to provide more than just pleasure and a disinterested sort of edification. On the contrary, in Havelock's words, they were viewed as a "vast encyclopedia" (1986:79). They were seen as handbooks for proper conduct, or *paideia,* since time immemorial, storehouses of true statements about men and the gods.[102] But in functioning as a continuous series of factual historical and ethical exempla, the epics perpetuated a situation in which the lines between history and myth were blurred.[103] This was because an oral culture's lack of

99. The emphasis here is on the word "exclusively," since reliance on acoustic evidence did not by any means disappear altogether. See Thomas 1989, 1992 for Greek evidence about the continued reliance on oral modes.

100. *Odyssey* 3.93–95; *Oedipus* 105; Herodotus 2.99, 147, 156; Thucydides 1.20.1, 73.2; 6.53.3, 60.1; cf. Thomas 1989:3 n. 3; Segal 1986:86.

101. It is interesting to note that this relationship between newfound literacy and theatrical representation is evident also in the emergence of aboriginal theatre in Canada. The use made by Native poets of actors and theatrical form, starting in the 1970s, has been described by one expert as "giv[ing] the oral tradition a *three-dimensional* context" (Petrone 1990:180).

102. Xenophanes frag. 10 (Lesher 1992); Jaeger 1960:35–56; Robb 1994:67.

103. The same point has been made for other oral cultures as well. In Canadian aboriginal society, for example, oral myths and legends and folk tales were not experienced as fictional. On the contrary, they functioned as indispensable repositories of cultural values

"hard copy" compels it to satisfy its need for the conservation of information by means of a medium that is by nature prone to continual change. As an inevitable result, an event such as the Flood, or the Sack of Troy, will enter the realm of myth nearly as soon as it occurs—that is, at the very moment of its entry into the unstable medium of oral tradition. As Rosalind Thomas has shown for family and state history as perpetuated in Greece (1989), factual material told and retold orally becomes very distorted. With no written account to refer to, even genuine memories of real events get "simplified" by oral modes of transmission. Acquiring "conventional or idealized elements, clichés and stereotyped form," they are gradually transformed into legendary material that bears "slight relation to the original material" (284). These falsifications are cumulative, and thus the telescoping, distortion, and simplification of oral transmission is "irreversible" (284). Anachronism is common, as is the tendency to endow events with a more "colourful" narrative character than they really possessed (285). The past is commonly altered to fit in with present values and beliefs, and whole blocks of history disappear altogether. Although such distortions are occasionally deliberate, in general they are a function of the mode of communication itself (284). Above all, it is exaggeration that is responsible in oral record keeping for turning historical fact into what Thomas calls "a timeless catalogue of heroic deeds"—in short, into myth (232).

Goody (1986, 1987) and Ong (1977, 1982) have found that this tendency toward the narrativization of experience is a feature common to all oral milieus, and it is easy to see why. Not until a fixed record, such as that of a Thucydides, can exist, will true history be able to detach itself from oral lore. As William V. Harris points out, Thucydides included actual transcriptions of key texts, and thus was able to separate history from the mythologizing tendencies of oral history, tendencies that are still very much present even in the work of Herodotus, who was content to record and accept as fact "what was said" (1989:80).[104] Thucydides, however, explicitly and repeatedly ridicules those who believe everything they hear, and proudly advertises himself, by way of contrast with such mythographers, as a contemporary of and eyewitness to many of the events he recounts. Moreover, because he was writing, he did not have to rely on the stylizations

---

and teachings (Petrone 1990:10). Songs and stories served as applied science, historical record, and religious practice all rolled into one: certain songs were used to heal the sick, others to attract animals, others to strengthen the hunter (10–19, 121). When Petrone lists the genres unknown in native Canadian culture before contact with writing, she tellingly names "fiction" along with drama (183).

104. The same point is made by Thomas 1992:112.

that had been the oral singer's only cure for forgetting.[105] In Thucydides, as Harris puts it, the logic of performance and invention was replaced by the logic of writing and documents (80), and history is differentiated from storytelling as a special kind of activity with its own rules and procedures.[106]

Writing for this reason has been credited with the emergence not only of historiography but also of fiction, as distinct, intentional activities separable from mythic recitation (Segal 1986:90). For as soon as a difference between tradition and truth can become perceptible, fiction can emerge as a distinct way of speaking about the world or the past. In Theagenes' sixth-century defence of Homer on allegorical grounds, we see the first awareness of this category of fiction in Greece: as Theagenes argued, a story may have value *even though* it is not literally true. And by Kallias' time, storytelling had detached itself so far from the record-keeping function of epic poetry that a play could be written about something as patently fictional as talking letters.

To Aristotle, in whose time literacy was much more deeply entrenched, the distinction between fiction and history was fairly obvious (*Poetics* 1451bf.). In the *Poetics* we see him drawing boundaries between such specialist disciplines, distinguishing poetry from history and history from philosophy. The category of fiction, of a poetic making which is altogether free from the record-keeping function of oral epic, was also securely established by this time, as we see from Aristotle's reference to the fact that, like Kallias, some dramatists make up their stories from scratch (1451b19–26).

In what Bowra calls "the strict tradition" of epic recitation, "any manifestation of individual idiosyncrasies" is usually rejected (1969:56).[107] But

---

105. These mnemotechnical stylizations included conventional formulas and epithets, parallel structures, regular meter, and exaggeration. Now, the memorable qualities of a statement such as "In fourteen-hundred and ninety-two, Columbus sailed the ocean blue" do not, it is true, seem to interfere with the historical accuracy of the saying. But in the recording of more complex and detailed historical verities, conventionality and exaggeration will seem to have their way. As proof of this, we need only remember the mythical qualities of Homer's telling of the events surrounding the Trojan War. So thoroughly did history become myth through oral transmission that scholars before Schliemann did not believe that there was any historical truth behind Homer's tales of Mycenae (see Chadwick 1990:6).

106. As Gordon Shrimpton (1997) has shown, however, Thucydides organized his history according to a seasonal principle in order to facilitate memorization, and thus still assumed that his readers read as a prelude to memorizing, not as a substitute.

107. Finnegan 1977 and Thomas 1992 stress that oral singers do tend to embellish stories and stamp them with their own style; deliberately changing meanings, however, is impermissible.

once the conservative function of storytelling was obviated by the existence of writing, "variation came to be accepted for its own sake" (Kirk 1985:103), a change that would further reinforce the emergence of fiction as a distinct linguistic category. Speaking about the "fresh meanings" introduced into traditional material by Aeschylus, Sophocles, and Euripides, G. S. Kirk says that "such drastic . . . reinterpretations usually presuppose a literate culture, both in Greece and elsewhere" (1985:109). For as long as stories function as collective memory, writes Albert Bates Lord, deliberate changes in the telling of them would be counterproductive, even dangerous to the survival of the tradition: oral bards accordingly always look on innovative interpretations or alterations as "wrong or awkward, or . . . a 'mistake' " (Lord 1960:130).[108] As Lord goes on to suggest, it is only in a literate context that conscious changes and departures are felt to be "right" and desirable (130). Thus, in what must have seemed a radical departure from the long-established rules of storytelling, the dramatists began to change the epic stories to suit their own personal intentions. In his fourth-century guide to the practice of playwriting, Aristotle confirms that the rules of poetry had changed in precisely this way: he says not that the dramatist "may," but that the dramatic poet "*must* show invention" in his use of the tradition (1453b11; my italics). The innovative, and in some places downright subversive, character of the tragedians' treatment of epic material can thus be attributed to a great extent to the freedom given them by a written version of traditional material: they were free to alter and criticize as much as they wanted without imperiling the survival of the tradition itself.

As a particularly powerful symbol of this new literate concern with narrative novelty, competition in drama, unlike rhapsodic contest, demanded the creation of large quantities of brand new poems, year after year. The oral poet must conserve; the literate poet, as Aristotle nagged, must show invention; he must offer his audience something *new*. And the very structure of the theatre festival, where original plays were expected every year, reflects this literate freedom from conservation, this freedom to change, innovate, rewrite stories of the past, even to invent new ones that have nothing to do with conservation at all.

Had the dramatists confined their innovations in storytelling to their irreverent handling of tradition, however, their art, while certainly much altered from oral epic, would not have differed from it in more than content.

108. Finnegan 1990:247 makes the same point.

Instead, they changed the mode of performance, too, and in so doing created an art that departed from its antecedent along fundamental generic lines.

The shift from a narrative to a dramatic mode was made by Thespis through his introduction of the mask. This was a radical innovation, and it must have left no doubt in the minds of sixth-century audiences that a new type of storytelling was being introduced. For masks had never been used in any epic or lyric performance up until that time; before Thespis, all narrative performance had been delivered *in propria persona*. Neither epic reciters nor dithyrambic choral singers wore masks, for neither had any need of disguise. Predramatic singers always spoke as themselves: as revelers, worshippers, inspired bards, or members of a competing tribe.[109] Thespis' radical departure from traditional poetic practice was so notable, in fact, that classicists were once at a loss to explain it. Some, like Jane Ellen Harrison, looked outside poetry to the sphere of religion, hoping to find in the common ritual use of animal and god masks an explanation or source for Thespis' unprecedented move toward corporeal impersonation (1991:568).[110] But the true explanation is both more obvious and more mundane. Thespis needed a mask for purely practical reasons, since storytellers had never before attempted what he was about to attempt: the telling of a story not through *propria persona* narration, but through *visual representation*.

It should be noted that even the predramatic rhapsode was expected to be something of an impersonator. From the *Ion* (530cff.) and from Aristotle (*Poetics* 1462a6–7), we know that Homer's reciters typically got carried away with the representation of their fictional characters' speeches, and were as apt to overdo their gestures in the process as actors. When rhapsodes such as Ion recited sections of the *Iliad* and the *Odyssey* at the Panathenaia, they, like actors, wore special costumes and impersonated the speech of their fictional characters. In fact, as John Herington has shown with a number of ancient sources, a good deal of what we have come to think of as "histrionic technique" had already been worked out by the rhapsodes of the sixth century (1985:7–13). Because of their impersonations, and because their perfor-

---

109. Flickinger 1973:10–11; Pickard-Cambridge 1962:50; Vernant and Vidal-Naquet 1990:23–24.

110. Harrison was of course a student of religion, not theatre, so her misguided efforts are understandable. By her own admission, Harrison was interested neither in art nor in theatre (Peacock 1991:173). She was similarly unapologetic about what she called her "dislike for history" (Schlesier 1991:201). Her "ritual hypothesis," that drama took its rise from orgiastic religious practices, has been discredited. See esp. Pickard-Cambridge 1962:189; Else 1965b:7; Vickers 1973:33ff.; Kirk 1985:223ff.

mances consisted of interpretations of poetic texts (*Ion* 530c3–4), Herington is justified to some extent in considering the actor's art a continuation of, rather than a radical break with, earlier genres of poetic performance.[111] But he is justified only to a certain extent, for there is a generic leap between merely reporting the various characters' speeches, as the rhapsode did, and actually pretending to stand in for one of them visually, as the actor came to do. The rhapsode did not change his identity or appearance: he always performed visually "as" himself, a rhapsode, merely telling his audience, with appropriate gestures, what other fictional figures said.

In drama however, and for the first time in poetry in Greece, the performer now pretended to have traded his own identity for the identity of a fictional figure. And because the direct physical representation of fictional characters was unprecedented in his time, Thespis had to think of something to show unequivocally that his performers were not mere rhapsodes, narrating the story, but were rather a new poetic species, performers whose own appearances and identities were to be ignored in favor of whatever visual illusion they might create of representing Homer's Achilleus, or Odysseus, or Clytaemestra, Medea, or Ajax. So Thespis experimented, first using white lead as a disguise, then flowers; but evidently these were not adequate, and he settled on a plain linen mask as a sign to the audience that they should focus not on the performer's own face or persona but instead imagine someone else's in its place.[112]

Thespis' experiments with disguise and eventual settling upon the mask were therefore probably a case of necessity being the mother of invention: the theatrical performer visually represents something other than himself, so the actor needs a disguising device. Yet it is still not clear how it came to pass that the actor became this kind of performer. Why had Thespis abandoned a narrative style in the first place? Why didn't he retain the *propria persona* voice of the rhapsode and bard?

It is distinctly possible that, having internalized the alphabet's mode of representation, the inventors of drama were able to conceive of an "alphabetical" representational style for performance too: as letters represent, so might the performer. Because it breaks the sounds of speech down into units on the individual or "atomic" level, alphabetical writing has been connected with the trend toward "atomization" in the Western intellectual tra-

111. Havelock makes the same point: "Whether recited and mimed by an epic rhapsodist who himself 'does' all the characters, or split up into parts done by different reciters who became actors," the two types of performance "differed in degree rather than in kind" (1963:48).

112. See Pickard-Cambridge 1968:190 for Thespis' experiments.

dition generally. In science, for example, this trend is visible in the fifth-century writings of Leucippus and Democritus, who conceived of individual "atoms" which "are compounded together and entangled . . . [to] create something" (Aristotle *On Generation and Corruption* 1.7, 325a30ff.).[113] Such thinking clearly reflects the alphabet's procedure of dividing unities into small, mobile units. This breakdown of speech into individual letters has also been associated by some cultural theorists with the breaking down of monolithic social and political structures. As Kristeva sees it, whereas "the ideogrammatical type of writing was often accompanied by a mode of production said to be 'Asian' (large productive and interdependent collectives, managed by a central organization without isolated, urban and 'democratic' . . . units . . .)," alphabetical systems tend to be accompanied by social systems in which the individual is given an autonomy analogous to that afforded to individual letters: "The Greek alphabetical system had as its correlative, on the sociological level, units of production that were isolated and closed on themselves, a development of individual consciousness in ideology, and a logic of non-contradiction in science" (1989:95). In the aesthetic sphere, the same analogy is visible: the "emancipation of the signifier" typical of alphabetical representation is echoed in the emancipation of the narrative figures typical of theatrical representation. Just as the alphabet represents speech by dividing the verbal world into a small number of repeatable visual shapes, or letters, so too does the dramatist proceed by dividing the storytelling world into a number of discrete, visible "characters."

In the *ABC Show* in particular, we see the continuity of activity between inscribing speech in writing and performing stories through the bodies of actors. For in the same way that the letters of the alphabet could be freely used in combination to represent the words of speech, so too were the bodies of actors—or young men singing in the chorus—given over to the task of representing the letters of the alphabet. We recall from my earlier discussion that the novelty of the alphabet was that letters represented sounds arbitrarily, unconnected to any meaning, and that it was this semantic indeterminacy that gave phonetic letters such flexibility in representing speech. Theatrical performers thus function like letters in this respect as well: their freedom from their own identities, or any particular identity, gives them the freedom to represent any other thing. This absolute representational mobility is ultimately what separates the actor from the bard or rhapsode, who remains always Homer or Ion even when he is relating what Achilleus said or did.

113. As translated by Kirk, Raven, and Schofield 1987:407.

The body of the actor, which functions explicitly as an unmotivated "letter" in the *ABC Show,* functions implicitly as an unmotivated sign (for a fictional character) in every other play. Unlike the epic *aoidos,* who sings the Muse's song in his own person, the theatrical performer has the semiotic freedom to stand in for anyone and anything. Whether representing a mythic hero or a contemporary Athenian slave, a god, or a frog, actors, who explicitly represent letters in Kallias' play, are those performers who, like letters, function primarily *by* representing, and have the semiotic freedom to represent potentially any meaning.

In this way, the stage could be said to have absorbed the signifying, alienating practice of writing, for the semiology of phoneticism was transferred from the letters of the alphabet to the bodies of performers on the stage. In theatrical representation, the performer is liberated from the bardic or rhapsodic "as-himself" and endowed with an (arbitrary, alphabetical) "as-anything." In all dramatic literature, there is perhaps no better description of this semiotic freedom than the analysis of the particular "manner" of theatrical "showing" provided by Shakespeare's Launce:

> Nay, I'll *show* you the manner of it. This shoe is my father; no, this left shoe is my father: no, no, this left shoe is my mother; nay, that cannot be so neither:—yes, it is so; it is so; it hath the worser sole. This shoe, with the hole in, is my mother, and this my father . . . this staff is my sister . . . : this hat is Nan, our maid: I am the dog; no, the dog is himself, and I am the dog,—O! the dog is me, and I am myself: ay, so, so.
> (*Two Gentlemen of Verona* 2.3.15–26)

Like Launce's shoes, the actor has the representational freedom to stand in for *anything* on the theatrical stage—even inanimate objects like Kallias' letters. Furthermore, the basic principle of semiotic mobility extends also to objects on the stage, where shoes and hats can stand for parents and maids.

The use of a body as a sign for something else obviously has predramatic precedents; but it is in drama that this basic semiotic activity is exploited consciously and fully for artistic ends. For example, in the *Odyssey* alone there are numerous cases of corporeal impersonation,[114] although it is usually the prerogative of a goddess, Athena, to arrange for someone's disguise (1.105, 2.383, 2.401, 8.8, 13.429–30). Not only does the fictional Odysseus dress up as a beggar as part of his homecoming scheme, but also the historical Solon, we are told, impersonated a mad messenger to deliver a

---

114. These cases of corporeal impersonation were not, of course, aesthetic performances, but rather functional expedients to accomplish a practical goal.

political poem in the marketplace (Else 1965b:41). In addition, the use of the body to represent animals or gods has been seen to accompany religious rituals and dances around the world.[115] As Aristotle suggested (*Poetics* 1448b5ff.), and as contemporary neurobiology confirms,[116] imitative role-playing comes naturally to humans and serves the practical function of adapting us to our cultures and teaching us how things are done in them. Children do it even before they have done much else, and continue to use their bodies to imitate other things throughout their lives. Humans apparently learn by imitation and role-playing, the utilitarian benefits of which always seem to include a measure of inherent pleasurability. So the use of the body and things for representing *other* bodies, things, or states of affairs clearly did not come into existence with the advent of dramatic form (let alone writing). But before theatre, there is no evidence that such role-playing had been fused with storytelling, nor had it emerged as a poetic genre proper. Before writing, storytelling was the province of a single speaker and that speaker's own deictically grounded identity. The various characters represented in his tale were all controlled and motivated by his single identity as composing/performing servant to the Muse. When the appearance of writing fractured this oral unity of composition and performance into two separate activities, the poet emerged as a writer who tells his story through the use of arbitrary signs rather than through his presence. And this semiotic method of storytelling, observable at the stage of poetic composition in the activity of inscription, was extended to the activity of performance as well, with actors rather than letters doing the representing. Arbitrary representation of this kind was not new to life, in other words, but new to the phenomenology of storytelling.

As a further consequence of the dramatist's ability to divide performance up alphabetically, it became possible to delegate storytelling to nonspecialists. In a literate world, performers were suddenly able to memorize a story written from start to finish by someone else, and to do so conceivably overnight, with no apprenticeship whatever. This in itself would have supported the move toward atomization in storytelling. With the contribution of each performer determined in advance and recorded in text, a communal storytelling effort would have become much easier to manage. But most significant of all, the preexistence of the story in written form made it possible for performative power to be delegated to those who had no special skills in improvisation or oral-formulaic technique. Once scripts exist, paradoxically

---

115. Hsu 1985:196–208; Lévi-Strauss 1982; Petrone 1990:17; Beck 1993.
116. See esp. Finkel 1988:66.

enough, the performer does not even need to know how to read (although it helps), because the fixity and repeatability of a written text makes rote memorization possible even for those who must learn their parts with help from another reader.[117] And so it is not insignificant that the earliest Greek actors were amateurs: in a notable departure from epic practice, actors had no specialized skills, nor were they in possession of a specially monopolized traditional style. Although actors' guilds and clubs, schools and techniques, were eventually to emerge and a "histrionic tradition" eventually to appear (and sometimes be passed on within families), none of these existed in the early days of dramatic performance (Slater 1990:385ff.).

This de-specialization of performance is fundamental to the representational style of the theatre, and has remained a distinguishing characteristic of dramatic performance to this day. For, in the final analysis, all the "methods" and theatrical families in existence cannot outweigh one fact: that more plays are enacted by amateurs than professionals. Whether in school plays or church plays or plays performed at home or at some local community center (Brownies, summer camp, Boys' and Girls' Clubs, and so on), ordinary citizens participate in thousands of theatrical performances every year throughout the Western world. Even individuals who have never set foot in a professional theatre are likely to have performed some part, in some play, at some time.

The liberation of the performer from the need to belong to an exclusive sect or special caste was achieved through the detachment of performative material from the body and physical memory of the initiate. Before writing, traditional stories existed solely within the mind and personal performance of culturally sanctioned specialists. Within the newly literate world, these songs now existed "on the outside," where they could be picked up and performed by "anybody." That this democratizing alienation of mythological material represented an alarmingly new state of affairs, at least to some observers, can be seen in Plato's *Ion*. Here the philosopher raises his concerns about the propriety of performances of important traditional material by those who had no legitimate or obviously special claims on it. Because Ion was just an "anybody" with a script,[118] Plato cast doubt on his legitimacy by

117. This is an important point, for it suggests that not all participants in a literate theatre would necessarily need to be skilled readers, or even literate themselves. See W. Harris 1989 for very conservative estimates of the number of readers in the various Greek periods.

118. Ion was clearly a very talented reciter of Homeric epics, so he was not just "anybody" in that sense. Plato's objections revolve rather around the fact that Ion was demonstrably not an expert in anything other than the memorization of another man's words. For evidence that rhapsodes like Ion used written texts, see Xenophon *Memorabilia* 4.2, 10; Sandys 1958:30; and Thomas 1992:119.

saying that he had neither sufficiently specialized *episteme* nor authentic *techne,* neither knowledge nor craft. What rhapsodes like Ion inaugurated by performing material that did not belong exclusively and properly to them, actors developed even further.

It is worth noting that Plato's resistance to amateurism in public performance cannot be wholly attributed to his particular philosophical outlook. Wherever performance has traditionally been the preserve of specialists, the figure of the actor, every inch the amateur, is bound to be welcomed onto the storytelling scene with all the warmth extended to the parvenu at the yacht club. As we see in Europe some centuries later, this was precisely what did happen when the popularity of amateur plays began to challenge the privileges of the professional minstrel. The monopoly on storytelling previously enjoyed by the minstrels was in fact so seriously threatened by the script-bearing amateur actor that the minstrels tried to have amateurs prohibited from giving performances (Child 1912:8). The ability of written stories to take storytelling out of the hands of a specialized group is thus attested both in antiquity and in the early days of secular drama in Europe.

But there is an additional issue here: in a theatrical performance, the story is not merely detached from the body of the tradition's proper representative, the *aoidos* or minstrel. It is detached also from the body of *any* single performer. In contrast to both bardic and rhapsodic performances, the story in a dramatic presentation is shared among a number of separate performers. As Niall Slater points out, it is when the story can no longer be told by the single body of any one performer (specialist or otherwise) that the actor is born (1990:385). Rather than embodying in himself the locus and control center of a single unified poetic monologue, as did the bard or rhapsode, the performer in drama becomes, like a letter, an atomized element in a larger semiotic structure, a systematic collective.[119]

Returning to Kallias' grammatical theory, we can now see the natural affinity of the actor for the alphabet, and vice versa. Instead of creating meaning for an audience through who he *is*—an *aoidos* inspired by the Muse of memory, or a rhapsode inspired by the memory of the *aoidos*—the actor creates meaning through whom or what he can arbitrarily *represent:* a

119. Gordon Shrimpton has suggested in conversation that the nature of rhapsodic competition may *itself* have suggested a dramatic style. Indeed, the sixth-century rule about sequential recitation determined that each competing rhapsode would, in effect, have been cooperating in telling a bigger story, and thus would have functioned as an actor in this respect—or in any case would have had a performative experience akin to the systematic storytelling of theatre. This is an intriguing possibility that had not occurred to me. Nevertheless, the contest rule that would have inaugurated this practice—the demand for sequential recitation of a "single" story by separate reciters—was itself a product of a literate approach to storytelling, as we saw earlier in this chapter.

Trojan woman, a cloud, the letter *O*. But the use of writing for poetic composition had also created a situation in which the story to be told no longer
inhered within the performer's body and his specialist technique. Instead, it
existed in a written version, a fixed, external form, separate from any particular performance technique. Although this disconnectedness from technique meant that a written story could be learned easily by anyone, it *did*
have to be learned—from scratch—because the literate demand for "invention" in storytelling meant that each story now had to be a *new* one. Unlike
the specializing bard, who was a bard precisely by virtue of the fact that he
already knew how to tell all the old stories, the amateur actor was the performer called upon to learn all the new ones. The actor's part had to be
"taught" to him, and new ones were taught each year.[120] And so it is altogether fitting that, in the *ABC Show*, the actors should be cast in the role of
students.

The alphabetical division of the story into separate characters determined that the poet could no longer tell it by himself; but the literate bias in
favor of originality guaranteed that no performer already knew it. The poet
now needed actors; but actors needed the poet's instructions. For this reason
the playwright was called *didaskalos,* the teacher of his poems, for his original stories could be properly told only by being taught to performers who
would not otherwise have known what to say or do.[121] In this way did the
alphabet bring the actor into existence and determine that he would be a
species of performer new to Greece: the grammar student, the memorizer of
text.

120. See Taplin 1977:12–14; also *Frogs* 1249ff.; *Birds* 749.
121. Taplin 1977:13; also *Thesmophoriazusae* 30, 88, and *Frogs* 1021.

CHAPTER 2

The Student Body

Yes, my dear, when you have first shown me
what it is you have in your left hand, under
your cloak. For I suspect you have the actual
text.   Plato

The abdomen is the reason why man does not
easily take himself for a god.
                                                   Nietzsche

O NE FINE DAY IN FIFTH-CENTURY ATHENS, OUTSIDE THE THEATRE OF
   Dionysus, the great philosophy teacher Socrates was delivering a lecture, and Plato chanced to hear him. Now Plato, barely twenty years old,
was already something of a poet by this time, having composed dithyrambs
and other lyrics; he had also just written a tragedy, and was planning to submit it to the upcoming contest in drama. Our source for this story does not
reveal the subject of Socrates' talk; but whatever it was, it must have had a
sensational effect on Plato, for as a result of it, he renounced playwriting
forever. We know nothing about what happened to Plato's work in the predramatic genres of choral and solo lyric; but the tragedy he had written for
submission to the theatre festival suffered a remarkable fate under Socrates'
pedagogical influence: Plato consigned it to the flames (Diogenes Laertius
Plato 3.5–6).

Plato went on, of course, to make his name as a writer of dialogues, a
literary form whose connections to drama are intriguing to say the least.
Like drama, the philosophical dialogue focuses on the speech of speakers at
the expense of almost all surrounding lexical and narrative material. Like
drama, its "stories" are cast in terms of an interlocutory situation. But the
difference between drama and the dialogue, as far as literary form goes, is
perhaps ultimately more significant still: what is implied by all dramatic
texts, the bodies of performers, is not required by the Platonic dialogue. Regardless of what Plato may have intended in composing them, his dialogues

have survived as objects for classroom study and private reading, and function self-sufficiently as pure literary texts—something that cannot be said of texts intended for performance in the theatre.

For theatre people, there is no more revealing story about the relationship between students and teachers than this one. In becoming a student, Plato had found it necessary to renounce not *all* aspects of dramatic form but only the bodies of performers. In burning his tragedy and composing dialogues instead, Plato is a powerful symbol of the trend in literate culture toward increasingly de-corporealized communication practices. For as Aristotle noted, the history of artistic genres, from oral epic through drama and toward the novel, is a gradual movement away from the body and toward communication "in bare prose" (*Poetics* 1447b). Under conditions of orality, verbal communication in the absence of a body is not an option; but when writing came on the scene, the choice could be made to do away with it and communicate by language alone. In short, with literacy came a new problem: what role should the body be given in a particular act of communication? Now, there is much in Socrates' own philosophy that could explain his student's decision to eliminate corporeality from his artistic output. Throughout the Socratic metaphysics as related by Plato, there is a generalized devaluation of the "sights and sounds" of sensible reality, sensory phenomena of which a performing human body would naturally be a prime example. But, as we shall see, there is something in *all* literate learning and teaching that separates itself from the body in this way. It was not only by virtue of his being Socrates' student that the body became a problem for Plato; it was by virtue of being a student, period.

The first thing we notice, however, when cogitating upon the nature of the fifth-century student is how closely theatrical practices resembled scholarly ones. Had Socrates' lecture taken place within the Theatre of Dionysus rather than outside it, he might have looked, to all appearances, like an actor rather than a teacher; and we know from Aristophanes' *Frogs* that plays were expected to *teach* as well as delight. Not only did fifth-century teachers of rhetoric and philosophy such as Lysias, Protagoras, and Prodicus dress in special costumes when they appeared before large festival audiences, but they are also known to have delivered their lessons from memorized written scripts.[1] In so doing, they performed much in the manner of actors, who similarly delivered written works to the public in an oral form. Like Plato's unperformed tragedy, the plays of the ancient theatre did not reach their public unless the text was learned and memorized by actors. For this reason the playwright was

---

1. *Phaedrus* 227d–228, 228d–229, 230e; *Theaetetus* 162a; Diogenes Laertius 9.50. See also O'Sullivan (1996:115–27) for the written nature of Sophistic teaching.

called *didaskalos* (*Thesmophoriasuzae* 30, 88; *Frogs* 1021), a teacher, and he must have functioned very much as did the fifth-century schoolmaster. "And as soon as his boys have learned their letters, and are in a condition to understand what is written . . . [the teacher] sets before them on their benches the works of good poets to read, and compels them to learn them by heart" (Plato *Protagoras* 325d–e). Indeed, as Richard Green and Eric Handley remind us, the word normally used to say that someone produced a play, *edidasken,* is the very same one used to describe teaching youngsters in a school (1995:33). If the playwright is the teacher of his poems, presumably that makes the actor his student; and learning a written text by heart certainly does seem a scholarly thing to do. When we consider the fact that, before writing and book-based schools, such activities were utterly unknown, the actor's likeness to the student becomes especially pronounced.

In fact, no matter where we look in stage history or dramatic literature, a connection between theatre and scholarship is visible. From Aristophanes' "Thinkery" to Molière's schools for husbands and wives, students and teachers are omnipresent in the repertory. As early as the century after Aristotle, theatre is explicitly singled out among the genres as having a special connection with attendance at school. In Herondas' mime *The Schoolmaster,* an irate mother complains that her truant son skips school so often that he cannot even recognize the letter *A;* and the proof of his delinquency is that he hasn't memorized a single line from a play!

> But when asked to say something from a play,
> As anybody might ask a schoolboy,
> . . . What trickles out, as if from a cracked jug?
> *Apollo the bright, a hunter was he!*
> Your old granny, I say, can recite that
> Without being able to read or write![2]

In other words, while even the schoolmaster's granny—or the student's great-grandmother—might have committed to memory a line of oral-formulaic poetry, like "any Phrygian slave in the street," it was a mark of a book-learned student that he would also know lines from a *play.*

The natural affinity Herondas sees between the theatre and the classroom has only strengthened through time. After centuries of the near-total abatement of organized theatrical activities in the Christian era, theatrical form was to make its first reappearance (ca. 900) in the school plays of Hroswitha, written for performance by her students. And the reemergence

2. From the Davenport translation (1981).

of a theatrical tradition in the Renaissance is unthinkable without the early experiments of scholars and schoolmasters whose adaptations of the classics for the classroom not only reminded Europe that such works were meant to be performed, but also stocked the nascent professional theatres with boy actors used to memorizing and acting in plays. From Hippolytos to Hamlet, Pheidippides to Faustus—and including such later-day students as Tesman, Constantine, and Oleanna—the Western stage has abounded with characters who are cast in obvious ways as book-toting students, and whose fates are intimately connected with their scholarly vocations. The grammar student of Kallias' dramatic imagination has clearly gone on to become one of the perennial images of our theatre.

Even for Antonin Artaud, centuries later, to whom the theatre's alliance with bookishness seemed an unholy one, the connection was nonetheless evident: because the Western theatre is built on a respect for "what has been written," its practitioners are vilified as "grammarians" and "graduate students" (1958:41). Theatre, for Artaud, is *too much* like school, and we find similar complaints about theatrical didacticism in twentieth-century theorists from Edward Gordon Craig (1956:35) to Patrice Pavis (1982:141). Judging from what we have seen so far of the shift from bardic expertise to actorly amateurism, such concerns do not seem altogether unfounded. In trading a virtuosic composition-in-performance technique for a mere "teacher's" text, the literate performer does seem, at least at first sight, to have lost creative autonomy in direct proportion with the adoption of scholarly models. For all the hysteria of his attack against the Western theatre's textual didacticism, Artaud may have been on to something.

Whether the theatre is indeed, as Artaud feared, too much like school is one of the questions toward which we will be working throughout this chapter. In answering it, we will also see something of what is at stake in Plato's schooldays rejection of theatre altogether. But for now we need to set the scene, historically, for the appearance of the first schools in Greece; for it appears that the first playwrights, beginning with Aeschylus, were among the very first poets in the Western tradition ever to go to school.

The archaeological record for schools in Greece is not easy to interpret, and there remains some uncertainty about when exactly it was that classroom instruction began. A very early wax-covered writing tablet has survived (ca. 650) with the alphabet written across the top as if for a student (Powell 1991:155 fig. 55), but there is nothing specifically to connect this teaching device to use in a school. A tradition does exist that dates schools in Greece all the way back to this time, the seventh century B.C.E., but the sources for it are late and have been deemed untrustworthy by some (cf. Beck 1964:77). Evidence for schools in the sixth century takes the form of the school laws attributed to Solon of Athens and Charondas of Catana; these stipulated that schooling was mandatory for all citizens' sons, and that the city must foot the bill (W. Harris 1989:21). The problem with these laws is that the sources for them, again, are centuries after the fact, by which time it had become something of a national pastime to attribute to Solon laws that actually came later. Concrete references to specific grammar schools (in Chios ca. 496, Astypalaea ca. 490) do not appear until the first decades of the fifth century. As William Harris notes, however, none of this evidence suggests that the teaching of letters in a classroom was any sort of innovation (1989:57). Herodotus refers only casually and in passing to the 119 children who were killed when the roof of their school collapsed on them while they were "learning their letters" (6.27). From such evidence, scholars such as Harris conclude that "there must already have been some [schools] in the sixth century" (57), and his opinion is shared by most of his colleagues.[3] By the 490s, it is fairly certain that "practically all prosperous Greeks, and some who were not, sent their sons to school" (58). The Douris Cup (ca. 485) represents a typical school scene from this period, and confirms iconographically the literary evidence, such as it exists. In summary, then, though in some ways ambiguous, the available evidence suggests one thing unmistakably: that the first grammar schools cannot be dated to any point after the 490s, since they were already widespread and well established by this time; and it would be wrong to date them much earlier than the birth of Aeschylus in the 520s, since there is no concrete proof of their existence so early. It appears, in other words, that book-based schooling came on the scene at some point between the end of the sixth and the beginning of the fifth centuries B.C.E., which means that Aeschylus may have been among the very first students ever to creep like snail unwillingly to school.

Is it really possible that poets before Aeschylus had no experience of classroom instruction? Was not Sappho famous for her school for girls in the Archaic period? As Susan Pomeroy reminds us, the image of Sappho as a schoolmistress is a modern invention, and one that is belied by both her poetry and all the stories told about her in antiquity (1975:53). The case of Sappho is nevertheless revelatory, for it reminds us how profoundly education was changed with the introduction of formal schooling. If Sappho's poems are "teachings," they are all addressed to the teacher's intimates, lovers, and

---

3. See Beck 1964, 1975; Burns 1981:375; Immerwahr 1964:17; cf. Havelock 1977:386 n. 4, who alone disagrees, dating schools somewhat later.

friends. Her love songs to Anactoria, Gongyla, Atthis, her daughter Cleis[4]—all these bespeak the kind of "passionate involvement" (53) that typified all learning and teaching before the advent of schools.

For book-based study radically altered the nature of learning in Greece. As Frederick Beck (1964) has pointed out, the word *didaskaleion,* or "school," does not exist at all in Homer, nor can it be found anywhere else in predramatic poetry. It makes its first appearance in the sense of "school" in the fifth century, in Herodotus (6.27), Sophocles (frag. 799), and Thucydides (7.29).[5] In predramatic literature it is more common to come across references to individual teachers, whose actions are described with the verb *trepho,* to "rear" (Beck 1964:49). Both from the context of Homer's and Hesiod's discussions of this brand of teaching, and from the word itself, it is clear that this preliterate "rearing" is a rather different thing from that which happens in schools. Speaking of the relationship that prevailed between a Cheiron or a Phoenix and his pupil, Beck summarizes as follows. The "rearer" in Homer and Hesiod "was responsible for the whole development of his pupil, moral, physical and intellectual, and not merely or solely for the imparting of specific aspects of knowledge" (49).

The preliterate teacher began his involvement with his charge more or less from birth, and might continue it for nearly a lifetime. Phoenix, for example, "reared" Achilleus "to be both a speaker of words and a doer of deeds" and did so "with [his] heart's love" (Iliad 9.435–43, 485). In preliterate education, as Beck describes it, "the pupil learns by imitating his teacher in all their joint activities" (60–61). Consequently, between such "rearers" and their charges there is a strong emotional bond, and learning is but the outcome of their intimate ongoing relationship and shared experience. Phoenix bounced Achilleus on his knee, cut up his meat into little pieces at table, and fed him wine (*Il.* 9.490ff.). As a result, the service of a preliterate teacher such as Phoenix is, in Werner Jaeger's words, "only a continuation of the almost paternal love which has always bound him" to his charge (1960, 1:28). The poems of Sappho confirm that this intimate relationship, this passionate lifelong attachment between teachers and their pupils, continued beyond the Homeric period and into the "lyric" age of Greece.[6]

A legendary teacher like Cheiron—evidence of whose reputation has come down to us through literary and archaeological material from the Archaic period—is, however, never represented as a teacher of letters (Beck

---

4. *Lyra Graeca* (Edmonds 1952), Sappho, 1.38, 45; 2.48, 81, 82, 83, 86, 108; 6.130.
5. See Beck 1964:78.
6. The Suda *Lexicon* is not sure what to call the subjects of Sappho's poems and affections, and so names them "pupils or disciples." See Edmonds 1952:147.

1975:10). For literacy was to put an end to the kind of one-on-one relationship that such teachers represented. Predictably enough, representations of Cheiron in Greek art begin to disappear with the establishment of formal literary schooling (Beck 1975:10). Whereas teachers and students had formerly enjoyed each other's company "in all their joint activities," fifth-century students were trundled off to learn their letters only for certain specific hours of the day. And when they arrived for their lessons, they appear, by all accounts, to have sat in classrooms in anonymous groups of between sixty and one hundred or more.[7] And whereas the tutor had formerly shared all the student's activities, Athenian grammar students apparently had separate specialist instructors for each class.[8]

From the fifth-century dramatists and from Plato we have learned a few general things about the nature of education in a newly literate world. From Sophocles and Euripides, who both feature *pedagogoi* in their *Elektra* plays, we learn that the rearing function of a Homeric teacher seems to have been taken over by a household servant called a *pedagogus;* he was a kind of nanny, caring for the children and taking them to school, but apparently not responsible for instructing his charges himself (Plato *Lysis* 208c). In Aristophanes' school in the *Clouds,* an actor representing the "Right" argument waxes nostalgic about the good old days when boys walked to school together decorously, when discipline in the classroom was strict, and the students learned good old-fashioned poetry by heart (961ff.). Right Argument describes the regular school curriculum of earlier fifth-century education as consisting of music and/or letters and gymnastics—an educational program that is confirmed in other literary sources as well.[9]

In Kallias' *ABC Show,* however, we are treated to an especially intimate portrait of the kind of book learning that the dramatists would have experienced themselves as boys.[10] They repeated. And they repeated verbatim: "Beta alpha: ba. Beta epsilon: be. Beta eta: bē." They did as the teacher bade them do: "You must pronounce alpha by itself, and secondly epsilon by itself. And you there, you will say the third vowel!" (frag. 31 Edmonds 1957). As archaeological evidence confirms, students learned their lessons in precisely this way. A piece of pottery has survived with grammar lessons in-

7. Herodotus 6.27.2; Thucydides 7.29; *scholion* on *Laws* 629a as cited by Burns 1981:375 and Beck 1964:77–89.

8. Jeffrey 1990:63; Burns 1981:375; Beck 1964:81.

9. *Knights* 188–90; Plato *Protagoras* 325d–e; also Harris 1989:57 n. 56.

10. From a few surviving vases and terra-cottas, we see that it was not only boys but also perhaps girls who went to school (Cole 1981; Beck 1975 plates 69 and 71 esp.), as Kallias' play suggests.

scribed upon it—"rha, rhē, rhi, rho, rhou, rhō, sa, sē," and so on—complete
with a mistake and the teacher's correction (Beck 1975:16). From literary references and contemporary representations in visual art, we know that poetry, largely Homer's, was a major component of the student's educational
diet (Beck 1975:14). And as the passage cited earlier from Plato shows, poetry was memorized the same way that the alphabet was: the student learned
it by heart from a written text placed before him on his bench (*Protagoras*
325d–e). Plato's account of epic memorization in the classroom is further
confirmed, iconographically, by the Douris Cup. It shows a student studying a (now lost) poem, the first line of which—"Moisa moi amphi Skaman-
dron eurron archom' aeindein"—is depicted on the scroll held by the
onlooking, seated teacher (Beck 1975:14).

In the year when the Douris Cup was decorated with this charming
teacher-student scene, Sophocles was nine years old. He would have been in
school himself at this time. An iconographic image from Aeschylus' school
days is unfortunately not available; can we perhaps provide one for ourselves? The teacher says, "You there, Aeschylus, recite this passage from Sappho's love poem." And the diligent student does, knowing all the while that
he is not a Sapphic lover, his teacher is not the beloved, nor is the classroom
either a festival or a symposium to which the other pupils have come for entertainment. In short, what is repeated by the student in the process of book
learning is not connected with his "here-and-now" experience in the classroom. In the preliterate one-on-one relation between tutor and friend, the
recitation of poetry would normally have had some direct grounding in the
interlocutors' shared experience. In Homer, songs about battle or homecoming are sung in related circumstances; Sapphic poems about love and
friendship were sung to lovers and friends. But between a roomful of students and an instructor who may be a virtual stranger to them, and a paid
professional to boot (Beck 1975:14), any direct relation between the content
of the lesson and the social context in which it is learned is precluded. Consequently, book learning demands the repetition of contextually irrelevant
material, material that is unmotivated by the context in which the speaker
finds himself. It requires the student to "bracket" or ignore the present being
lived—ignore, that is, the concrete social relations inherent in the present
interlocutory situation.

This tendency of literate study to detach readers from the concrete circumstances that surround them is comically demonstrated by Aristophanes
in the *Frogs*. Reading from a written text of Euripides' *Andromeda* while
aboard a ship, Dionysus loses all sense of context and proper action. He is
supposed to be fighting the enemy under his captain Cleisthenes, but is carried elsewhere by his reading, first mentally, and then physically, as he basi-

cally deserts the fleet in order to seek out the author (52–53). A similar loss of contact with the physical "here-and-now" is attributed by Aristophanes to the bookish Sophists: in the *Clouds,* Socrates is presented as so oblivious to his immediate surroundings that he wouldn't notice a lizard sitting over his head unless it actually shat in his eye (16off.). And in the *Phaedrus,* Phaedrus' book is likened to a drug which makes its readers heedless of their surroundings: like the mythical Oreithyia, whose preoccupation with Pharmacea got in the way of her noticing a dangerous wind, so too may a reader of books have his senses distracted from prevailing physical circumstances.[11]

In conditions of orality, it is hard to imagine anything teachable that would not be taught within a concrete sphere of action: fishing is taught to the apprentice in midstream, religion to the initiate during a ceremony, recitation to bards-hopeful during a recitation, proverbs to grandchildren in contexts to which the proverb applies. But learning a poem by heart in a classroom is clearly not of this kind. Like all other book-based classroom activities, it is characterized by a high degree of abstraction and decontextualization. As Werner Jaeger has pointed out, students before writing learned everything in situ and by physical imitation in a 360° context of action (1945 1:29); a student who is learning from a book, by contrast, is confined to a specialized "abstract" space and encouraged to develop a unidirectional gaze at a writing tablet or book roll.[12] What were the effects of this new pedagogical model on its first students? Might their exposure to this novel teaching style have influenced their poetic output as adults, particularly insofar as their contributions to the nascent art of drama is concerned? For as we have seen in our time, it is largely through their experiences in the classroom that literates absorb the kinds of practices and models which mark them as "literate" in comparison with their "oral" counterparts. Modern psychological studies and tests have demonstrated that it is an individual's exposure to the classroom that, more than any other factor, causes the changes in his or her attitudes and mental habits which we have come to associate with the effects of literacy.[13]

For a start, the *Phaedrus* suggests that the decontextualizing of book-

11. This reading of the myth is suggested by Steiner (1994:213–14).

12. This point was made to me by Derrick de Kerckhove in a personal exchange. Jesper Svenbro takes the idea further by suggesting that this readerly, scholarly disposition—passive, unidirectional viewing in an autonomous, abstract space—is precisely the one that theatre assumes and calls upon in its audiences. Svenbro (1990:365–84), however, does not connect such skills to schooling per se. His concern is with the skills acquired through reading itself, particularly *silent* reading.

13. See esp. Scribner and Cole 1981; also Taylor 1988.

based study is a bit of an effort, not the natural impulse when students and teachers get together. But apparently it is an effort that needs to be made if literate teaching and learning are to proceed. In order to avoid succumbing to the charms of his student's physical presence, immersing himself in the present context, Socrates finds that he must go so far as to keep his head and eyes covered (237a5). Socrates is determined to compete as a teacher with Lysias and discourse upon the subject of love. But Lysias, "the cleverest of present writers," has worked on his composition "at his leisure" and over a long stretch of time (228); in order to compete in cleverness with such a polished speech, Socrates must immunize himself against the physical realities of the interlocutory situation in which he finds himself.

Phaedrus begins by reading out the written lecture of Lysias in the hope of convincing Socrates of its excellence. Expecting, no doubt, to prove his theory about the weaknesses of writing and the superiority of oral modes of instruction, Socrates counters by attempting to improvise a speech on the same subject orally. But what he finds is that oral performance *cannot* compete with the special kind of teaching that writing makes possible, that in fact oral performance interferes with thought. Before he knows what has happened, he has started speaking "in hexameters," the language of epic poetry (241e). He has become "possessed," not just by his student but by the beauties of the place to which his student has "exposed" him (241e). He gets carried away by his talk about the appetites of love, and, perhaps noticing the extent to which the content of his speech and the social context of its delivery have coincided—for Phaedrus is many times referred to as a bewitching creature—Socrates stops his speech in the middle, unable or unwilling to go further (241d–e). In allowing the present situation to intrude upon his lesson, Socrates has not only lapsed into the language of the inspired bard but has also replicated the bard's compositional style: he recites episodically, with no proper structure, no ending, and he interrupts his discourse with vocatives to his audience (238c–d). Worse still, he has missed the mark of truth. In speaking extemporaneously about the interestedness of a lover, he has become interested himself *as* a lover, and in consequence delivers a "dreadful speech" of which he is ashamed and for which he refuses to take responsibility (242c–d). So completely did the presence of his interlocutor determine his lesson that he thrice attributes the speech to Phaedrus, his student and listener, rather than to himself (238d, 242d, e).

Like Lysias' written speech, which asserts the superiority of the disinterested lover (231–34d), the dialogue as a whole has many positive things to say about the advantages of disinterestedness in learning and teaching. Bodily based conversation, with its immersion in present contexts, is shown to risk "[leading] us in a wrong direction" (265b–c), taking us astray "like an animal" (235e). By contrast, the disinterested, phenomenally disengaged character of literate study is shown—and not just in this work but through-out Plato's oeuvre—to have enormous advantages over a practically embed-ded model of learning. Taking utterances and information out of contexts enables one to reflect on them consciously and at leisure, to view their premises and hidden assumptions, to expose the prejudices that support them and the illogicalities that they hide. Mental structures, social para-digms, and inherited values can be pulled into the light of abstract reason, and inconsistencies, contradictions, and injustices drawn out. By "bracket-ing" the sights and sounds of sensible reality, one is less likely to mistake fleeting desires, illusions, or mere opinions for truth. This literate bracketing of one's physical context is also associated in the *Phaedrus* with the qualities that make for clear thinking and speaking generally: self-consistency, syn-thesis, clarity, definition of terms, the breaking up of entities into con-stituent parts, "divisions and collections," and especially a unified organic structure (264c, 266c). Although these are qualities that "even . . . the worst writer" is not likely to fail in mastering (235e), they prove to be qualities be-yond the reach of the oral improviser, whose involvement in his context must siphon attention away from his proper study. As the representative of the "old school" remembers in the *Clouds,* the proper learning of the boys' lessons meant "on *no* account pressing their thighs together" while memo-rizing epic texts, nor leaving bum prints in the sand during gym class (969ff.). When it comes to study in the classroom, the body just gets in the way.

In Platonic philosophy, particularly as explained in the *Republic,* this effort-ful detachment from sensible reality is described as a precondition for free-ing oneself from mere opinions about the world and approaching ideal forms of thought. But poetry, too, was a beneficiary of this bookish practice of detachment from contexts, for dramatic form no less than philosophy re-flects the "drawing away" or abstraction of the body from engagement in acts of performance.

In Chapter 1 we looked at some of the changes to poetic composition that followed on the use of the alphabet. The literate poet, freed of the con-servative function of the oral bard, suddenly had greater leeway in making his own contribution. Instead of being expected mainly to preserve the tra-dition, he came to be expected to "show invention" in his use of it (*Poetics*

1453b11). Unburdened by text of his obligation to serve the Muse of memory, the poet came to be viewed as an inventor of fictional stories instead.[14] The ability to see the beginning, middle, and end of a composition simultaneously further reinforced the emergence of the literate category of fiction: narrative closure, thematic structure, and organic form became poetic virtues in their own right, connected with compositional skill but not with the needs of any particular audience.[15] Having been reduced to writing, the epic tradition of the Greeks came to be redefined as a storehouse of stories amenable to division and alteration, criticism and innovation. Whereas the lyric poet Stesichorus was believed to have been struck blind in punishment for having "sinned in matters of mythology" (*Phaedrus* 243), the dramatists of the fifth century had gained the freedom through literacy to treat the epic tradition more or less as they pleased.

The alienating atmosphere of literacy puts inherited mythology, and the formulas that contained it, at a distance from poets and performers alike. For this reason, a general "interrogatory" stance—both toward inherited material and toward the values carried by it—has been linked by many scholars to the use of writing.[16] The development of a generalized skepticism is especially dependent on the use of writing, for without written records that can be accumulated and compared, doubts about inherited wisdom cannot be followed up and will tend to be overwhelmed by the longevity of the tradition itself (Goody 1986:31). The strength of the tradition over and against the individual derives mainly from the fact, observed

14. From the descriptions in the *Odyssey* of the practice of Phemios (1.325) and Demodokos (8.43ff.), it is clear that the bard's song was not considered fictional: it was history and news in one. Telemachos, hearing reports of Orestes' matricide, says it will soon be a "theme for bards," confirming that the instantaneous passage between history and myth that I mentioned previously was a smooth one (*Od.* 1.350–52; see also Beck 1964:29). The bards were "the historians of their time, having the double function of recording and teaching history" (Beck 1964:30). What they sang was inspired by the Muse, authorized by the collective memory over which she presided, and was therefore true. By the literate dramatic age, however, traditional material had become simply the "raw ingredients" of fiction, to be divided up and used for various pleasurable effects which were unrelated to any record-keeping function (*Poetics* 1450b8–1451b3).

15. A performance of epic material, on the contrary, was shaped according to the needs of the audience. As we see from the opening invocations of the *Iliad* and the *Odyssey*, and from Demodokos' own procedure (*Od.* 8.500), the singer starts up at potentially any point in the cycle, and ends equally arbitrarily, usually when someone interrupts him, as Alkinoos and Penelope do (7.97; 1.340). In fact, as Albert Bates Lord found from his field research in the former Yugoslavia, stories are rarely sung to the end; they simply stop for one reason or another (1960:30).

16. See esp. Winchester 1985:34; Goody 1987:279.

in Africa by Jack Goody, that the "embeddedness of speech and action" in concrete contexts produces an atmosphere in which meanings, norms, and values tend to be immanent in one's way of life. Until ideas and practices take on an existence outside a particular lived context (i.e., when they get written down in texts), they tend not to be experienced as having any existential limits or boundaries. Until a practice is "drawn away" or abstracted from the doer by being written down, it is not an "object" for a "subject" to view but a constituent of his being (Bauman 1986:44). With no difference delineated between speaker and spoken or actor and thing done, members of a nonliterate society have been observed to have no experience of, for example, religious ritual as a distinct category of action. As Goody puts it: to be an Asante is to be necessarily in an existential state where such-and-such things are said and done (1986:3–12). Ritual doings, such as mimetic sacrifice, and traditional sayings, such as mourning songs and prayers, are ontologically merged with the doer and sayer's own identity. It is consequently a feature of many preliterate practices that they are compulsory. Any question as to whether or not something culturally mandated should or should not be performed or said by an individual will tend not to emerge.

Greek poetry before drama is clearly marked by these two oral features: identity between speaker and spoken and the presence of compulsory ritual elements. The Homeric bard is described as a "divine singer" whose special identity as the gods' elect is affirmed throughout, both in epithets and by his blindness, as a sign of his sacred office (*Odyssey* 1.335; 7.62–64). In the choral lyrics that are said by Aristotle to have given rise to drama, poetic content is identical to performative context: a song about Agido and her cousin Hagesichora is sung by Agido and her cousin Hagesichora (Alcman 1 35–95 Edmonds 1952). Epic recitation is also marked by the presence of a compulsory ritual element: the invocation to the Muse at the start. A fixed ritual invocation is also included at the beginning of many modern Yugoslavian songs as well (Lord 1960:45).

These features of predramatic performance can also be seen in more recent examples of oral practices. A piece of oratory has been recorded from a West Coast Native tribe of Canada which is cast in the form of a responsive choral song. A bereaved chief exhorts his tribe not to mourn any more; they repeatedly respond, "We do not mourn any more" (Petrone 1990:22). A modern reader or anthropologist might be inclined to see in this dialogue between chief and tribe a dramatic speech practice. But to do so would be to take literacy practices so much for granted as to forget that, in this mourning ritual, speaker and spoken are ontologically merged. These words are not "performed" for viewers, in the dramatic sense. They are a necessary consequence of who the speakers are (a mourning chief and his tribe). Similarly in Greece, the predramatic poetic genres were a direct expression of the identities of the speakers. Brides sang bridal songs, and the descendants of Homer's heroes sang the praises of their forefathers. For the epics, too, functioned as affirmations of the identities of the singers and their audiences. To be a post-Mycenaean Greek was necessarily to sing the praises of one's ancestors, to celebrate one's own lineage as recorded in the epic catalogues of men and their illustrious deeds.

In literate contexts, however, Goody has found that speech practices become decontextualized to the point where they are optional; not only does the compulsion of ritual disappear, but also performance is no longer an extension of identity.[17] Accordingly, in drama all compulsory ritual sayings and doings have disappeared. Despite what Arthur Pickard-Cambridge has called the "unscrupulous" fantasies of members of the myth-and-ritual school, classical scholars have been unable to find any evidence of fixed and compulsory ritual elements in the ancient Greek plays.[18] And as we saw in Chapter 1, the identity of speaker and spoken which typically characterizes nonliterate practices is visibly sundered in theatrical representation: a chorus of Trojan women is performed by Athenian ephebes (Winkler 1990:20–62); young boys represent women who represent letters of the alphabet. Plato could choose to compose a tragedy or not, go to the theatre festival, or attend a Socratic lecture instead.

These new freedoms in performance—from the duty of conservation and its attendant constraints, from the constraints of proper identity, and from the compulsion of ritual—can all be connected in one way or another with the existence of fixed texts. It is certainly paradoxical that textual fixity should have such liberating effects. But both in Greece and again in the

17. Goody 1986:14; 1987:69.

18. I am speaking here about the contents of the plays. The only religious ritual performed in the theatre was apparently the immolation of a piglet to purify the space; but as this action was also performed in the Assembly to purify the seats of the Prytanes, it can hardly be considered a ritual with any special connections to theatrical performance. See Else 1965b:3–17; Pickard-Cambridge 1968:x–58; Taplin 1978:161, 191 n. 3; Gernet 1981:57; Herington 1985:5–7; Segal 1986; Vernant and Vidal-Naquet 1990:16–23; Csapo and Slater 1995:103–7. Winkler's hypothesis that the chorus was made up of young men in military training is not evidence for the existence of ritual elements in the plays themselves; even if this does connect tragic performance to a rite of passage for some, it was hardly a ritual, since only the best singers were chosen, and thus not all ephebes would have gone through it (1990:57–60). A ritual in the sense I mean is compulsory and must be repeated exactly the same way every time to function properly. See Vickers for the absence of ritual elements in the earliest drama (1973:33–42). The theatre festival itself staged a number of civic and military rituals in addition to the dramas; these will be discussed in Chapter 4.

Middle Ages, book-based study tended to loosen up ossified poetic habits: not only was its unprecedented control by writing what allowed drama to be the first poetic genre to make deliberate use of colloquial speech (Ong 1977:72), but also it was the most "sophisticated . . . schoolmen" who pioneered the use of vernaculars in the poetry of the Middle Ages (Clanchy 1979:170).

When a customary saying or practice gets written down, a number of things happen. First, it loses its "invisible" or transparent and borderless equivalence with life as lived. It is made a visibly concrete, distinct thing on the page, but it also becomes an intellectual challenge insofar as it becomes a thinkable thing with limits. In an oral society man stands, in Walter Ong's words, at the center of a 360-degree sound-life: he is part of it and contained within it. Once aspects of this sound-life are put on paper, they can be viewed, as it were, from without. The individual's unidirectional gaze at a page—be it papyrus, parchment, or waxed tablet—puts him in a new relation to cultural material. No longer contained "within" a speech or social practice, he is availed of the position of an "outsider," a viewer whose gaze is separated from involvement.

This outsideness of a literate's relation to a text not only introduces the possibility of taking an individualized stance toward the language or custom, be it dissent or active endorsement, but also to some extent necessitates a redefinition of oneself as an individual, perceiving subject. For as long as engagement is one's mode of being in relation to a given practice, the practice is equivalent with one's participation as a member of the group. It is probably for this reason that even elementary literacy has been tied to the likelihood of an individual's separating himself or herself from local traditions, imagining an alternative reality, and actually seeking it elsewhere (Winchester 1985:47), just as Dionysus does after reading the *Andromeda*. Literacy's tendency to separate individuals from their unexamined immersion in cultural practices and to encourage their individualized responses was implicitly recognized by Plato, who criticized literates precisely for their tendency to be difficult to manage (*Phaedrus* 274–75). In the *Clouds*, Aristophanes exaggerates this tendency, suggesting that students are prone to reject traditional ways of life to the extent of beating their parents!

The separation of speaker and spoken that writing accomplishes means that epic material now exists "outside" the poet, and he stands outside of it. This "outsideness" can be credited directly with one of the central poetic innovations that dramatic form represented in its time. Oral epic is a genre that praises the past deeds of heroes. The epic bard had a single rigid mandate: to preserve and increase "the glories of men" (Jaeger 1945 1:40). The bard Phemios is described as "the speaker of fame," and the glorifying function of the epic singer is made clear elsewhere as well (*Od.* 1.338, 8.73; *Il.* 9.189). As Jaeger observes, epic is so strictly limited to praise that "everything low, contemptible, and ugly is banished from the world of the epic" (1945 1:42). In the words of the ancient rhetor Dio of Prusa: "Homer praised almost everything—animals and plants, water and earth, weapons and horses. He passed over nothing without somehow honouring and glorifying it. Even the one man whom he abused, Thersites, he called a *clear-voiced speaker.*" [19]

As Gregory Nagy has shown (1986:89–102), the genre of praise poetry to which the Homeric epic belongs is practised around the world. Ruth Finnegan has described the context of this genre as practised in parts of Africa: the bard travels from town to town, taking up his position in the marketplace and singing the praises of a rich or influential townsman until he gets money or some other gift (1990:250). From descriptions in the *Odyssey,* we find confirmation of this practice: Demodokos is fetched by a herald to come and sing the praises of an illustrious house and be fed (8.43ff.). And Pindar, too, made his living by peripatetic flattery: "My plainest rule, when I arrive in this isle, is to shower it with praises" (*Isthmians* 6, 20f.).[20] Now, in African praise poetry the panegyric turns to invective if the singer is ignored. As we see here clearly, praise and abuse are related as antithetical speech types; but most important is the fact that both are motivated directly by the context in which the performance occurs. One praises in expectation of one's supper and abuses when it is not provided.

In a preliterate milieu there is no sustained abstraction possible of content from context: to sing the epics is necessarily to be performing a particular concrete action, namely, praising heroes. But when writing allows composition to be separated from performance, poetry comes out from under the control of specific performative contexts. It can be composed outside of these contexts (alone and at home, for example), and new options can emerge. In predramatic poetry each genre had its own specific performative function and its own distinctive musical meter. The praise poetry of a Pindar, for example, would be written in the appropriate meter, such as Aeolic or dactylo-epitrite. Epic praise was confined to dactylic hexameters and invectives to iambics. Within oral performance, this melopoetic consistency served both the needs of the singers and dancers and the pragmatics of the song itself, whose function had to be made manifestly clear. In praising

19. Dio Prusensis *Or* 33,2, cited in Jaeger 1960 1:42.
20. As cited and translated by Kirk 1985:102.

an athlete in an epicinian ode, for example, one could not very well lapse into iambics, the meter used for invective. But because the advance of literacy was increasingly making poetry an object for analysis rather than contextual performance alone, it became possible to contemplate these compositional norms and to overturn them.

Thus, whereas predramatic poetry was locked by orality into the use of a single homogenizing musical and metrical mode, drama became, under literacy's tutelage, the first genuinely heterogeneous genre. In dispensing with dactylic hexameter and introducing iambics (among other meters) in its place, dramatic composition was able to exploit the potential of the alphabet for recording speech. By including iambics in its storytelling, drama was able to bring poetry closer to the sounds and rhythms of everyday speech, as Aristotle acknowledged (*Poetics* 1449a18).[21] But equally pronounced was the effect that this hybridizing must have had on the nature of the story and of performance itself. Singing the legendary deeds of one's ancestors in *iambics?* This was new indeed. What must the poet think of Homeric material if he writes about it in the meter reserved for invective?

According to a well-known anecdote, Solon berated Thespis for standing in front of so many people and telling such blatant lies in his play (Plutarch *Solon* 29). Now, this story is usually interpreted to mean that Solon was shocked at the duplicity inherent in Thespis' chosen form, that is, in pretending to be someone he was not. But a closer look tells us something else. It was certainly not Thespis' *impersonation* that shocked him, for Solon was in fact well known for at least one such poetic impersonation of his own (*Solon* 8.2). A more plausible explanation lies elsewhere.

Unfortunately, we have none of Thespis' plays. But drama from Aeschylus onward is specially marked by its tendency to set inherited material on its ear. All the plays that treat of mythological material (and that is most of them) share a distinct taste for criticizing, altering, questioning, and transforming the traditional stories they treat. Dramatic texts tell the story of a Greek military victory from the point of view of the losers, who turn out not to be "barbarians" at all; Iphigenia was never actually sacrificed on the altar by the Greeks, as legend had it, but got a job elsewhere, sacrificing the Greeks themselves; the glorious hero Ajax is portrayed in the theatre as a demented and decidedly unheroic torturer of sheep; the great and famous archer Philoctetes is depicted as a smelly, pathetic, whining invalid; Helen is portrayed with any number of contrasting personalities, and flies off to Egypt instead of Troy; Orestes is delirious, if not clinically insane; the mur-

21. See also Herington 1985:119–20.

der of Agamemnon was masterminded and carried out not just by the tyrant Aegisthus but by Agamemnon's own wife; heroes are exiled or executed for political reasons rather than dying magnificently in battle, or simply go about in "rags and tatters" rather than in the shining armor and strong greaves that Homer dresses them in. The all-seeing Zeus is portrayed as a paranoid, typical sixth-century tyrant, Athena as a recognizable fifth-century citizen, casting her ballot capriciously in the *dikasteria*. As G. S. Kirk notes, Euripides' Princess Elektra is married off to a "virgin peasant" and herself becomes a "condescending psychopathic shrew"; Jason is both cowardly *and* unfaithful; and the god Apollo is a bungler (1985:103–4). On the theatrical stage, as Geoffrey Bakewell (1997b) has shown, traditionally awe-inspiring figures such as the Eumenides and Oedipus are demoted to the status of metics, the fifth-century Athenian equivalent of green card holders; the stories of such gods and kings are recast in drama and described partly in terms of decidedly inglorious immigration problems. In drama, Homeric deities and heroes are no longer the extratemporal, godlike stuff of praise poetry but, essentially, contemporary Athenians subject to ridicule and abuse, and to representation in iambics. If Thespis' plays were anything like this, it is no wonder that Solon was shocked.

Comedy's connection with iambics, or lampoons, was well known to the ancients (*Poetics* 1448b10ff.); but rarely do scholars today accept how close tragedy, too, must have been in its early days to the humor of the lampoon. Because one of the novelties of tragedy was to represent even epic heroes in nonheroic meters, tragedy can be seen today, as the ancients themselves saw it, as sharing a common origin with comedy. As G. F. Else records, Plutarch wrote in his *Proverbs of the Alexandrians* (30) that tragedy and comedy both arose "out of laughter" (1965b:24), and Aristotle clearly shared this view, for he says that tragedy only "acquired seriousness late," being initially composed of "short plots and comical diction" (*Poetics* 1449a17–18).

The tendency of orality to lock composers into a single poetic mode and meter also afflicted performers, of course. As far as the worldview and technique of epic is concerned, this remained the case even after writing had replaced the improvising bard with the reciting rhapsode. In the *Ion*, it is clear that even as late as the fifth century B.C.E., the performer of epic material remained confined to a contextually embedded pragmatics of praise. Throughout this dialogue the rhapsode describes his activity, and is described by Socrates, as *praising* Homer, even when he is explaining him (536c–d, 541e). In fact, Plato speaks of both poets and performers in *all* the predramatic genres as "in bondage" to a single metrical muse:

Each is able to do well only that to which the Muse has impelled him—one to make dithyrambs, another panegyric odes, another choral songs, another epic poems, another iambs. In all the rest, each one is poor. . . .

So the worshipping corybantes have a lively feeling for that strain alone which is that of the deity by whom they are possessed, and for that melody are well supplied with attitudes and utterances, and heed no others. (534c; 536c–d)

Like Ion and Homer, predramatic performers and poets of all kinds are each "held" by a single muse (536b). Ion is skilled "only in regard to Homer" and the speech genre of praise (531). As we shall see, this "bondage" of the performer to his poetic material disappears in the actor, who, like the dramatic poet, is freed by writing from immersion in any particular type of contextual speech.

In separating spoken content from speech context, literacy makes shocking and socially unconventional speech acts more likely to occur. Whereas heroes must, so to speak, always be praised in oral epic recitation, they can be subjected to novel interpretations when creation has been separated from performance. Indeed, in the hybrid literary art of the fifth century, what Solon called "lies" were not merely tolerated but actually sanctioned. As Simon Goldhill (1990) has shown, ancient drama expresses its nature—its rewriting of tradition and subversion of norms—both within the plays and between the plays and the festival context in which they were performed. According to Goldhill, tragedy and comedy were "genres of transgression" in the most expanded definition of the term, for their targets were not only the heroic values of the Homeric worldview,[22] but also the norms and values so grandiloquently displayed at the Great Dionysia itself. The performative context of the theatre festival—with its display of allied tributes, its awards to citizens for outstanding service to the polis, and its parade of the orphans of war—was meant to celebrate Athenian civic-military virtues and to advertise them abroad. Considering the dramatic festival as a "speech act" of a global kind, one could say that it was a genre of praise for Athens. But the plays themselves actively probe and even undermine the civic and military virtues that are championed by the social setting in which they appeared (Goldhill 1990:97–129). For this reason, Goldhill is almost alone among classicists today in maintaining that there was in fact a more than circum-

22. See Goldhill 1986: chap. 6.

stantial connection between theatre and its patron deity, Dionysus.[23] Contrary to the ancients' own favorite dictum, that it had "nothing to do with Dionysus,"[24] Goldhill suggests that it was this specially theatrical transgression of context by content that made dramatic performance an "essentially Dionysiac event" (129).

But in addition to its daring use of iambics for singing of heroes, drama distinguished itself from previous poetic practice by combining in itself practically all the meters that had traditionally been kept distinct. As M. S. Silk and J. P. Stern remind us, the various poetic meters available in Greece from the eighth century B.C.E. to the birth of drama were roughly equivalent not only to the various rhythms of Greek music, but to separate poetic genres as well (1981:139–40). Add to this the fact that these poetic species had associations with separate localities and even different dialects (Herington 1985:112–13), and we can begin to get an idea of the radical heterogeneity that drama introduced. Before drama, the poetic and musical modes had not been allowed, as it were, to "converse" with one another; with writing they could be brought into contact, into a hybridized state of mutual interanimation. Speaking of drama's incorporation of previously unrelated poetic material, Aristophanes wrote in the *Frogs:* "What is this phlatothrat? Was it from Marathon that you collected these rope-winder's songs, or from where?" (1296). Of Euripides he writes: "He gets his honey from anywhere—from porn songs, from the drinking songs of Meletus, from Carian oboe tunes, from keenings, from the dance-halls" (1301). In Aristoxenus' words, tragedy was "a *mixture*" (Herington 1985:110).

Drama's thoroughgoing language heteroglossia shows just how complete a disjunction literacy had effected between speech content and speech context. Euripides could put porn songs and ritual lamentations into "dialogue" in a single poetic composition, and put them both together on the

23. Compare the more representative conclusion of Louis Gernet that there is "no primary and fundamental relationship" between "Dionysus and the literary genre which circumstances ended up placing under his patronage" (1981:57). See also Jaeger: "Tragedy, too, owes both its traditional material and its ethical and educational spirit to epic, not to its own Dionysiac origin" (1960 1:42). Vernant and Vidal-Naquet write similarly: "The 'truth' of tragedy is not to be found in an obscure, more or less 'primitive' or 'mystical' past secretly haunting the theatre stage" (1990:185). Rather, it is "a literary genre with its own rules and characteristics" which must, "from the point of view of art, social institutions, and human psychology, be regarded as an invention" (23). Or, as R. C. Flickinger writes, it is only by "transgress[ing] good philological practice" that one could trace tragedy back to any sort of religious ritual (1973:6).

24. This motto was originally uttered in connection with either Epigenes' tragic composition, or Thespis'. See Flickinger 1973:11.

stage, because thanks to literacy's alienation, both had lost their necessary connection to particular performative actions and contexts. A Sapphic love poem, when recited in the classroom, is no longer an *instance* of love but just a poem of a certain genre in a certain meter. The existence of such poetic genres in writing meant that a "keening" was no longer something that was necessarily and exclusively done over a dead body; it was now just one poetic language among many. As an alienated (decontextualized) language with no inviolable connection to any particular action, it could be "staged" in juxtaposition with a porn song without excessive impropriety. Standing outside of direct involvement with any concrete speech context, the literate playwright could bring languages into novel combinations, representing them freely on the stage as objects for contemplation.[25]

Throughout his oeuvre Mikhail Bakhtin argues that it is only when discourses are seen from "without" that they lose their sacrosanct and inviolable character. When this happens, social languages, and the practices that go with them, are relativized to the point where they can no longer lay claim to any absolute metaphysical truth. They are forced instead simply to compete with one another in the "marketplace" of heteroglossia. The emergence of this condition of linguistic free enterprise in Greece cannot, of course, be attributed solely to the study of poetry in school. Certainly Athens's growing cosmopolitanism under the Peisistratids, as well as Greek colonialism and commerce generally, would have made their own contributions to this process by "physically" bringing various languages into relativizing contact with one another. But the radical heteroglossia of language that drama reflects is also liable to have been encouraged in the classroom, where poetry was abstracted from its normal contexts and studied in a disinterested, objectifying way.

Book-based study is also characterized by a tendency toward debate and contest. At least this is what we see in the *Phaedrus* and the *Protagoras*, both of which dialogues show Socrates, with surprisingly little success, competing against rival teachers and their interpretations of various subjects. And it should not be wondered at that bookish pursuits should lead to such intellectual contests. For not only does the cutting loose of discourse from its embeddedness in contexts of action give rise to an individual "subject" who can treat a discourse as an "object", but by the same token, it also must lead to the possibility of conflicting views of that same object. For this reason,

25. Vernant and Vidal-Naquet stress the difference between doing something and staging it: on stage, a ritual lamentation or sacrifice becomes "simply a representation" (1990:16).

the emergence of an individual perspective on, as opposed to a group participation within, cultural activities has also been linked with a shift "from
worldview to ideology." As Goody notes, "writing, the presence of the text
of the word in addition to its utterance, favours a partly independent role
for ideology, giving it a measure of 'structural autonomy' which it doesn't
possess in oral societies" (1986:22).

The most significant consequence of the emergence of an independent
ideology is that by its nature it will be perceived in opposition to other ide-
ologies. For example, in fixing the worldview of Homeric orality in writing,
the technology of script detaches its value system from particular lived performative contexts (the celebration of the deeds and *arete* of heroes), and establishes it as an abstract, non–context dependent "universal" dictate.
Through the now visible dialectical difference between textual universals and
lived particulars, an ideological conflict emerges. But writing goes further: it
establishes what Goody calls a "semi-permanent platform" (1986:31) for those
aspects of experience that conflict with these now universalized ideas. In so
doing, writing allows the dissenting voice of the ideological "other" to be
heard over longer stretches of time, long enough to establish itself as a different interpretation of reality. For example, we begin to hear, in the poetry
of Archilochus (ca. 650), the occasional challenge sent out to the traditionally esteemed Homeric notion of the glory of a hero's death in battle. In
Archilochus a coward proclaims *his* virtue, the love of life. This is a proclamation that thumbs its nose at an entire worldview—the Homeric culture of
kleos (acoustic renown). But in Euripides, Archilochus' personal, lyric rejection of the heroic ideal has been detached from the mouth of any one singer
and instead appears within the context of multiple views of the same subject.
When in drama a character says that "it is better that we live ever so miser-
ably than die in glory" (*Iphigenia at Aulis* 1250), one competing point of view
among many is receiving a generalizable expression, and one that does not
depend on the identity of any particular speaker. In short, interpersonal conflict is now ideological in nature, and discourse is its medium. And because
each discourse is equally alienated, and representative of a different interpretation of reality, there is no resolution possible, only winning and losing.

As we have seen, the Homeric worldview did not exist in a fixed written version for long before ideological debate over its values appeared: Xenophanes
attacked it on a number of grounds; Stesichorus (ca. 640–555) denied the ve-
racity of Homer's version of events;[26] and rhapsodes performing the textual

---

26. As we learn from his *Palinode;* see Plato *Phaedrus* 243a.

Homer were, accordingly, forced to defend him ideologically, some resorting to allegorical arguments. From at least the sixth century on, Greek poetic and intellectual life was dominated by this polemical spirit, this
agonistic claim and counterclaim by individuals against other individuals.
Stories of the famous "contest" of Homer and Hesiod go back to the sixth
century (Pfeiffer 1968:11), as does the institution of contests in epic, dithyrambic, and dramatic poetry.[27] In the fifth century, Sophists attacked one
another, philosophers attacked the Sophists, and by Aristophanes' time,
playwrights were accusing one another on stage of being "frauds" (*Frogs*
909). These polemics only escalated into Aristotle's time, when arguments
"Against X" were the order of the day (Pfeiffer 1968:49–131). In other words,
Homeric praise was increasingly replaced by ideological contest, a discursive
shift that also manifested itself in the innovations of theatrical form. As Vernant and Vidal-Naquet put it, "The legendary hero, extolled in epic, becomes a subject of debate now that he is transferred to the theatrical stage"
(1990:186).[28]

The agonistic style of literate Greek discourse has been usefully discussed by G. E. R. Lloyd (1990), who finds the conflictual ad hominem argument at work in spurring on many of the finest humanistic achievements
of Greek science and philosophy. But where storytelling is concerned, the
literate shift from worldview to ideology proved equally productive. Between the eighth and the sixth centuries B.C.E., as writing began to be used
for increasingly elaborate poetic compositions, the idea emerged that a poet
of mythological material could be a single creative individual. Consistent
with the earliest uses to which it was ever put,[29] writing thus became a mark
of poetic "personal property." In the fifth century, as we see from Aristophanes' *Frogs,* storytelling had become a site of personal ideological conflict. By contrast, the rhapsode, as depicted in Plato's *Ion,* was but one link
in a chain of inspiration which bound the performer to an impersonal tradition. But the dramatist was expected to fight it out personally, bringing to
bear not just his poetic technique but the full weight of his individualized
interpretation of the world. As a powerful symbol of the ad hominem nature of this contest in theatrical performance, the central seat in the Theatre

27. See Csapo and Slater, who point out that whereas dithyrambic singing has a long
history as a choral genre, it seems not always to have been a *competitive* genre (1995:106–7).

28. See also Peter Arnott, who notes that "debate" predominates in both tragedy and
comedy, even at the expense of "action," and serves "more often than not [as] the heart of
the play" (1989:105).

29. See Schmandt-Besserat 1989:27–42 for writing generally, W. Harris 1989:46 for
eighth-century Greece.

of Dionysus was decorated on both sides with an image of fighting cocks (Winkler 1990:49). For John J. Winkler, the cockfight captures perfectly the "zero-sum" reckoning system of the Greek agon in this period, for to win always meant to defeat one's opponent. And indeed, when the teachers go head-to-head in the *Protagoras,* surrounded by "partisan" students on chairs and benches egging their favorites on and even applauding the nice hits (337–38), they exemplify the same kind of agonistic spirit that enlivened the battle of poetic identities staged every year at the theatre festival.

Dramatic form reflects this shift to ideological contest in two crucial ways. In the first place, poetry in the theatre had become ideologized insofar as it had become *dialogic.* I have spoken of the poetic heteroglossia that drama inaugurated by combining within itself meters and dialect characteristics that had been used only separately before (see Herington 1985:114). There is one poetic feature, however, that drama does not appear to have borrowed from anywhere: the stichomythia (Herington 1985:140). This rapid-fire interchange of statement and counterstatement is the epitome of the special kind of ideological debate that writing fosters. Swift but sustained dialogic exchanges between speakers was not used anywhere that we know of in predramatic poetry—and could not have been practiced in poetic composition without the aid of writing. This is because, in stichomythia, meaning is created between speakers. In isolation, the utterances are incomplete; the meaning of each is absolutely dependent on its position in the two-part exchange. The locutions of dialogue are interrelated, codependent on one another to the extent that the whole exchange stands or falls on the inclusion of each and every element in sequence. This is not the kind of poetic composition that one can improvise spontaneously in the manner of an oral bard. The verbal fabric is so tight that every word, in exact sequence, counts for the intelligibility of the whole. In other words, its exact verbatim repeatability is a precondition of stichomythian dialogue, which means, in effect, that the use of writing is a precondition for both its creation and its performance.

Stichomythia is an interchange not only of utterances but also, necessarily, of *voices.* Dramatic dialogue, which thus marks the breakup of the unified time-space context in which poetic discourse used to be located, is for this reason a clear aesthetic reflection of the ideologically conflictual tenor of literate society. By using writing in the first place, the dramatist is untying his discourse from the time-space context in which he produced it. But in using dialogic form in particular, the playwright goes further. The dramatist is the poet who can no longer perform his own work by himself, and thus the very act of writing is inclusive of others, and of the separate time-space contexts which they inhabit. Dramatic poetry not only implies others but needs them as well.

The contest that writing opens up between inheritors of the same poetic tradition is thus reflected, on the level of dramatic form, by a textual gap—and, potentially, another contest—between creator and performer. Just as two literate poets will differ in their interpretation of the same mythological material, and pit these differing visions one against the other on the stage as the fifth-century dramatists did, so too may the poet and his performers come into conflict over the interpretation of the role as written. Stories of such interpretive contests between actors and playwrights are numerous in our time; but even in Aristotle's time there is evidence that, as Plato predicted, literacy would make students—and the actors who were their aesthetic corollaries—"difficult to get along with."

The contest between performers and poets that written study helps make possible is an important one to keep in mind. For it is not just the literate poet such as Aeschylus who accrues to himself all the benefits of literate decontextualization; the performer benefits in the same way. Critics of text-based learning and teaching from Plato to Artaud—and there is no shortage of them even today—presuppose that a system of verbatim memorization will inculcate a superficial, parrot-like mentality and discourage true wisdom, real art, all good things in proportion as it is adopted. No longer accustomed or allowed to improvise in the manner of an oral bard, the performer is imagined to have lost all creative freedom. The text, which must be memorized word for word, is seen as a tyrant, a dictator, bringing to bear on performers all the authority of a bad teacher.

The actor's textual lesson, however, is not of this kind. Both for reasons having to do with the historical context of drama's emergence, and because of certain features of all writing, the student of a dramatic *didaskalos* enjoys, if anything, greater liberty in his performance than his poetic antecedents. Representing a radical contrast to the "bondage" of the rhapsode, who is magnetically "held" in obedience to Homer and compelled always to "praise" him (*Phaedrus* 534e, 536d–e), the actor's study snips the chain of "possession" that enthralled previous performers, and puts debate, disagreement, and even opposition in its place.

Unlike the oral bard, the student-actor repeats verbatim. But because the words he repeats come from a book and not from another performer's mouth, what he repeats has a special character. Like musical notation, written speech cannot record the performance itself. As theorists of language such as Mikhail Bakhtin (1981, 1986) and Paul Ricoeur (1981) have taught, writing cannot even record *meaning* by itself (i.e., without interpretation).

In speech, linguistic meaning derives mainly from extraverbal factors: from conditions prevailing in the context of the utterance; from the inner intentions, knowledge, and beliefs of the speakers; from the nature of their relationship in terms of social status; from their gestures, tones of voice, and facial expressions (Lakoff 1972:926). In speech, in fact, the verbal component constitutes a relatively small percentage of all meaning-generating elements.

To use the speech act vocabulary of J. L. Austin (1975; orig. pub. 1962) and J. R. Searle (1992; orig. pub. 1969), writing can record only the locution of the said. The locution gives us, essentially, a string of syntactically arranged words whose *possible* individual meanings can be looked up in a dictionary. But that, of course, does not give us a meaning for the utterance as a whole. This is because writing has no means of recording either the illocutionary intentions of the speaker (a desire to frighten, inform, or to arouse the listener), or the perlocutionary effects the utterance was meant to generate (causing the listener to do, feel, or think something as a result of the utterance). The dramatic text, composed as it is almost exclusively of direct first-person utterances without surrounding lexical material, is therefore especially ill equipped to convey the meaning of its locutions.

Nicholas Udall, who with *Ralph Roister Doister* wrote perhaps the first genuine comedy of the English Renaissance, understood the inherent ambiguity of such texts. As headmaster of Eton, he appears to have written the play at some point between 1534 and 1541 for performance by his students. The play features the famous letter incident, where Ralph Roister Doister's (purchased) love letter is read aloud on stage, twice, each time with an opposite meaning. In terms of the pedagogical relation between Udall and his actor-students, the play would have provided a superb example of what the decontextualization of language in writing can do. Indeed, when one of Udall's students went on to publish his own book, *Rule of Reason* (1553), he inserted Ralph's letter into the text as an example of ambiguity.

Udall's pupil Thomas Wilson certainly learned this lesson well, whether from his classroom studies or his acting one cannot say. But Ralph's delightfully ambiguous letter is a paradigmatic document for the theatre as well as the classroom. Before speaking what has been written, one needs to decide what type of speech act it is: is it a humble and charming love letter, or the offensive blather of a self-aggrandizing blockhead? As Robin Lakoff puts it: "It is normally true in all languages that one must somehow make clear the type of speech act involved: are you asking a question, making a statement, or giving an order?" (1972:926). Are you being ironical, or serious, professing your love, or merely being kind? In written speech, the "type of speech act involved" is not provided.[30]

When a performer learns a poem from the mouth of an oral bard, language comes complete with its bodily dimension intact. Words are accompanied by appropriate gestures, and the "type of speech act involved" is implicit in the context. In memorizing a text, however, one can internalize only what the text provides. And what the text provides is the locution. In order for the text to be spoken, to make sense as an act of speech, the actor must decide what type of speech act it is. In other words, per- and illocutionary intentions must be added. Consequently, in turning a decontextualized locution into a speech act, the actor must contribute "more" than he is given.[31] Not only must he decide what type of speech act to supply, but he must also add all the extraverbal elements which in life would normally accompany a speech act of the kind he has decided to perform. These extraverbal elements, without which the actor may be uttering just a list of ambiguous words, will range from rate of delivery, to tones of voice, to facial expression, to physical action and deportment, even through to an imaginary positing of a "context," which may involve appropriate clothing and the use of objects.[32]

The difficult position into which writing thrusts its performers has been effectively described by David Olson: "While writing solved the problem of storage of information, it created . . . the 'meaning' or 'interpreta-

30. This deficiency of written language is of course less apparent in inflected languages such as Greek, which goes further than English in expressing the mood of an utterance.

31. Interpretive contributions of this kind are obviously not literally quantifiable. But as the example of Ralph's letter (or, better still, very bad acting) proves, it is possible to reduce the comprehensibility of a written utterance to near zero—a fact which suggests that the actor's contribution must be accepted as decisively large.

32. The situation is of course made even more complex by the fact that the speech act which the actor has devised on the basis of the written locution is not in fact destined for reception by the listener to whom the locution is addressed in the text. That addressee is a fictional character, and exists only as another textual locution or set of locutions. Rather, the speech act is destined, initially in rehearsal, for reception by the actor's fellow performer(s), and ultimately in performance for an audience of spectators, many of whom may be barely within earshot. Therefore, in addition to creating a meaningful corporeal speech act, the actor must devise a way to communicate his conception to a great many people who may be watching and listening from a distance. Depending on the circumstances, this may require that he add features to the conception, amplify it, or modify the whole in some other way. It is clear, then, that the verbatim memorization of a textual locution is in fact but the very beginning of a complex interpretive process which far exceeds the model on which it is based.

tion' problem" by inaugurating a visible distinction "between what a text says and what it means" (1988:425, 429). Out of this difference comes the possibility of taking a variety of different mental attitudes to verbal content: "One can hear the propositional content and then decide whether to believe or doubt it, or one can hear an utterance and then think whether it was meant literally or metaphorically. One can, as we say, begin to reflect on text rather than merely remembering it" (435). Thus, compared to the type of repetition an oral performer might practice, that of the text-bearing actor is more philosophical and ultimately more personal: philosophical because it involves the interpretation of an abstracted, decontextualized locution, personal because textual locutions are by nature ambiguous and will admit of divergent interpretations. Interpretation not only gives scope for an individual's own tastes, values, beliefs, and desires, but in fact demands that the full range of these personal criteria be brought to bear. In short, verbatim repetition, when used in the service of performance, is not at all the same thing as parrot-like copying, and may in fact discourage it.

In his discussion of the nature of writing, Plato implicitly acknowledges this feature of written speech. In a much-discussed passage in the *Phaedrus*, Socrates laments the fatherlessness of all writing. Cut off from its author, a text "has no power to protect or help itself" when "ill-treated" (275e). By ill-treatment, Plato did not of course have in mind the interpretive liberties that actors are wont to take with their texts; but because their study is a written one, actors learning a role are dealing not with the tyrant of Artaud's imagination but with the "orphan" of Plato's. While the text's inability to "answer back" disables it, to Plato's mind, as an effective teacher, this same fatherlessness gives the actor performative liberties not enjoyed by his poetic antecedents. The members of the Homer Society were not by accident called the "sons" of Homer, for the rhapsode's allegiance to his bard approaches the filial in its irrational exclusivity. Ion confesses that Homer alone inspires his love, obedience, and reverence; Hesiod and Archilochus only make him fall asleep (530–31). The fifth-century actor, by contrast, was the heir of no one poet, being instead assigned to dramatic poets randomly, by the luck of a drawn lot. And this disconnectedness of the actor from any one poet was made even more palpable in the fourth century, when the best actors were required to appear in all three dramatists' plays.

Whereas the most that a rhapsode might do in personalizing his recitation of Homer was to "overdo his gestures" (*Poetics* 1462a6), the ancient actor quickly distinguished himself, and became notorious, for playing fast and loose with his text. As Denys Page suggests, surveying the hundreds of known or suspected changes made to tragic texts in performance, "We can be certain that actors made themselves free of the play and altered it repeatedly" (1987:10). They appear to have added lines, cut speeches, altered stage directions, written their own prologues, changed sad endings to happy ones, transposed speeches from one character to another and even from one play or other written work to a separate piece. Aristotle mentions, among other things, the penchant of actors such as Neoptolemos and Theodorus for deliberately giving "new significance to old sentences" (Page 1987:16), and Theodorus apparently "would not allow any other actor . . . to enter before himself," regardless of the order of entrances called for in the text (*Politics* 1336b27). Aristotle also mentions the tendency of actors to "put in something of their own" (*Poetics* 1461b3–4). The actor who was to play the Phrygian slave in *Orestes* is believed to have flatly refused to jump off the roof for his entrance as the text demands, evidently insisting that lines be added to support his preference for entering normally, through the door (Page 1987:42). Given the penchant of the ancient theatre's "students" for thus contradicting the "teachings" of their texts, Page concludes that our founding thespians may have been almost as cavalier with their texts as Garrick was with *Hamlet* or Hamlet was, for that matter, with *The Murder of Gonzago*.

In fact, the kind of textual liberties attributed by Aristotle to Neoptolemos were apparently taken so often and so generally that the Athenians actually felt compelled to pass a law against such irreverent behavior.[33] Copies of the three great tragedians' work were installed "in public," presumably in the city archives or Metroön, and actors were legally bound not to deviate from them. Now, the act of installing plays in the archives is symptomatic of a typically literate tendency to endow certain much-beloved works with a "classic" status and to protect them from any changes thereafter. This happened to the Homeric poems soon after they were written down, as we saw in Chapter 1, and performers of Homer from that point forth were bound to be "very precise about the exact words" (Xenophon *Memorabilia* 4.2, 10). Once a consciousness of the canonical nature of a given text has set in (as we know, with the passing of the Lykurgan law, that it had by the fourth century in Greece), it does indeed become increasingly difficult to alter a text in performance. Or does it?

One need not look very long or hard at theatre history to see how futile are all attempts to protect the integrity of even the most canonical texts. Father Shakespeare never could say anything about the happy endings added to *Lear* and *Romeo and Juliet* by later actors, and not just because of his

---

33. Plutarch *Lives* 10, *Orat. Lyc.* 841f. as cited by Thomas 1989:48.

death. Nothing prevented the first performers of *A Doll's House* in Germany
from abusing the play, within Ibsen's lifetime, to the point where Nora decides not to leave her husband after all. If the actors of the ancient theatre
took advantage of the fatherlessness of their texts in performance, they were
certainly not doing anything that all actors haven't made a profession of
doing since.

The formal feature of drama which all but guarantees the taking of such
liberties—a textual separation between composer and performer—has also
determined the subject of many plays. Mention of the Lykurgan law puts
us instantly in mind of the many plays of Shakespeare which, like *Hamlet,*
depict a character's attempts to control his actors, forestall nonauthorial
additions, or make alterations to a given play. The clearest example of all,
of course, is *Measure for Measure,* which shows Angelo as a Renaissance
Lykurgus, trying to legislate the citizen body into obedience. But as he
learns, the body, always outside the text, in one way or another resists
all such attempts at didactic proscription. Neither Angelo's legal text, nor
Isabella's religious text, nor ultimately the Duke's dramatic text proves
able to bring the performing body into obedience: Barnardine's body refuses
to obey the schedule and die at the prescribed time (4.3.59); Angelo's sex
organs fill up with "strong and swelling" blood in the middle of an anti-
sex lecture (2.2.142ff.); and Isabella's body can barely be stopped from
further seducing and "breed[ing]" with practically the first man she sets eyes
on when on furlough from the nunnery (2.2.40ff.). Everyone's "codpiece,"
as Lucio puts it, will "rebel" of itself, irrespective of all discursive dictates
(3.2.124).

We can be quite sure that Lykurgus' law against textual liberties on
stage was about as effective as Angelo's law against fornication out of wed-
lock. The proof of this is to be found in the ancient plays themselves, which
are forever reinforcing the idea that the body escapes all written prescript.

Although it is not about texts specifically, the *Philoctetes* provides a useful introduction to the nature of didacticism as a fifth-century dramatist saw it.
As a story about a *didaskalos,* it may tell us something about how Sophocles
viewed his role in this capacity. The play begins with Odysseus giving Neoptolemos some very schoolmasterish, decontextualized instruction, teaching
him in the manner of a Sophist what to say and how to say it. As we know
both from Aristophanes' *Clouds* and from Plato's *Protagoras,* the Sophists
were marked as teachers precisely by their skill in teaching citizens how to
use words for "gain;" and Odysseus, in justifying his teaching, defends his
lesson in just this way, in the name of "gain" (111). He in fact directs his stu-

dent in an elaborate play-within-a-play, explaining the actor's objectives, and even offering him a possible "motivation" with which to make his performance appear more credible.

Neoptolemos goes on to give an excellent recitation for the poor susceptible Philoctetes—at least initially. He begins by doing as all obedient student/actors must: he "brackets" his own contextual reality, suppresses his own motivatedness *in propria persona,* and functions like a sign in Odysseus' story. He represents the embittered warrior, wronged by the Atridae, on his way home. But his cooperation in Odysseus' plan to "ensnare the soul of Philoctetes with . . . words" ultimately crashes to the ground like a stack of writing tablets when the bottom is pulled out. The bottom, literally, for what he faces is that against which no lesson is proof: the grotesque body of his interlocutor. As is the case elsewhere in Greek literature, it is the foot and not the buttocks which takes on the burden of all that is lowest in man; and Philoctetes' foot is as grotesque as can be imagined. Gushing pus and foulest stench, it reduces the body connected to it to that powerless state of surrender to biological reality so typical of physical illness or decay. This is human life before civilization, during that period of servitude to a "state of nature" wherein life is but the grinding round of pain, sleep, the struggle to feed oneself and drag one's imprisoning carcass into shelter. Face to face with this suppurating flesh, this man as "the thing itself," Neoptolemos, from the point of view of his own physical, experiential reality, must reevaluate his semiotic intentions in the midst of his performance. He takes off his mask, speaks unscripted lines, and shows *himself.* And Sophocles criticizes the "shabby, slit-eyed soul" of Odysseus precisely for its life-denying didacticism: he criticizes him for teaching Neoptolemos "step by step" how to act "against his nature" (*Philoctetes* 1013).

What we find here is a contest between teacher and student in which the battle lines are drawn between the content of the lesson and the lower bodily reality of the performer's own experiential context—the student's "gut" reaction. We have already had a glimpse of this text-body contest in the *Phaedrus.* When Socrates greets the book-toting Phaedrus by asking what he's got protruding from under his cloak, he sounds rather like Mae West demanding to know whether the bulge in her interlocutor's trousers is a pistol or a sign that he's "happy to see" her. When he wants to subvert the loftiness of his ascent into tales of mythic nymphs, Socrates brings the discussion down to the level of his feet (230b7). In fact, he uses foot-related tropes twice in this dialogue (250e4–5), both times referring either to "descent" into animalistic pleasures ("surrendering himself to pleasure does his best to go on four feet") or a descending return to the physical reality of the present context ("to judge by my foot"). Whereas, according to Socrates, bookish pursuits elevate writers to the status of immortal gods (258c), face-to-face instruction thrusts speakers down to their lower bodily parts. In fact, the whole dialogue is an implicit comparison between the elevation of texts, the high-minded pursuit of disinterested truth, and the downward pull of the lower body—sexual appetite, impregnation, birth, eating, sickness. By the dialogue's end, Plato has come down in favor of entry, impregnation, and the propagation of one's ideas, or "seeds," in the physical body of a listener (276–7b). Although real knowledge, for Socrates, can perhaps be gained only through physically disengaged means, to stay alive it must keep planting itself physically into present bodies. If we plant our ideas only in books, he says, we will be sowing them ineffectually, that is, our words will bear no fruit (276e). We must on the contrary sow what we know physically in our listeners, keep seducing them in the flesh and impregnating them with a love of wisdom. The superiority of face-to-face instruction therefore ultimately rests on the fact that it is *procreative* (276e).[34]

The same association between texts and sterility is drawn in the *Hippolytos,* a play that features a student second in fame only to Phaedrus. Hippolytos is introduced as a "pupil" (11), an obsessive reader of books (953–54); but his bookishness has immunized him to the calls of the flesh. Not only has he forsworn the flesh literally, in the vegetarianism which he flaunts so shamelessly (952), but he scorns Aphrodite too, spurning the bed of love and marriage (14). His hatred of women (612–52) and allegiance to chastity, even his devotion to the hunt, are all presented in this play as consequences of his bookish "high heart" (730). And because of all of these denials of bodily life, "the doors of death" must open for Hippolytos (56): Aphrodite, or love itself, will "lay [him] by the heels" (9), crush him to death under the feet of trampling horses.

In both the *Phaedrus* and *Hippolytos,* we find similar conceptions of book-based study. Books are associated with height and high-mindedness, but also with barrenness, and contrasted with "lower" realities of the body, particularly the feet. In Aristophanes' lampoon of the Air-worshipping residents of the "Reflectory" in the *Clouds,* we again see this association of scholarship with elevation and height: Socrates flies onto the stage suspended aloft from the god's machine, and walks around with his head in the clouds (200–235). When Aristophanes wants to criticize the physical gag

---

34. Oral teaching is described as "taking a fitting soul" and planting and sowing in it "words accompanied by knowledge, which are able to help themselves and the man who planted them, and are not without fruit but contain a seed, from which others grow in other soils."

artistry, the reliance on giant phalloi, that characterizes the comedy of his competitors, he explicitly contrasts the lowness of such techniques with the highness of his own, more bookish ones (*Clouds* 520–64; *Wasps* 65). And when he wants to ridicule the pretensions of high-mindedness, he lowers the discussion to "the lowest reaches" (192) of the student anatomy, the asshole (185–95). In fact, once we have seen the outlines of this contest between high texts and low bodies, we begin to find it everywhere, functioning as a central organizing principle of many fifth-century plays.

For example, Oedipus may not often be associated with scholarship, but we should remember that in Sophocles' lifetime, the Sphinx was depicted iconographically as reading from a book. In solving her riddle, Oedipus would thus have been seen by Sophocles as exemplifying, if not a skill for textual exegesis, then at least a general kind of literate braininess. But Oedipus knows nothing about himself physically, cannot recognize his father's body, his mother's womb, the truth about his own desire. And, as we might expect from the reliance we find elsewhere on the feet as symbols for low corporeality, Oedipus' high textual mastery is explicitly contrasted with the brute lowness of his "swollen foot."

In fact, the lower body "puts its foot down" against high textual aspirations throughout the plays of the fifth century. Like Odysseus' didactic stratagems, which are thrust earthward by a disgustingly odoriferous disease in the archer's foot, the high justice of written law in the *Oresteia* is contested and opposed by the grotesque bodies of the Furies, who ooze bodily fluids on the ground. In the *Women of Trachis,* overweening confidence in the interpretation of oracular texts is countered with grisly physical agony. In the *Antigone,* Creon tries to set "written laws" over and above the needs of a dead body, but Antigone, answering instead to the call of the lower, chthonic orders, will not be instructed. In another typical subversion of textual height by bodily lowness, Philocleon of the *Wasps* starts the play addicted to writing out sentences and penalties in the law courts, and ends the play, cured, dancing drunkenly around the stage with a naked flute girl. This play is an especially interesting example, since the low-bodily triumph over textuality refers directly to the performance of drama itself: the debased dikast speaks distinctly of "the feet of Euripides" (1414) and the dance steps, leg kicks, belly slaps, and bum splits of Thespis and Phrynichus (1480, 1492, 1524–25). In the *Knights,* the reading of oracle books is brought into direct contrast on stage with the guzzling of a bellyful of wine. Pentheus' official state cleverness is also "taught a lesson" by the low animalistic forces of physical ecstasy in the *Bacchai.* And what, in the end, is the great answer to the Sphinx's riddle? It is of course the *feet* of man as he ages, his physical reality, which, like Oedipus' "swollen foot," can be punctured and wounded, which decays and really dies—but only once.[35]

What all these dramatic characters learn to find "below" their written lessons is the body, for better or worse. And it is a discovery that dramatic characters were still being forced to make centuries later. Beneath their religious and legal dictates, Angelo and Isabella, too, discover what "the flesh . . . shall better determine" (2.2.273–75): that to be frozen into textual absolutes (1.4.58–67; 2.2.45; 3.2.106) is to "be absolute for death" (3.1.5, 118). All attempts to legislate the body into strict obedience must fail. The "voice of recorded law" (2.4.61) may attempt to control the body, but short of "geld[ing] and splay[ing] all the youth of the city," they "will to't" nonetheless.

The contest between high and low that we see in these plays is characteristic of literate cultures everywhere. As scholars of literacy such as Jack Goody (1968, 1986, 1987), M. T. Clanchy (1979), and Gerd Baumann (1986) have shown, even in newly and only partly literate societies, bookish activities quickly establish themselves as "higher" than orally embedded ones. Goody describes how schools and/or religious sects—be they of the Egyptian temple scribes, medieval scriptoria, or other types of academy—actively perpetuate this high/low binarism, this socially polarized high/low "diglossia" (Baumann 1986:42). Characteristic of this valued split is its tendency to spread out both horizontally and vertically: it will have the effect of classing occupations as well as gender in a social hierarchy. Those who work and learn with their hands, or speak only the "mother tongue," will lose status proportionately as scholarship establishes itself.

Where does this high/low binarism come from, and why does literacy tend to introduce it? Historical explanations might be found, such as the early use of writing for charting the movements of heavenly bodies, or the fact that a given culture is likely to have learned writing from one that seems to be "superior." In some places it might seem attributable to the use made of writing by the "upper levels" of a given social hierarchy (government, clergy). These explanations will not do for ancient Greece, however. Not only did the Greeks believe themselves culturally superior to all of their lettered neighbors (Steiner 1994), but writing was first used in Greece by private individuals, and never appeared to be the prerogative of any elite, religious or governmental. It may rather be the case that the high/low con-

35. See Vernant's discussion of the riddle (1978:485).

test originates in a more fundamental and universal experience in the bodily life of literates.

Just as all people must experience their head, eyes, and brain as "higher" than their lower regions of feet, anus, gut, and genitals, so too, perhaps by a kind of primal existential analogy, will intellection, sight, and imagination be deemed higher functions than walking, making, copulation, digestion, and defecation. Peter Stallybrass and Allon White (1986:3) have provided a useful description of how, in general, "cultures 'think themselves' in the most immediate and effective ways through the combined symbolisms" of a geographic hierarchy (mountaintop versus valley), a corporeal hierarchy (upper versus lower orifices, protrusions, and organs); a hierarchy of the social plane (king versus beggar) and of psychic forms (high philosophical, theological, or "classic" literary genres versus low physical crafts, "popular" entertainment, etc.) [36]

In one of his characteristic attempts to interfere with such rigid binary thinking, Nietzsche famously claimed that the only thoughts worth having come *while walking;* but the communication of thoughts through writing is by definition an activity of the "upper" realms. With no alphabetical equivalent for the physical presences of speech, what writing leaves out is, in Roland Barthes's words, "quite simply, *the body*" (1985:5). It is still a body that writes, and a body that reads; but reading and writing cannot be corporeal in the same way that speaking and listening are. Passionate readers and writers might disagree. After all, as Euripides shows in *Iphigenia in Aulis,* even writers moan, wail, and pull out their hair in the act of writing a letter. But there is a limit to the extent to which writing can serve as conduit for the body. Punctuation and other graphic and lexical devices can substitute themselves somewhat for the signs the body uses in speaking (grimaces, eye movements, hand gestures); but there is one side of bodily input into speech for which there is absolutely no analogue in writing. How does one even describe it in writing? Following Walter Benjamin, Barthes refers to the "aura" of an individual body, the obtuseness and uniqueness of its brute surfaces, none of which can be mechanically reproduced or even properly contained within language at all. But Bakhtin possibly puts it more usefully by speaking about the "grotesque body," the body experienced as full of secreting orifices and pregnant protrusions, the body that burps and farts, laughs and

36. A writer in the twelfth century C.E. contrasts the lowness of "trifling mummers in vulgar rhymes" with the height of literary works such as the *Aeneid* (Clanchy 1979:157); Aristophanes elevates his intellectual writings over "vulgar low comedy" (*Wasps* 66).

gets pregnant, putrefies and dies. In terms of the symbolically generative hierarchy just mentioned, this is the *low* body, the body as lower order, the body as base. In eliminating all traces of this grotesque aspect of bodily life from written communication, writing "elevates" itself over speech. Writing thus makes all texts appear "high" in comparison with the grotesque bodily realities of speech. But of course Plato has as much as suggested this explanation already: in the absence of a real speaker's body, physical entry and fecundation cannot take place.

The high textual/low bodily polarity pursued so far owes a great deal to Bakhtin's concept of the carnivalesque (1968). In Bakhtin's view, the grotesque body represents the body of "the people" which resists all attempts by official culture to control its actions and centralize its verbal-ideological reality. Bakhtin conceives of "carnivalesque degradation," which manifests itself in popular-festive forms of social interaction such as theatre, as subversive of the attempts made by the high forces of serious, literate culture to impose their sacred books and transcendent doctrines throughout the verbal-ideological world:

> The carnivalesque spirit . . . destroys this limited seriousness and all pretense of an extratemporal meaning.
> The essential principal of [this] grotesque realism is . . . the lowering of all that is high, spiritual, ideal, abstract; it is a transfer to the material level, to the sphere of earth and body. (20)

For Bakhtin, carnivalesque degradation is a double movement down: it both "bring[s] down to earth," and "turn[s] [its] subjects into flesh" (20). In the cosmic dimension, "downward" is earth, "upward" is heaven, while in the bodily aspect, "which is not," according to Bakhtin, "clearly distinct from the cosmic, the upper part is the face or the head and the lower part is the genital organs, the belly, the buttocks" (21). Or the feet, we might add, which were and which remain in many Mediterranean countries the "lowest," rudest part of the anatomy. Bakhtin was chiefly interested in the incorporation of carnivalesque imagery by the novel, and he did not pursue the relation between carnival and theatre.[37] But like Nietzsche's Apollonian/Dionysian contest, by which it was certainly influenced (Wise 1989), Bakhtin's high/low binary has obvious uses in theatrical theory. Indeed, all the plays we have looked at in this chapter are carnivalesque in the Bakhtinian sense, even the tragedies. For no matter whether the end is a happy or sad one, an ecstatic drunken dance or an ecstasy of death and de-

37. See Bristol 1985, who did.

struction, the body always wins. All high textual aspirations are turned into flesh by the end.

Literally: for drama is a genre in which real grotesque bodies are always given the last word. Theatre is itself a kind of generic acknowledgment of the lesson about literacy taught in the plays I have described: that the body must have some input into any interpretation of what is good and right, human or inhuman, virtuous or evil. The lesson about literate study that these plays teach thus amounts to a kind of critique of literacy, a warning about its dangers. Many such critiques of didactic prescription appear in the repertory, and all of them, when performed, must succeed in a way that cannot be matched elsewhere in literature, even by the most self-critical of novels. We cannot say, of course, whether the actor Neoptolemos was inspired by the Sophoclean hero of that name, but what we learn from each of these pupils is the same: the literate student body will rebel. As a literary form, drama is uniquely well equipped to teach this lesson again and again, to actors, poets, and audiences alike.

The actor who has conned his part considers himself "off book," an accurate description if ever there was one. In his analysis of the actor's interpretive procedure, David Cole (1992) argues that the actor interprets his text while alone, and then defends his reading against the solitary readings of other actors in rehearsal. In reality, the process is not as masturbatory and "readerly" as that. For in the particular type of textual understanding that characterizes the actor's work, the bodies of others actively enter into the interpretation process, where they become both hermeneutical device and final court of appeal. In the theatre, the creation of meaningful utterances out of textual locutions happens in a context of direct intercourse between bodies. Meanings generated from play texts are thus the products not solely of isolated literary interpretations, but also of the actual effects that bodies have on one another. In rehearsal no less than in performance, the ear for speech that the text provides is augmented by an eye for what the grotesque body *does*. A suddenly dilated pupil or rush of blood to the skin tells the actor something new about the relation of this language to these bodies; perspiration, revulsion, or desire may come unbidden and add to understanding. The actor, as memorizer and repeater of already written texts, thus starts out like the Athenian grammar student with a poem set on his bench. But as a performer who speaks to listeners in person, he is also like Phaedrus, the lover who affects his interlocutor with his lower body. To borrow the imagery that Plato used throughout his dialogue about writing and teaching, a performer of this type is thus subject to both decontextual *and* sexual models of communication. If the theatre is a classroom, it is therefore one in which the student learns as much from bodies as he does from texts.

As a performed art of texts and bodies, drama can reveal the limitations of textuality and *mean it.* What dramatic critiques such as *Philoctetes* or *Measure for Measure* represent, in writing, is also necessarily what actors do themselves in rehearsal and performance: they both study their parts *and* show themselves in ways that may contradict textual dictates. Dramatic texts as lessons thus have a built-in generic safeguard against the possibility that any text may turn out to be the product of a "slit-eyed soul" in light of new physical evidence. All actors may begin like Neoptolemos, dutifully learning their lessons, but they are also generically sanctioned, nay, forced, to do as he does in going beyond and "below" them.

What does an actor find "below" his text? In Bakhtin, the textually re-pressed lower order is characterized, to use Michael Bristol's words, as "insis-tently cheerful and hopeful" (1985:23). It is the fecundating principle of the Platonic body as described in the *Phaedrus.* To Bakhtin's mind, the lower material bodily realm is forever affirming the indestructible vitality of life, the indomitable spirit of the people, the ever-regenerating power of nature. In carnival as Bakhtin sees it, the barriers separating man from man are joy-fully broken down and a spirit of universal brotherhood prevails. Not sur-prisingly, Bakhtin's vision of bodily life has since been characterized as "naively idyllic, vague and even silly" (Bristol 1985:23).

But Nietzsche, who first sketched in the outlines of this theory, knew better. The populist orgiastic rituals which for Nietzsche represented the an-tithesis of high Apollonian control threatened even their participants with savage violence and death. If we can trust Euripides' account in the *Bacchai,* Nietzsche was closer to the ancients' own view of the matter. Indeed, the blind destructiveness of the bacchantes' revels in the *Baccha* stands as a per-petual caveat against any temptation to view the body and its low domain in simplistic, idyllic terms. The bodily principle in *Hippolytos, Oedipus, Antigone,* and *Women of Trachis* is similarly shown to bring painful disfigure-ment, entombment, and death.

As far as the history of literate culture is concerned, Bakhtin was largely right. Populist corporeal doings *do* tend to be banished, denigrated, and ide-ologically demonized by high, official culture in its efforts to establish itself as sovereign over cultural life. And all texts do banish the grotesque body, naturally and inevitably, from the elevated spheres of writing and reading. Historically, the theatre certainly has suffered, over lengthy stretches of time, from just such attempts to repress the lower bodily realm. These at-tempts have taken the form not only of the antitheatrical tracts written in such numbers by the early Church Fathers, but also of the many hierarchizing statements by modern literary theorists who demote theatre in status as a vulgar or "impure" form.

But it would be wrong to reverse the snobbery, so to speak, and view all nonliterary activities as transcendently, transhistorically true, good, and humane. As Stallybrass and White remind us, carnivalesque orgies are just as likely to manifest their grotesque bodily impulses in the stoning of pigs, or Jews, or adulteresses, in the slaughtering of animals, or "witches," or Turks, or in the ideologically motivated destruction of any other group marked out for a ritualistic "cleansing." Pentheus was not the first nor will he have been the last to be ripped apart by reveling mobs.[38]

The lower material bodily stratum certainly stands opposed to literate modes, insofar as it marks the limit of what texts can represent and what they can compel. But there is no justification for positing the existence of any single bodily truth, from "universal harmony" to "the fecundating goodness of nature." If we are to take the body seriously in the theatre, and the genre obviously demands that we do, we must take it seriously on its own terms. To do so means taking it as, primarily, a material substance in human history. And just as any other aspect of material nature is affected by culture and reflects its ongoing changes and trends, so too must the body be seen as subject to more or less precisely locatable historical values and assumptions.[39] The female body for example, as I think most would now agree, has been perceived throughout history in various different ways. Images of "womanhood," however they are generated, become the lenses through which spectators view female bodies on the stage, even through which actors view their own bodies (Diamond 1992:390ff.). The body is *also* a "medium of culture,"[40] and it will be perceived and even experienced according to available models. To take just one example, T. B. L. Webster noticed that seventh-century B.C.E. sculptures of the human form were to some extent determined by literary models. The Homeric body, with its emphasis on eyes and knees, is what artists came to see when looking at real bodies: their human forms privilege eyes and knees accordingly (1959:44). Such historically determined perceptions of the body may be invisible at the time, and those who represent the body through history may claim that they are simply seeing the body as it really, or naturally, is. But the verbal-

38. To say nothing about the more prosaic fact that the lower body can also be, and in our time especially has been, a carrier of disease, suffering, and death.

39. In particular, see Purdy 1992:5 for a discussion of the body as "a primary site for ideological inscription."

40. Susan Bordo as cited by Forte 1992:249.

ideological content of such representations (i.e., "eyes and knees")[41] becomes increasingly obvious over time. In short, the relation between "the 'material' body and the body in representation" is not a simple one (Forte 1992:249).

The relation between text and body is rather a dialectical one which the theatre simply keeps alive. In the *Philoctetes,* Sophocles all but admits to the undecidability of the contest between high and low by bringing on a deus ex machina at the end of the play. The battle between Odysseus' clever mouth and Philoctetes' grotesque foot, in the midst of which the actor-student Neoptolemos finds himself, is not the kind of contest that should be decided once and for all in favor of either. Neither foot nor mouth has a greater claim to truth as far as the human anatomy is concerned: an absolute decision either way is amputation, or censorship, of the most arbitrary kind. As far as the theatre as sociohistorical institution is concerned, Philoctetes' foot, as a stage image, will take its meaning for audiences and actors alike from the historical context in which they are all embedded. For the Greeks—who in spite of their many cures for diseases (*Antigone* 398) had no antibiotics or CAT scans—the decay of the archer's flesh would probably have represented a genuine threat to bodily health and a descent, ultimately, into the realm of the inhuman. To us today, it might represent no more than a quaint reminder that we are composed of flesh and blood after all, in spite of our many machines. The important thing is that, as both a literary and a corporeal art, drama can explore the text/body dialectic without peremptorily annulling the "lower" half—something that obviously cannot be said of the philosophical dialogue. Having ruled out a role for the performing body in his writings, Plato ensured that in Platonic texts the body is never grotesque and rebellious. All that is left is an abstract literary *idea* of the body.

The spread of literacy, both in post-Homeric Greece and in early Renaissance Europe, does seem to have inaugurated precisely the kind of split in cultural life that both Bakhtin and Nietzsche describe: on the one hand, urban, Apollonian forces tend to put centripetal pressure on cultural life, textualizing and universalizing it; on the other hand, rural, Dionysian involvements, with their popular oral traditions and orgiastic rituals, dances, and animal acts, tend to function centrifugally, pulling it apart and down to the lower regions of the grotesque body. In such periods of transition from

41. The "eyes and knees" of Homeric epic might be compared to the "tits and ass" of the modern American musical comedy; see the song of that name in *A Chorus Line.*

oral-traditional to high-literate culture, when centrifugal and centripetal forces are both simultaneously at peak levels of vitality and influence, a special species of art could be said to emerge. The period between Homer and Socrates must number among these transitional times, as must that between late medieval and early Renaissance Europe. And the genre of poetry that emerges under these conditions is one that could not have been produced by either oral or literate modes by themselves, but is rather a kind of offspring that, as Nietzsche would say, requires the participation of both parents.

Furthermore, what has been said about literate culture in the Renaissance could be said with equal justification about the context of drama's birth (and of other literate civilizations as well): that literacy is a city phenomenon (Goody 1987:300). It is to the cities that intellectuals and poets gravitate, and it is from the city that writing emanates in the form of decrees, laws, levies, treaties, books. To inhabitants of the city—with its tendencies toward enlightenment, erudition, and verbal-ideological centralization—the country—with its illiterates, its stronger connections with ancient rituals, animal life, and other bodily doings—often appears base, backward, low. At Athens, a ham actor is told to take his small verbal technique and big bodily brawn to the rural festivals, where a "lower" form of art prevailed.[42] Socrates had no use for the country; the only thing that could lure him beyond the city walls were "speeches in books" (*Phaedrus* 230d5–230e). Illiterates represented in the dramas and fragments are generally from the country, as I mentioned earlier; and Socrates of the *Clouds* dismisses his hopeless old student as an ignorant rustic (628). And when characters try to escape the city in the *Birds,* the city comes after them in the form of books and more books. Peisistratus is said to have brought poets from all parts of Greece to the Athenian city court, within which urban literate milieu drama was developed (Herington 1985:61).[43]

We have already seen something of this marriage of high and low in the intrapoetic dialogue that drama established between the praise of epic and the blame of iambics. To this carnivalesque generic novelty we might also

42. Pickard-Cambridge 1968:168; Aristotle *Rhetoric* 3.12.1413b12f.; cf. Dover 1972: 12 n. 3.

43. Similar circumstances can be seen to have been instrumental in the development of aboriginal theatre in Canada. Theatre was "foreign" to aboriginal culture before writing (Brask 1992:142; Brask and Morgan 1992:x, xii, xiv; Wheeler 1992:43), but playwright Tomson Highway, born in rural Manitoba, says that it first occurred to him to dramatize traditional Native stories during his sojourn, after a university degree, on the city streets of Toronto (quoted in Morgan 1992:130).

add the story about Arion of Methymna, who, although supposedly rescued at sea by dolphins, was also believed, by Herodotus at least, to have written a tragedy before Thespis. If true, the legend supports my depiction of drama as a generic combination of high and low. For Arion is said to have come up with the idea of tragedy by bringing some low, concupiscent satyrs—the embodiment of everything bodily, rural, and debased—onto the stage in the middle of a high choral praise poem.[44]

But whatever intermediate stages poetic performance went through on the way to the invention of dramatic form, there is no doubt that a "satyric," or carnivalesque, lowering of all that is high has remained the main distinguishing characteristic of theatre among the literary genres. This has tended to brand it with a more or less disreputable image within high-literate culture.[45] Always implicitly threatening the highest ideals of scholarship with "debasement," the theatre has also had a checkered career as far as its membership in the hierarchy of genres is concerned. In ancient Greece as in Renaissance Europe, however, literary standards were very high, but never so all-encompassing as to foreclose inclusion of the grotesque body in literate compositions. For this reason, despite their various historical distortions and idealizations, both Nietzsche's and Bakhtin's generic theories are not altogether wrong in connecting the birth of genres to precise historical moments.

For the inventors of drama, bookish elevation was still something of a novelty. When Aristophanes quips that "either Prodicus, or a book, has been the ruin of *him*" (frag. 490 Edmonds 1957), he is giving voice to a widespread belief that books are just bad news, and bad for the city.[46] In fact, nearly all Aristophanic scenes that feature writing criticize it as a "nuisance" of one form or another (*Birds* 1037). Whether maligned for its sterility (Plato), its secrecy (Herodotus), its tendency to effeminize citizens (*Clouds*) or empower the rabble (*Birds*), it is clear that in the fifth century, in the first "round" of this contest between the student body and text, the text was *not* the favorite.[47]

44. Herodotus *History* 1.23; Webster 1959:68, 76 n. 36; Else 1965b:17–24; Pickard-Cambridge 1962:131f.

45. The most exhaustive study of the theatre's low reputation within literate culture is Jonas Barish, *The Antitheatrical Prejudice* (1981).

46. See Steiner 1994, who makes the same point for Herodotus.

47. Rosalind Thomas confirms the non-controlling nature of writing as used by the Greeks through all phases with much discussion and evidence (1992:128ff.). Turner (1951:15–23) discusses fifth-century critiques of writing; Slater discusses those of Old Comedy (1996:99–112).

For the fifth century was still a period of literary history in which what was said and done mattered more than what was written. This is especially true of poetry. Playwrights, we must remember, won or lost on the basis of what happened on stage during performance; their plays were not judged in the festival as texts (Page 1987:108). When Dionysus, in Hades, has settled on the poet best equipped to save the city and the theatre festival, he does not want merely to bring a text back up with him; he wants a poet in the flesh (*Frogs* 1419). As Rosalind Thomas (1989, 1992), William Harris (1989), and Deborah Steiner (1994) have shown, Greek society in the fifth century continued, despite the presence of a growing number of literate activities, to be organized primarily around face-to-face communication, whether in the form of speeches in the Assembly, testimony and argument in the law courts, gossip in the marketplace, or poetic performance, which was still the expected method of disseminating verbal art. From Aristophanes' depiction of Dionysus sitting on board a ship reading his own copy of Euripides' *Andromeda,* and from other remarks about everyone having a book "in his hands" (*Frogs* 52, 1114), we have to conclude that plays were available to the public in written form, at least from the end of the fifth century. But available not as holy writ, as it were, for bodily performance was still the main goal. By contrast, literate activities in our time have come to dominate civic and artistic life to an extent that would have been unimaginable to the first playwrights. And so a historical leap is required to imagine what "the text" meant for the inventors of drama: it was not an ossified dictator but a part of an ongoing oral process.

What the playwright presented in competition on stage obviously consisted of the performers' own corporeal speech acts. And since, for all we know, the first published version of a given play was based on one specific and highly interpolated performance, such actorly input may itself have *become* the official text.[48] In the context of theatre's emergence, the literate preference for authorized versions, canonical texts, and narrative closure had

48. As for the difficult question of exactly how the dramatic texts were copied and circulated among the public, very little is known for certain. L. D. Reynolds and N. G. Wilson find enough evidence to date the existence of a "book trade" to the middle of the fifth century (1968:2). References to the part of the Athenian market where books could be bought (Eupolis, frag. 304 cited by Reynolds and Wilson 1968:2), plus Socrates' statement about the price of philosophy texts (*Apology* 26), would lead us to assume that the public got copies of plays by likewise buying them. Whether the copies were made by the playwright, the actors, or entrepreneurial booksellers and scribes is not known. See Page 1987 and Hadas 1954.

not yet taken the extreme form to which students are accustomed today.[49] Intending both memorization *and* performance, the dramatic text that emerged under these conditions of literacy has, as a result, retained what Bakhtin would have called a "loop-hole," a bodily escape hatch which ultimately distinguishes plays from other products of literacy. It should not therefore be surprising to find that classicists are in agreement that the texts of the three great tragedians have come down to us in irredeemably "corrupt" versions. And what was true of ancient Greek tragedies is true of Shakespeare and plays in modernity as well: Which text could lay claim to being the "authorized" Shakespeare (see esp. Orgel 1988:1)? Which version of a Beckett play is the "original"? Although playwrights such as Jonson[50] and Shaw[51] have occasionally appeared as exceptions to this rule, it is more typical of dramatic writing from Aeschylus to the present that the dramatic text does not possess the kind of textual purity and fixity up against which scholarized standards for "original authority" and "absolute allegiance" can meaningfully be held.

It is fascinating to see that the particular attitude to text that we find in the fifth century has managed to survive within the theatre to this day, and perhaps there alone, despite all pressure from other spheres of literary endeavor to enshrine texts as unchangeable. Even the actor's book bespeaks the irreverent attitude of theatre to its texts. Unlike the books of many other types of students, the actor's text looks more like a scroll than a book from spending so much time in a pocket during rehearsal; it is covered with markings on every page, from the arrows and squiggles that indicate blocking, to coffee stains, to underlinings, to marginal notes of every kind. It quickly becomes a fairly dog-eared palimpsest of the actor's physical experience during the preparation of the show. Used book stores tell the same tale in another way. Except perhaps for gift-box sets of Shakespeare, the volumes in the play section are invariably smaller, cheaper, and in general more disreputable-looking than the objects one sees on the history, religion, and

49. Thomas provides copious evidence that improvisation was still highly valued in the fifth century and beyond (1992:124), and that written records never developed the kind of "controlling" power over Greek life that some moderns associate with literacy (129ff.). Thomas cites Lévi-Strauss as an example (128), a modern writer whose misunderstanding of literacy's effects parallel Artaud's almost exactly.

50. Jonson supervised the printing of his plays and cared deeply about the published version.

51. Shaw's obsessiveness about the printing of his plays extended even to the spelling of particular words and included an almost novelistic concern with the finer details of decor and clothing.

philosophy shelves. This may seem a trivial point, but it is an accurate reflection of the theatre's relation to its books. That is to say, even the theatre's high texts are somewhat base, grotesque, "corrupted" by traces of lower, material, bodily life. When we consider players' manuscripts from the late Middle Ages, we see just how significant this fact is. The oldest extant secular play in English, the *Interludium de Clerico et Puella,* written in approximately 1260—and abducted from the British Museum in 1971—survived into our century in a tiny, palm-sized roll (Clanchy 1979:113). Like other players' manuscripts of the time, it is a physical record of the contexts in which it was used. As Erich Auerbach points out, these texts, written for use by actors, survive so sparsely in libraries precisely because they were actively, physically carried around in palms and pockets and simply fell apart. Those that survived are generally poorly executed and very badly worn (1965:288–89).

As Jiri Veltrusky remarked about the possibility of a genre's remaining "the same" over time: "A literary genre is not 'timeless' because it does not change but because it preserves its identity through all the changes it undergoes" (1977:7). The identity of drama as a literary genre thus resides in its maintenance of a certain freedom from itself *qua* literary text. As Thomas (1989 and 1992) suggests, the standard of absolute textual authority which the scholarly community was destined eventually to champion, and which in art we are more justified in associating with novels than with plays, had to wait for its fulfillment for the invention of the printing press. By Artaud's time, theatre's scholarly associations had come to seem shameful and constricting. So "high" indeed had bookishness become over the centuries that bodily performance itself had been eliminated entirely from many spheres of public and scholarly life. But the tyrannical text of the twentieth-century theorist's diatribes, while perhaps always a fear, was never a reality for fifth-century playwrights and performers, who esteemed a dramatist's belly slaps and bum splits on an equal level with his words.

Two conclusions are inevitable. First, if the theatre involves a kind of learning in which the student profits equally from an intercourse with texts *and* with bodies, then theatre as a literary genre is not one that is likely to endear itself to teachers convinced of the inviolability of textual messages. Scholarly anxieties about textual spuriousness and corruption are bound to be at their most acute in studies of drama, for it is a type of writing that does not lose its contact with bodily realities, with new performative contexts that leave their marks upon it. If literate culture must cast the body as low, theatre is almost guaranteed to retain its somewhat disreputable position as far as the hierarchy of literary genres is concerned.[52] We have seen how the decontextualizing atmosphere of the newly established classroom may have facilitated fresh operations on poetic material, operations that determined both the generic form and many of the perennial thematic concerns of drama. But as literacy and scholarship went on to entrench themselves as increasingly sovereign over cultural life, the very decontextualizing activities that brought theatrical form into existence in the first place became ever more well positioned to banish theatre's "Neoptolemean" inclinations from the ranks of serious study.

The second conclusion is that the dramatic text, by a felicity of history, is not the bad teacher that Artaud imagined it to be, for it is both written and "unfinished" at the same time.[53] Because it intends performance by contemporary bodies, the dramatic text must be weighed in the corporeal scales of actors' lived experience of the present, and made answerable to their live speech contexts on an ongoing basis. If its wedding gowns are experienced as ideological straitjackets, or its heroic-militaristic ideals as paralyzing suits of armor, then the actor can exercise his or her generically mandated prerogative for casting such textual garments off. Using a Bakhtinian figure, we might say that drama is a kind of textual acknowledgment that, when it comes to the student-performer's body and the fabric of the text, "all existing clothes are always too tight" (1981:37). Despite the fact that drama has surely benefited from its high intellectual standards, the practice of book learning has not made the theatre too much like a school. For unlike Plato's preferred literary genre, the philosophical dialogue, the dramatic text does *not* "always say the same thing" (*Phaedrus* 275d).

And so we return to Plato, whose rejection of theatre launched our inquiry into the nature of the student. The final message of the *Phaedrus* is that while intellectual errors will no doubt come of our surrender to live speech acts, it is a risk that must be taken, for the very madnesses and transports that produce poetry and wisdom in the first place cannot feed but on real flesh. Too bad this teacher did not heed his own lesson. Had he done so, he'd have written plays.

52. Sir Thomas Bodley's thinking when it came to establishing his library at Oxford in 1612 is typical: all plays were to be excluded from his collection of books. He considered them all unworthy "baggage" (Stone and Kahrl 1979:168).

53. It is fascinating, if perplexing, to observe the frequency with which literary theorists arrogate this quality of "unfinishedness" to the novel, a genre that, more completely than any other, reflects the fixed and finished tendency of print literacy. See Bakhtin 1981 and 1986, and the discussions of Friedrich Schlegel's theory of genre in Szondi 1986:75–94.

CHAPTER 3

Courtroom Dramas

This can't be Athens; I don't see any law courts.
Aristophanes

For the law of writ and the liberty . . .
Shakespeare

W HEN THE HEROES OF HOMER'S WORLD COLLIDE, THEY SULK IN THEIR tents, nurse grievances, steal one another's prizes, go on strike, slaughter the suitors. They receive embassies of reconciliation, advice from elders, offers of settlement from rivals and kings; but they feel free to reject all such arbitration in their disputes, preferring to take justice into their own hands and arms against their troubles. Had Homer's heroes lived in the literate age of drama, they would have taken one another to court.

For the Athens of Aeschylus' time was a highly litigious place. Aristophanes never tired of ridiculing his fellow Athenians' mania for public prosecution, their addiction to jury trials. And with six thousand citizens registered for jury duty every year, Aristophanes' quip in the *Birds* appears less hyperbolic than simply descriptive: if they're Athenians, they must be jurymen (108–9). Like Shakespeare's London, always noisily "buzzing with lawyers and their litigious clients" (Thomson 1994:84), fifth-century Athens was a hive of disputatious wasps from which no one was safe. Having been hauled before the courts himself "for having ridiculed magistrates . . . as well as Kleon, in the presence of foreigners" (*Acharnians* 377–82), Aristophanes knew the workings of the city's legal system from painful firsthand experience. But in this he was not alone among his playwriting predecessors and contemporaries: Phrynichus was tried and found guilty of insulting the city with his play *The Capture of Miletus*, for which crime of bad taste he was fined one thousand drachmas; Aeschylus was prosecuted, but acquitted, for violating secrecy laws of the state religion (Aristotle, *Nicomachean Ethics* 3.1.1111a6–10); and Sophocles was accused of incompetence by his son, although the charges were read and dismissed after the preliminary hearing

(Bieber 1961:28–29). Born into a world newly altered by books and class-rooms, the playwrights of the fifth century B.C.E. grew to adulthood in a city not long since revolutionized by the courtroom. As a result, disagree-ments between fathers and sons, sons and suitors, suitors and wives, wives and husbands were no longer occasions for private revenge, curses, murder, and abduction, but had come to be seen as public matters, requiring public legal redress. Unlike disputes in Archaic times, human conflicts in the fifth century were resolved at law, staged in public before an assembled citizen jury.

Like the book-based school, the *didaskalion,* the law court is a social phenomenon that is conspicuously absent from the world of the epic. But the law court, again like the literate classroom, is highly visible in both the dramatic age at large and in dramatic works in particular. Aeschylus, Sopho-cles, Euripides, and Aristophanes each wrote at least one play on the subject of written law and the jury system; of Aeschylus' surviving works at least four are concerned with it. If Athens's democratic legal system was so often discussed on the stage of the theatre, this was the case for a simple reason: the theatre, as a mode of public speech, was organized along the same lines as the popular jury courts, and is in fact unthinkable without them. With-out the advent of written law, Athens's particular brand of litigiousness could not have emerged; and in the absence of this peculiarly *literate* attitude to conflict resolution, neither would the storytelling style of the theatre.

Of course, legal processes of one sort or another exist in most human societies that have been observed and described throughout history; but legal procedures in preliterate societies do appear to share certain features that distinguish them from the practice and function of law in societies with writing (Gagarin 1986:8, 9). The workings of preliterate justice have often been studied before, both as depicted throughout the Homeric epics and as manifested in a variety of nonliterate cultures around the world.[1] The many obvious parallels between Homer's version of oral law and the proto-legal procedures typical of other oral cultures suggest that the bard's picture of justice before writing is a reliable source of information about conflict reso-lution in Greece during the oral period.[2] In comparing the representation of human conflict in the epics with the theatre's treatment of such discord, however, we see a number of significant differences—differences that accu-rately reflect the generic shift from epic to dramatic form.

1. O'Barr 1982:10; Beck 1993; Humphreys 1985:316; Gagarin 1986:2–6, 23, 29–30.
2. Bowra 1969:32; Humphreys 1985:316; Powell 1991.

The picture that Homer provides of the workings of preliterate justice is also corroborated by Hesiod, who was himself involved in a legal wrangle with his brother Perses. Both from Homer's most detailed descriptions of conflict resolution (*Iliad* 18.497–508 and *Odyssey* 11.568–71) and from Hesiod (*Works and Days* 27–39), we find a conception of justice as "straight *dike*," as a "straight" settlement that is spoken by the noble elders, called kings (see *Il.* 23.571–95). These hereditary kings are described as sitting in judgment, either individually or in an elders' circle, and suggesting mutually agreeable compromises to the disputants. From Hesiod (*Theogony* 80–93 and *Works and Days* 213–85), we know that proposing solutions of this kind was one of the central duties of the hereditary kings, and that giving such judgments was largely a matter of persuading the parties to accept the offered solution. From Homer's description of the arbitration of the blood feud on Achilleus' shield, we see that the elder who proposed the "straightest *dike*" was rewarded with "two golden measures," a prize or gift paid by the disputants. Not surprisingly, these kings were also said to be "gift-devouring" (*Works and Days* 27–39), for favorable judgments had to be paid for in gifts. In the absence of a code of written law, justice thus resides within the body of the king or magistrate, and the judge's authority derives also from his body, as it were, for he is a king and spokesman for justice by virtue of blood ties and class inheritance.

Other features of preliterate justice can be found throughout the *Iliad* and *Odyssey*. Among the most important from our perspective is that legal redress was not available universally, and in many respects remained a private (as opposed to a public) affair. In the case of homicide, for example, it was the duty of the victim's family to enforce the traditional punishment, which was generally exile (or possibly blood money; cf. *Il.* 18.497ff.). The epics show that this reliance on family meant that murder went unpunished in many cases. For example, as Michael Gagarin points out, Heracles could kill a foreigner without legal consequences, for a foreigner has no family to enforce the customary penalty (1986:14; *Od.* 21.24–30). Or, as Gagarin further reminds us, Homer's Oedipus could commit patricide with impunity, and continue to rule Thebes even after knowledge of his deed had come to light (1986:14; *Od.* 11.271–80; *Il.* 23.679–80). With legal process a private, familial affair, it was, in effect, optional and dependent on the existence of individual families, and on their will and power to enforce punishment. This meant that suppliants, women, noncitizens, or any other members of society without strong kinship or clan ties would necessarily find themselves excluded from the customary avenues for legal action. Moreover, because justice in the absence of legal codes consists of mutually acceptable compromises (Gagarin 1986:105), disputants are in a sense free to determine whether even customary legal rules will pertain or not. For example, Eurymachus suggests a settlement in the *Odyssey* (22.54–59) which Odysseus appears to be at liberty to reject; he accepts no restitution from the suitors and slaughters them instead. All the Achaians agree that Agamemnon should accept the ransom offered by the priest as settlement for Chryseis, but he rejects the proposal out of hand (*Il.* 1.20–34). The private and personally discretionary character of preliterate justice is also evidenced in Achilleus' rejection of Nestor's proposed settlement in Book 1 of the *Iliad* and in other disputes throughout the same work (23.543–54, 571–95, 787–92).[3]

Indeed, the narrative of the *Odyssey* as a whole validates the ad hoc workings of private hereditary justice. Odysseus is presented as praiseworthy in his murder of the suitors, and, as Richmond Lattimore reminds us, the example of Orestes, in his decisive murder of Aegisthus, is held up to the procrastinating Telemachus as a positive one (Grene and Lattimore 1991:8). In the absence of written laws of the state, blood ties will tend to empower individuals to make their own family-rooted rules: as legitimate hereditary kings, Odysseus and Orestes can also claim "legitimacy" for any bloody deeds that preserve their royal houses. The dispute between Achilleus and Agamemnon which forms the plot of the *Iliad*, despite the proposals of men in council, is also finally settled on a purely personal basis: Achilleus simply refocuses his wrath toward the enemy, and gives up punishing his own co-combatants. As Gagarin points out, in the absence of systematic legal rules and binding penalties, disputes will tend to be settled in a way that leaves the conflict itself intact (105). For example, the "resolution" of the conflict between Achilleus and Agamemnon makes no decision for the future about rival claims for status; within the heroic worldview, each combatant had little choice but to assert his own. Similarly with homicide: if families are obligated to exact extralegal justice for such crimes, then they are obligated to take turns in doing so ad infinitum—a point made by Aeschylus throughout the *Oresteia*. As long as blood crimes are resolved as if they were private offenses against individual families, there is no end to murder.

Gagarin, who has analyzed all of these Homeric disputes (and others in Hesiod), concluded that it is not an exaggeration to say that law as we understand it came into existence with writing. There existed, to be sure, many traditional maxims and orally repeated codes of conduct before writing. But as our Homeric examples show, traditional proto-legalistic sayings have the illocutionary force of pieces of advice; they are invoked to justify a certain

---

3. See Gagarin's excellent analyses of these episodes (1986:39–41).

line of conduct, but do not have the force of determining behavioral choices in the first place (55). They are statements of what people usually do, or have traditionally done, and are used as rhetorical support for advice. Unlike written laws, they do not apply necessarily and universally; and they are, in any case, sponsored by particular speakers whose advice may well be rejected.

The one exception to the notion that law is equatable with writing is often said to be the case of the Icelandic "lawspeakers." Like the early Irish bards, who are said to have memorized and recited collections of laws, the Icelandic lawspeakers possessed a body of laws which they recited in full every three years. But as the historian Knut Gjerset has shown (1924:29–48) and Gagarin has argued (10), in places where such "law" is confined to the oral register and remains in the possession of specially authorized individuals (lawspeakers or hereditary magistrates), it fails to produce "legal behavior." Such laws, because they remain connected with the body of the king or lawspeaker, do not inspire general obedience. As Gjerset notes, civic life in preliterate Iceland continued to be ruled by private custom, for regular citizens did not view this arcane specialist knowledge as having any relevance to them personally (46). Most significantly, when the Icelandic laws were written down circa 1118 C.E., they were still subject to a kind of private possession, the consequence of which was that for several centuries no official version of them existed. Between the various copies possessed by individual lawyers for their own use, there were substantive variations. The net effect of this condition, of course, is that justice remains "oral" in principle: the voice of the law is still rooted in a particular speaker's body.

The physical rootedness of (preliterate) legalistic utterances in the concrete circumstances of their delivery is reflected in their formal structure. Traditional spoken maxims will tend to take the form of a second-person imperative: "Do unto others," for example (Gagarin 1986:55). Speech of this type implies a close physical proximity between "me" and "you," between the giver and receiver of the oral counsel. Interestingly, the implied co-presence of speakers which characterizes proto-legal advice also characterizes epic speech. The epic singer addresses the Muse directly in a second-person imperative: "Sing, goddess, the anger of Peleus' son"; "Tell me, Muse, of the man of many ways."[4] This is speech from "me" to "you," and the deictic structure of the opening invocation is repeated in the works themselves, with the characters sometimes taking on the position of the "you" (e.g.,

---

4. Lattimore trans. (Grene and Lattimore 1991). Cf. the imperative mood of the line of epic verse inscribed upon the Douris Cup (see Chapter 2).

"Then, O swineherd Eumaios, you said to him in answer . . ." *Od.* 14.165, 360, 442; *Il.* 20.2). The speech act of epic could thus be described as "I sing to you about him," or "You (the Muse) sing to me about him." But in either case it is a speech exchange between a present "me" and a present "you."

In the type of speech that structures written law, however, the situation is different. Unlike oral advice, a law generally takes the form of a third-person conditional statement: "If anyone does X, Y will happen" (Gagarin 1986:55). In the first place, the utterance is in the conditional: "if . . ." or "when . . ." Who is now speaking? The lack of deictic grounding for the speaker in a conditional utterance is further emphasized by the lack of a specific addressee: Who is the intended listener or receiver? The subject of the legal utterance is "anyone" or "the man who . . ." Whereas both proto-legal advice and epic song are grounded in a specific speech situation—between "me" and "you"—and refer to the identity of a specific absent "him"—Orestes and his exemplary deed—a written legal utterance is abstracted away from any and all particular speakers, listeners, and subjects. Like the dramatic text as I described it in the previous chapter, written laws are thus "nonspecialist" utterances: they are addressed to anyone and everyone, but no one in particular. According to Dennis Kurzon's speech-act analysis of legal utterances (1986), the illocutionary force of a law is "to enact." But since the law being enacted depends upon future conditions (*if* anyone commits X), such utterances may more accurately be called "potential performatives" (40). To enact themselves, they depend on the fulfillment of certain "post-conditions." Kurzon claims that such potential speech acts do not occur outside of legal texts. But as a global speech act, the dramatic text stands as an exception to this rule, if it is one. Precisely like a legal text, the dramatic text as a whole is a conditional third-person utterance: "If anyone performs this play, this is what the actors shall say." As in the case of such legal performatives as wills and marriage ceremonies, which depend on future actions for their legal enactment (death or consummation), the dramatic text is a potential enactment contingent on future extratextual events. Like traditional maxims and proto-legal advice, the Homeric epic has an "I" declaring to a "you" what has happened in the past; like literate legal utterances, the dramatic text is a third-person "potential performative" awaiting enactment in the future by "anyone."

The earliest extant written law, found in Dreros, Crete, has been dated roughly to the middle or second half of the seventh century (Jeffrey 1990:311). It begins with the formula "the city has thus decided," and goes on to stipulate that if a man has held a certain public office, he shall not be able to hold the same office again for ten years. Carved in stone on the wall of a temple, this law is our earliest record of the growing trend toward public legislation that was soon to manifest itself throughout Greece. Whether written on *axones,* or wooden blocks, as they were initially in Athens (Jeffrey 1990:58–59), or cut in stone, as in Crete, the law codes of seventh- and sixth-century Greece had a number of features in common: they were self-consciously public, they applied to everyone, they were specifically *legal* in nature, and they were officially authorized and recognized as such by the polis as a whole. The homicide law of Draco (ca. 620), of which some fragments have survived (Gagarin 1986:52), is especially interesting in this regard. As perhaps the very first law on murder, the Draconian statute, merely by being written down, made murder a public offense.[5] As Kurzon says about such criminal codes, they are really "laws" only when they are addressed to everyone; "the *publication* of statutes is [thus] an integral part of the promulgation of legislation" (27; my italics). Or, as the legal theorist George M. Calhoun puts it, it is only with written law that legal rules and changes "become distinctly perceptible, and when made have to be made consciously and intentionally. . . . And so begins a long process which matures in a fully developed system of statute law, with permanent legislative machinery and provisions for periodic revision, and gradually transforms the esoteric legal lore of the aristocracy into legal science" (1944:22–23).

The first steps toward the establishment of a truly legal order seem to have been taken by the writing down of "ancestral *thesmia*" by lawgivers, *thesmothetai,* who recorded decisions for their own use.[6] But with the publication throughout Greece of written laws, or *nomoi,* law took on a different character. Their detached, public status, and the fact that highly specific penalties were stipulated, took such laws out of the hands of individuals and removed them from the sphere of personal discretion. With the establishment of an abstract entity such as "the city" as the agent of justice, a genuinely legal atmosphere was in effect inaugurated. As we saw in the Homeric examples, a crime might come to light yet remain unpunished in the absence of an aggrieved relative. But in a *legal* dispute there must necessarily be two parties. With the city now speaking the law rather than an individual, even those crimes that were suffered privately, because the plaintiff

5. Because, even after the reforms of Ephialtes, murder continued to be tried by the closed hereditary court of the Areopagus, one could argue that homicide continued to be a "private" suit (cf. Humphreys 1985). But the laws of Draco, which made legal procedure *compulsory* and closely regulated by public statute, had the effect of removing homicide remedies from the private realm of family self-help, making them in essence a "public" issue (Gagarin 1986:114).

6. Aristotle *Constitution of Athens* 3.4, 16.10; Gagarin 1986:56, 130.

had no champion, were brought within a public legal sphere. With laws now officially authorized by a *place,* they were for the first time addressed to everyone who lived in that place. Thus, even crimes within various "non-city" spheres, such as the family or religion, were soon brought under the Solonian "shield" of such universal city laws (Ostwald 1986:139, 145).

As Gagarin points out, the very act of enacting a set of laws for a particular place would have had the effect of redefining individuals as *citizens* rather than merely as members of families (1986:80). Aeschylus clearly acknowledges this effect in the *Suppliants:* individuals are now subject to the laws of their states, which, despite ancestral customs, may be different from one place to the next ("According to laws at home you must plead . . ." 390). And this new conflict between state law and family custom is featured prominently in other dramas as well (*Antigone,* the *Oresteia*). In fact, there seems to be a relationship between *all* theatre and this consciousness of citizenship. As Per Brask and William Morgan have observed of Amerindian, Inuit, and other aboriginal communities, theatrical performance "seems to have evolved in the context of the rise of state-level societies" (1992:x). Of the appearance of drama in Greek antiquity, Jean-Pierre Vernant and Pierre Vidal-Naquet have similarly observed (paraphrasing Walter Nestle), "Tragedy is born when myth starts to be considered from the point of view of a *citizen*" (1990:33).

The public inscription of law had another, equally significant effect: social rules were now visibly separated into laws and non-laws. This is important, for as Gagarin notes, societies without writing have rules, but no method for recognizing rules, no legal infrastructure for distinguishing rules from other types of social utterances. For this reason, it is fair to say that the Greeks' decision to write down a set of laws "was in effect a decision to enact legislation" (1986:136).

With written law, an abstraction—"the city"—now regulates the behavior of "everybody," another abstraction. Somewhat surprisingly, however, public prosecutors were unknown. With the city now authorizing the law but not actually representing it in court, it might appear that the legal rule requiring two parties in any dispute could not be upheld. But Solon enacted a law code in the first decade of the sixth century at Athens which was to have the effect of guaranteeing public prosecution. He introduced "the right of any person to take legal action in behalf of the injured party" (Ostwald 1986:9; *Constitution of Athens* 9.1). Legalizing an action of this sort, which came to be called a *graphé,* meant that legal redress became available even to those who, either by citizenship laws or by some other obstacle, were prevented from pleading their case in person. By permitting injured parties to be *represented* in this way by written accusations, the Solonian code changed the whole nature of justice. Because litigants no longer had to be *embodied* litigants, that is, particular flesh-and-blood litigants, justice was now something that even an abstract litigant could claim. This representational structure proved to be a democratizing one, for now cases could be submitted on behalf of "the people" as a whole, and crimes by magistrates or other civic officials could be prosecuted with "the people" as the injured party (Ostwald 1986:9; Gagarin 1986:69).

With even magistrates now subject to prosecution, the Homeric scenario, where two disputants bring their case before the judge, was rewritten. The judge was no longer the outside arbiter of private conflicts who possessed legal procedure within himself. He was now pulled within the legal sphere as a potential disputant. As a corollary of this new state of affairs, Solon enacted a law of impeachment (*Const. Ath.* 8.4.), and established what appears to have been a public law court, the *heliaia,* and an appeals procedure for hearing disputed judgments of the magistrates (*Const. Ath.* 9.1).[7]

There is a great deal of uncertainty about the finer details of the Solonian reforms, for the sources for them, Aristotle and Plutarch, are very late. But the written laws of the seventh and sixth centuries, whether intentionally or not,[8] indisputably started a shift toward an increasingly democratic legal system (Ostwald 1986:203). By establishing an appeals procedure and a public court composed of regular citizens chosen by lot irrespective of wealth, Solonian law sketched in the main outline of the populist jury courts of the fifth century which Aristophanes immortalized in the *Wasps.* Aristotle considered these law courts, or *dikasteria,* the main repositories of popular power in Athens.[9] The right of *isegoria*—the right of every citizen to have his say regardless of social position—was only further enshrined by Solon's followers, Cleisthenes and Ephialtes.[10] Although I have so far spoken of Athens as a cosmopolitan meeting ground for poetic dialects and metrical types and the place where the "mixed" genre of drama was invented, Athenians were even prouder, perhaps, of their other "mixing" policies: the mixing of the speech of rich and poor, powerful and powerless, in a single voice of binding legal authority.[11]

---

7. See Ostwald 1986:9.

8. That these legal reforms probably did not intend to have the effects they did is a point made repeatedly by Ostwald (1986) and Gagarin (1986). We shall be returning to this idea shortly.

9. *Politics* 2.12.1273b35–74a5; *Const. Ath.* 9.1, 41.2.

10. Ostwald 1986:48, 203, 461–62.

11. *Const. Ath.* 21.4; Ostwald 1986:15–20.

This pride in *isegoria,* in the mixed speech of the whole people, was surely shared by Aeschylus, whose *Suppliants* is a kind of sustained celebration of the glories of popular sovereignty. Performed, it seems, in 463 B.C.E.,[12] this play shows how, in a country where law has admitted into itself the principle of representation, even weak noncitizens can receive a fair public hearing. The suppliant women from Egypt seek refuge in Argos (which is really fifth-century Athens disguised), and throw themselves on the altars of the local deities for protection. But as Aeschylus shows, it is not by customary religious practices that the suppliants are saved but by a legally binding vote of the assembled people. The daughters of Danaus are described as exiles from a less democratic state, to whom the notion of popular sovereignty is quite alien. They know nothing of the empowerment of the people to make authorized decisions for the polis as a whole. Reflecting a prelegalistic concept of kingship, the Chorus, urging King Pelasgus to make a judgment in his own person, says: "You are, yes, the city, the people / A prince is not judged. / The land, the hearth, the altar you rule / With the single vote and scepter" (369–72). But Pelasgus, king in a democracy, must "share all with the citizens"; he refuses to "act / Alone, apart from the people" (367–68, 398–99). By "representing" the suit of the daughters of Danaus before the assembled citizens of Argos, Pelasgus wins for them an authorized *city* remedy against the customary violence of their pursuing cousins. As I mentioned before, a suppliant escaping the "self-help" of a family in its private disputes would have had no hope of protection from any higher public law before the Draconian code. In the *Suppliants,* this victory for the weak through legal means is a double one, however. Not only are otherwise helpless plaintiffs given protection from family vengeance, but also women, shown throughout Homer to be mere chattels or "prizes" for men to dispose of as they wish, are legally protected in their desire not to be "household-slave[s] to Egyptus' sons" (334). As the Chorus stresses, the citizen jury of Argos honored them even as women, not "cast[ing] their votes / On the side of men" (643–44), as would have been customary.

Although the publication of the Draconian and Solonian law codes did not necessarily intend this, the effect of writing on legal process was to give the Greeks a distinct taste for the precise kind of public accountability that Aeschylus celebrates in the *Suppliants.* In Ronald Stroud's words, the early Greeks were in fact "obsessed" with public accountability (1989:103–19). At the base of many Greek legal inscriptions we find the phrase "So that anyone who wishes may read" (Harvey 1966:600). That writing (in a script that

12. Podlecki 1966:43.

could be easily read by the public at large)[13] was the precondition for such juridical accountability is not merely the view of modern historians and theorists of law such as Gagarin, Kurzon, Ostwald, and Calhoun; it was the belief of the ancients themselves.

We find direct causal connections drawn between written law and democratic government in Aristotle[14] and implicitly in Aeschylus.[15] But Euripides perhaps stated it best: the public inscription of law is the great equalizer.

> In early days, before laws were common,
> One man has power to make the law his own:
> Equality is not yet. With written laws,
> People of small resources and the rich
> Both have the same recourse to justice. Now
> A man of means, if badly spoken of,
> Will have no better standing than the weak;
> And if the little man is right, he wins
> Against the great. This is the call of freedom:
> "What man has good advice to give the city,
> And wishes to make it known?"
>
> . . . .
>
> For the city, what can be more fair than that? (*Suppl.* 432–43)

This speech explicitly compares written law with preliterate conflictual speech: written law upholds the rights of weaker individuals, and does so by validating their verbal claims. Before writing, the rich man could be "badly spoken of" by one with "small resources," without effect. Writing comes to the aid of speech, under this view, for without it, disputes remain contests of identities in which the great will win.

The abstracting of justice away from the body of the judges and disputants alike made personal conflicts into decontextualized "cases" for public hearing. In the legal context that bred drama, conflicts and kingly decisions which were once hidden from common view went public: they became theatricalized.[16] Etymologically, the theatre was a place for viewing, the place

13. For estimates of how many members of the Greek population were able to read these inscriptions, see W. Harris 1989 and Thomas 1992.

14. *Politics* 1270b28ff.; Thomas 1989:60.

15. *Suppliants* 942–49; see also Burns 1981:377.

16. Vernant and Vidal-Naquet make a similar point when they write that tragedy "could be said to be a manifestation of the city turning itself into theatre, presenting itself on stage before its assembled citizens" (1990:185).

where citizens went to see, to contemplate and judge the musical *agones,* or competitions. What they saw on stage once dramas were performed there was very similar to what they saw on Athens' other public stages, in the Assembly and the law courts. In the courts they watched as cases were argued, self-justifications offered, events recounted, and verdicts passed on the guilty. They heard the claims and counterclaims of witnesses and the mutually contradictory statements of the litigants. They heard cross-examinations and denials, and observed the relentless drive to get to the bottom of things, to the truth. Judging from the earliest extant dramas of the fifth century, that is also precisely what they saw in the theatre in its glorious first century. In the Theatre of Dionysus no less than in the *dikasteria,* regular citizens watched as "great men" faced public prosecution, interrogation, and indictment on various charges. In drama, the great figures of mythology and public life were forced, like ordinary criminals, to stand public trial and justify themselves in speech. Orestes must defend himself against murder charges; Oedipus must prosecute "anyone" guilty of crimes against the state, with "anyone" proving inclusive even of himself; Antigone must stand interrogation for violating the state's written laws by Creon, who must in turn justify his own lawlessness; and Prometheus, sentenced to a term in the stocks for traitorous actions against a tyrant, justifies his man-loving crimes in a fashion at once typically dramatic and typically forensic: in speech, in argument, in rebuttal and explanation. That Prometheus is immobilized on a rock makes his recourse to verbal self-justification especially poignant.[17] But in appearing on stage before the assembled citizen audience as an accused criminal whose "case" is being heard, Prometheus is not in principle different from any other dramatic figure. And just as it was written law that gave the public the ability to bring even the strong man to justice, so too is Prometheus' criminal case connected with writing in the theatre. Prometheus' crime involved giving writing to mankind, an act conceptualized explicitly as a democratizing threat to the lawlessness of the tyrant Zeus, who rules without public accountability ("he . . . rules without having to give account" Aeschylus *Prometheus Bound* 324).

As Werner Jaeger has observed, the climaxes of the action in the *Iliad* are always "Tales of Prowess," or *aristeiai* (1960 1:44). Similarly, all the episodes in the *Odyssey* are aimed toward the *aristeia* in which Odysseus, together with his son, at last vanquishes the suitors. In Homer, the consequences of such great deeds are never so important as the doing of them. But even in the earliest dramas, we see a wholly different attitude to human

---

17. But not unusual in theatrical literature; see esp. Samuel Beckett's *Play.*

action. Here, the climax of the action is not the deed but the verbal justification of it after the fact. When Aristotle lists all the possible permutations of
a tragic plot, he admits that there can be only these: either the deed was
done or it was not, and if done, either knowingly or not (*Poetics* 1453b15–16).
The focus in a tragic plot, in other words, has shifted away from a recount-
ing of the prowess of deeds and toward a determination of their lawfulness.
Did the doer have criminal intent? Did he in fact even commit the crime of
which he stands accused? The types of plots Aristotle specifies for drama,
based as they all are on retrospective investigation of the mental state of a
protagonist, are of course completely incompatible with epic storytelling, in
which such deeds are long anticipated and then at last simply celebrated.
But when the action in drama begins, Ajax has already slaughtered the
sheep, Oedipus has already broken all the laws, the Danaids have already
disobeyed, and the Persians have long since built their unholy bridges. In
some cases, it is true, the crime is not actually committed until the second
scene or, as in *Medea,* much later. But delays in these cases usually exist only
to establish that the doer is acting knowingly and on purpose. Antigone and
Clytaemestra, for example, make their first entrances as purposeful criminals, despite having not yet actually committed the crime. Dramatic form
put all such mythic heroes on stage, not to watch them in action but to
cross-examine them.[18]

The startling similarities between public hearings in the legal sphere
and those that were staged before citizens in the theatre have often been remarked on.[19] Court cases were heard before mass audiences of hundreds or
thousands of listeners;[20] the audiences at dramatic presentations also num-
bered in the thousands, as we see from the size of surviving theatres. Furthermore, many scholars believe that even the seating for both types of
"hearings" was arranged according to the same rules.[21] The casting of a ballot by judges was the climax toward which both legal and theatrical specta-

18. The number of plays in the theatrical repertory that feature actual cross-
examination scenes is of course noteworthy in itself: the *Eumenides, Pierre Pathelin, Merchant of Venice, Much Ado, Measure for Measure,* Kleist's *Broken Jug, The Bells, Caucasian
Chalk Circle, Saint Joan, Our Country's Good* (to say nothing of *Witness for the Prosecution,
Inherit the Wind, Twelve Angry Men,* and other courtroom dramas).

19. See esp. Ober and Strauss 1990:237ff.; Henderson 1990:271–313; and Vernant and
Vidal-Naquet 1990:32–33, who write: "Tragedy is not only an art-form; it is also a social institution that the city, by establishing competitions in tragedies, set up alongside its political and legal institutions."

20. Humphreys 1985:316, 357 n. 20; Sommerstein 1983:xvi; Ostwald 1986:205.

21. Winkler 1990:22–23; Henderson 1990:286; Ober and Strauss 1990:238. See also
Pickard-Cambridge 1968:269–70.

cles aimed: both agonistic performances aimed toward a majority decision about the winner. Furthermore, playwrights and oratorical speech writers were described by their contemporaries as doing the exact same thing: both were writers of "tetralogies," a term that originated in reference to the delivery in court of four speeches concerned with the same case (Pickard-Cambridge 1968:80). The Greek word *agonizomai* refers equally to "going to law" and competing on stage for the prize in a play.[22] And finally, the length of the contestants' speeches was regulated at law *and* on stage (before the fourth century) in the exact same way: by the water clock (*Poetics* 1451a12).[23]

Philokleon of the *Wasps* describes the courts as "a mighty power that allows us to mock at wealth" (575); Euripides describes writing as an aid in this process of criticizing the "great man." In legal procedure of the fifth century, writing was used for this purpose in a particularly concrete way. The "complaints" that formed the preliminary hearings of a court case were submitted to the *anakrisis* in the form of writing, *graphé:* "to hand in an accusation" against someone was *graphen apopherein*.[24] This use of writing to criticize the great was equally palpable in the sphere of fifth-century poetry, for the dramatists *also* brought their work to an archon for a "preliminary hearing" prior to the theatre festival. This poetic *anakrisis* would likewise determine whether the case would receive a public hearing or not. For this reason, the act of submitting a play for performance was identical in structure to the act of submitting a legal complaint for trial: when Euripides handed in, say, the *Hippolytos* or the *Medea* for consideration for the theatre festival, he was in effect "handing in an accusation" against these noble-blooded mythological figures, these great men and women. To my earlier conclusions about the "unfinished" nature of the dramatic text, one might add this insight, drawn from legal procedure of the time: the dramatic text remains open precisely because, like the *graphé* of a complaint against the great, it awaits its day in court. It is the written accusation, not the judgment itself. Is Hippolytos an insufferable misogynist prude, or an innocent victim of a false *graphé* (in this case a literal one, submitted by his stepmother)? Is Medea a victim of a monstrous society or a monster herself? Is

22. See Liddell and Scott (1983:10): "to contend for the prize on the stage, act" and "to contend against in a law suit."

23. There is a problem with the manuscript at this point in the *Poetics;* Rudolph Kassel in his 1965 text marks it with obelisks. If the text as we have it is correct, however, it was believed by Aristotle's contemporaries that plays were "once in other days" regulated by the water clock, a device that unquestionably was used in the courts. For evidence of the practice in pre–fourth-century theatre, Aristotle cites only common opinion ("they say").

24. *Wasps* 846; Thomas 1989:42; Stockton 1990:99.

Orestes guilty as charged or innocent? What about Oedipus? Antigone? Verdicts of this type are made on the basis of performance alone. The case is not decided until it comes to court—and may, in any case, not make it past the preliminary hearing.

If and when such cases did come before the public, the audience, whether of jurors or of playgoers, was conscious of its role as a decision maker. And both in the theatre and in the law courts, Athenians relied on writing as an aid in reaching their decisions. Philokleon comes home from the law courts "plastered with wax beneath his fingernails" from marking the litigants' penalties on writing tablets (*Wasps* 109, 165); and when Bdelykleon acts the part of juror, he calls instantly for his writing tablets so that he might make a note of the main points of the testimony (538, 559, 576–77: "That's now the second point of yours I'm writing down."). Likewise, in the "great debate" that Aristophanes says took place in the theatre, and which he gives us a glimpse of in the *Frogs*, the "jurors" apparently came "armed for action" as well: "Everyone's holding his little book, so he can follow the subtle points" (1114). Whether he meant, by "little book," the texts of the plays being judged or tablets for writing down the good points of the debate is impossible to tell.[25] But certainly when it came to the final decision, theatrical judges voted by inscribing the name of their chosen poet in writing.[26]

Nevertheless, and despite the use made of writing by jurors and theatregoers alike, contests at law and in the theatre were decided primarily on an oral basis, at least in the fifth century. Admittedly, the role of writing in the jurisprudential process grew thereafter: from 378–77 B.C.E., witnesses merely confirmed their prepared written testimonies, and cross-examination was eliminated (Humphreys 1985:316). And by Aristotle's time, playwrights, too, were showing signs of retreat into pure textuality, writing plays "suitable for reading" alone.[27] But before this time, legal and dramatic trials were won or lost on an oral basis, according to the speakers' ability to win the audience's favor. When we remember that the six thousand jurors who passed judgment in the Athenian law courts were ordinary nonspecialist citizens who had received no training in law whatsoever, we can appreciate the full extent of the similarity between dramatic and forensic speech: "The presiding magistrate did not sum up the arguments made by the two parties or give authoritative rulings on legal issues" (Humphreys 1985:323). Nor did

25. See Pickard-Cambridge, who discusses the ambiguity of the line and the difficulty in determining exactly what Aristophanes meant by *biblion* in this context (1968:276).

26. See the evidence about literate voting practices in Csapo and Slater 1995:160.

27. Aristotle *Rhetoric* 3.12.1413b12f.; see also Pfeiffer 1986:29 and Taplin 1977:13 n. 1.

the jurors deliberate; they heard the oral performances and dropped their voting pebble in an urn. Similarly in the theatre, the judges listened, and voted then and there. Thus we see why her study of Athenian legal procedure led Sally Humphreys to conclude that the law courts and theatre were related "urban institutions": "Both put the audience in the position of judge; both made extensive use of competitions in argument" (323).

The same went, of course, for the popular Assembly, where arguments were similarly staged, put in contest, and voted on. The Theatre of Dionysus near Munychia was used on at least one occasion for such political Assembly meetings (Ostwald 1986:394), and of course the Theatre of Dionysus at Athens was used every year as an assembly hall, as a place for hearing complaints about behavior during the festival, after the plays had all been seen.[28] As in the law courts and theatre, performative speech in the Assembly, too, was preceded by a written document;[29] but the "end" of all these activities was an oral performance whose aim was to gain a lay audience's favor, that is, to *win*.

The chorus in the *Frogs* addresses the whole citizen audience as the "judge" of the musical competition. And, like the jurors of Athens' legal system, the judges of the theatre festival were chosen by lot.[30] In the theatre, admittedly, only ten spectators were officially allowed to perform the judging function, to pick the winners and cast written ballots on behalf of the whole audience; but Simon Goldhill is convinced that their voting was deeply affected by general audience response, by the sympathies of the mass theatrical "jury" as a whole (1990:100). Eric Csapo and William Slater similarly conclude on the basis of available evidence that theatrical judges not only were swayed by the crowd, but were expected to be swayed (1995:160). And as the story about Alcibiades' unpopular victory over Taureas shows, the audience made its preferences clear.[31] One ancient but much later writer reports that the audience at the *Clouds* shouted to the judges, "Write no other name but Aristophanes!"[32] In writing the winner's name, or voicing their approval or condemnation in the form of shouts, applause, or footstomping, theatrical audiences thus functioned essentially as jurors in a court of law. And as Jeffrey Henderson has demonstrated at length

28. Demosthenes *Against Meidias* 8–10, as discussed in Pickard-Cambridge 1968:64–68.

29. That is, by draft proposals prepared by the Council; see Stockton 1990:88; Ostwald 1986:77.

30. Pickard-Cambridge 1968:95–96; Ostwald 1986:462.

31. Pickard-Cambridge 1968:273.

32. Aelian *Varia Historia* 2.13, as cited and discussed by Csapo and Slater 1995:160.

(1990:271–313), the identity between these two activities was obvious even to the participants at the time.

Of course, what similarities there are between the "hearing" of a text-based case in the theatre and Pnyx or *dikasteria* conceal one major difference. A successful speech in the Assembly may send thousands of men off to their deaths in battle, whereas a successful tetralogy in the theatre causes nothing directly to happen outside of the addition of the victors' names to the list of winners.[33] But as a "literacy event,"[34] theatrical performance is structured like a jury trial, where a written accusation is judged by a mass audience in performance.[35]

The new written status of law thus created a social atmosphere, for plaintiffs and poets alike, in which the "great men" of public life and mythology could be conceived of as susceptible to public prosecution for their crimes. The stories told by the fifth-century dramatists clearly reflect this reconceptualization of human behavior, crime, and conflict. Heroes who in Homer get off scot-free are called to justice in drama. But they are called to justice in a particular way. For the future-oriented, conditional structure of properly legal utterances guaranteed that the mere accusation of guilt cannot be the end of the story. Oral, proto-legal utterances, with their first-person imperative structure and reference to the past, tend to exhaust themselves within the present context of their delivery. But the potential performatives of written law and theatre, with their conditional, abstracted structure, *require* a future trial, both for determining whether the "conditions" have in fact been met, and for applying the abstract rule about "anyone" to this particular case, these particular litigants. And because written law is authorized as law by the city as a whole, its application to particular cases through trial must involve the city, must take a civic form. A secret trial would have been as pointless and objectionable in Athens' literate legal system as would a private performance of the plays written for the theatre, and for the same reasons. Not only has the structure of written law deter-

33. Although basically valid and worth making, this distinction, between the real consequences of forensic speech and the unreal consequences from dramatic speech, is not absolute. Some of Aristophanes' poetic suggestions seem actually to have been instituted in reality. See Henderson 1990:271–313.

34. Brian Street discusses Heath's definition of a "literacy event" as "any occasion in which a piece of writing is integral to the nature of the participants' interactions and their interpretive processes" (1988:61).

35. The Greek preference for a mass decision over that of an individual gets powerful corroboration from Aristotle's insistence, even in the more bookish and specialist fourth century, that the opinion of a mass audience is more valuable than the judgment of a single critic (*Politics* 3.1281b7). See Pickard-Cambridge 1968:277.

mined that the city itself must hear and judge each new application of legal abstractions to particular individuals, but also the nature of written law, having made possible equitable representation for both plaintiff and defendant in any dispute, has guaranteed that hearings in the literate age will, and must, consist of dialogic argument.

Unfortunately, most of the works that originally made up the full tetralogy of the dramatic accusations are lost. Had more complete dramatic case hearings survived, it is certain that the legalistic essence of early theatre would be more readily apparent. Discussions of ancient tragedy in our time are more likely to emphasize Aristotelian notions of "catharsis" and "tragic flaws."[36] But the legal associations even of these terms have somehow been obscured in modernity. By Aristotle's time, the former had come to have strong associations with medical practice; by our time, the latter in particular has come to be associated with anachronistic Christian values. In the century before the invention of drama, however, in the legal inscription from Dreros, Crete, we find that *katharos* has something to do with the kind of purification one achieves by swearing an oath in court (Gagarin 1986:86). And *hubris* as we find it in Hesiod is not a tragic flaw, moral failing, sin, or any other abstract or merely personal ethical trait, but the bad outcome of a crooked lawsuit (*Works and Days* 224–85). The opposite of *hubris* is not modesty or goodness but *justice* and straight settlements in the arbitration of disputes (Gagarin 1986:49). When Aristophanes was indicted by Kleon with a crime against the state (*demos*), he was charged specifically with having committed "an act of *hubris*," an "outrage" against the people.[37] From Demosthenes' remarks somewhat later, it is clear that *hubris* for the ancients was practically synonymous with "anything illegal": "If anyone commits an act of hubris against anyone else, whether child, woman, or man, whether free or slave, or does anything illegal against any of these, let anyone who wishes, of those entitled, lay an indictment."[38] Anyone might bring such a lawsuit, not just the one wronged, because, as Isocrates declared at the end of the fifth century, "the matter of hubris [is] a matter of *public concern*."[39] We cannot hope to grasp the meaning of hubris today unless we recognize

36. Brian Vickers discusses the widespread misinterpretation and mistaken use by modern theorists of critical terms from antiquity (1973:26–31).

37. *Scholion* to *Acharnians* 378, as translated and discussed by Csapo and Slater 1995:178.

38. *Against Meidas* 31–33, mid-fourth century, translated by Csapo and Slater 1995:180.

39. *Against Lochites* 20.2–3, as translated by Csapo and Slater 1995:180; my italics.

that written law had made such outrages "a matter of public concern," and that hubris was therefore primarily a *legal* problem.

In the prosecution of Aeschylus for impiety we find further confirmation of how much more the early theatre had in common with law than with religion. Not only have the specifically legal meanings of *hubris* been eroded in modernity, but the extrareligious nature of the theatre itself is often denied by moderns altogether. Along with Megacles, Aeschylus shares the distinction of having been the first citizen to be charged with a religious crime against the state. He was accused of revealing religious secrets of the Eleusinian mysteries in a play, secrets that should have been known only to initiates.[40] Aeschylus was apparently acquitted by a *dikasterion;* his defense, according to Aristotle, was that he did not know they were secrets when he staged them in a play.

So far from "being" a religious spectacle, tragedy was legally prohibited even from *staging* religious mysteries. In the dramatic age, religious cults, which had traditionally been under the control of the old families, came under the jurisdiction of the state. The hereditary priesthoods were upheld by public legislation (Ostwald 1986:145), but their essentially private and secretive character was affirmed as well. In fact, in the first years of the fifth century, two particular family-run priesthoods were ordered by public decree to perform initiations *individually;* initiating in groups would be punishable by a fine of one thousand drachmas (Ostwald 1986:140). Therefore, while true religious practices were supposed to be individualistic, private, and secret in nature, what dramatists such as Aeschylus did in staging plays was the virtual opposite: public, communal, open, unhidden.[41] Theatre was not an initiation "into" anything; it was, like a legal spectacle, a public bringing-to-light, a show, a "hearing." Aeschylus' surviving three-part "case" against Orestes gives us perhaps the best glimpse we have of the legalistic nature of dramatic composition; and in subjecting his tragic hero to public prosecution in a play, Aeschylus was making use of a ready-made model for investigating public crimes and solving conflicts, and one to which he had been subjected himself.

As had so many dramatists: Herodotus (*History* 6.21.2) reports that the tragedian Phrynicus was also forced to stand trial in the courts, where he was

40. Aristotle *Nicomachean Ethics* 3.1.1116a–10; Ostwald 1986:528. This anecdote reminds one instantly of the trouble Mozart is said to have gotten into for revealing secrets of the Masonic temple cult in his *Magic Flute.*

41. See esp. Padel 1990:336ff. and Seale 1982 passim for discussions of Greek drama as that which reveals, brings to light, makes public.

not as lucky as Aeschylus. In 492 B.C.E. or thereabouts, he was sentenced to a fine of one thousand drachmas and prohibited from re-performing his *Capture of Miletus* on the grounds that it had reminded the Athenians of their recent and traumatic loss of that city. It seems that there were limits to what could be shown on stage: religious secrets were taboo, as were, apparently, too-fresh miseries. Sophocles was publicly charged by his son with incompetence; the accusation was read in court and the playwright was acquitted (Bieber 1961:28–29). After a performance of the *Babylonians* at the City Dionysia in 426, Kleon submitted a *graphé* against Aristophanes "for having ridiculed magistrates . . . as well as Kleon, in the presence of foreigners" (*Acharnians* 377–82).[42] This action seems not to have made it beyond the preliminary hearing; nevertheless, Aristophanes says that the filthy suit almost killed him anyway (370–82).[43] Aristophanes really seems to deserve some sort of prize, in fact, perhaps a Golden Wasp, as the poet most often "stung" at Athens. If we can trust our sources, he was also charged with "wrongful acquisition of citizen rights," a false accusation against which he was nevertheless forced to defend himself a second and a third time.[44]

That a particular legal system will tend to suggest, to the poets living under it, a corresponding type of storytelling is confirmed by Sally Humphreys's (1985) study of the social relations implicit in various legal systems. In China, for example, where magistrates were brought in from elsewhere to judge cases in social contexts that were unfamiliar to them, bringing the truth to light in court was a labyrinthine and hazardous task. To Humphreys it is therefore not surprising that the detective story, which explores the "outsider's" navigation through an alien, clue-strewn environment, was invented in China (315). But in Athens, where citizens sat in public judgment over fellow citizens, a forensic form of storytelling was invented instead.[45] In Greece's dramatic age, and under the influence of literacy, interpersonal conflict had become legalized and theatricalized, and dramatic form represents this state of affairs in its very structure.

In addition to its organization as a third-person conditional utterance oriented toward a public, performed "hearing," dramatic form reflects the legal atmosphere in which it materialized in other ways as well. Foremost among these is the stichomythia, which, while absent from epic speech, is

42. See esp. Henderson 1990.

43. Ostwald 1986:207 n. 33; see also Henderson 1990.

44. Scholion to *Acharnians* 378 and *Life of Aristophanes* 19–26, as translated by Csapo and Slater 1985:178.

45. See also Padel, who says that in Athens "the assembly and the law courts were a kind of theatre, and the theatre an assembly-place, a court" (1990:338).

typical of drama. In the dispute between Achilleus and Agamemnon in the *Iliad*, for example, the epic bard represents the speech of each disputant as separate and self-contained. In the space of 132 lines, only nine monologic speeches are represented, and each one is fairly long, ranging from seven to twenty-three lines of uninterrupted discourse. In epic storytelling, verbal contest consists of autonomous set speeches which do not intersect directly at any point. Because the bard introduces each speaker in the bard's own voice, the characters speaking never respond to one another directly; their speeches do not come into contact but are buffered by transitional narrative segments spoken by the bard.

In drama, however, a new type of verbal debate makes its appearance. The paradigmatic example comes from the interrogation of Orestes in the *Eumenides:*

> Chorus: Say first, did you kill your mother or did you not?
> Orestes: Yes, I killed her. There shall be no denial of that.
> Chorus: There are three falls in the match and one has gone to us.
> Orestes: So you say. But you have not even thrown your man.
> Chorus: So. Then how did you kill her? you are bound to say.
> Orestes: I do. With drawn sword in my hand I cut her throat.
> Chorus: By whose persuasion and advice did you do this?
> Orestes: By order of this god, here. So he testifies.
> Chorus: The Prophet guided you into this matricide?
> Orestes: Yes. I have never complained of this. I do not now.
> Chorus: When sentence seizes you, you will talk a different way.
> Orestes: I have no fear. My father will aid me from the grave.
> Chorus: Kill your mother, then put trust in a corpse! Trust on.
> (587–99)

In thirteen lines, thirteen separate statements, each responding directly and inextricably to the one before. I spoke earlier about why this type of interchange would require the use of writing, for both composition and performance. As a poetic mode of representing human speech, however, it owes an equal debt to the model of forensic speech which developed out of written law. Aeschylus was of course deliberately staging a legal cross-examination in this scene, as Aristophanes was to do later in the *Wasps,* where a trial of the family pet is staged with kitchen utensils for witnesses (908–80). Nevertheless, a forensic speech style is exhibited also by dramatic characters who are not visibly competing in a court of law. In a grove outside Argos, the daughters of Danaus are challenged to provide verbal proof of the "truth" of their "tale" that they claim Argive ancestry (*Suppl.* 270–80):

Chorus: Wasn't Io once in Argos charged with Hera's temple?
King: Io was, the tale is prevalent.
Chorus: And wasn't Zeus to a mortal joined?
King: Which was from Hera unconcealed.
Chorus: How end these royal jealousies?
King: A goddess changed a woman to a cow.
Chorus: And Zeus, did he approach the horned cow?
King: Zeus became a bull, they say.

. . . .

Chorus: But what did Hera appoint for ill-omened Io?
King: A gnatlike goad it was, or driving sting.
Chorus: That the Nile-dwellers call the gadfly.
King: That drove her from Argos.
Chorus: It confirms my tale.
(291–310)

When Aristotle was later to draw up rules for the effective interrogation of opponents in his *Rhetoric,* it was to the dramatists he looked for examples of forensic speech no less than to the orators themselves. He would have approved of the Chorus's strategy here of leading the witness by asking a series of short questions. As he puts it, interrogation is an effective device "when one premise of an argument is obviously true, and you can see that your opponent must say 'yes' if you ask him whether the other is true" (1419a6ff.). He goes on in this vein, advising further that, as the audience will be unable to follow "a series" of questions posed at once, the successful orator will ask one compact question at a time—precisely as the Chorus does here (1419a17–20). This forensic dialogue structure is apparent throughout Sophoclean drama as well. One sees a lengthy cross-examination, made up of short questions and replies, in the *Oedipus* (986–1045), *Ajax* (95–120), *Antigone* (786–815), and *Philoctetes* (100–122); the very terse dialogic exchange between the sisters in *Oedipus at Colonus* (1957ff.) is also structured as an interrogation.

Even when modern theorists acknowledge the forensic style of theatrical speech, rarely does it seem to occur to anyone that there might be concrete historical reasons for this peculiarity of theatrical form. For example, Manfred Pfister's *Theory and Analysis of Drama* is a thoroughgoing account of the special structure of the dramatic text. Pfister notes here that the direct speech of characters, especially their dialogical speech, "constitutes the predominant verbal matrix used in dramatic texts" (1988:5). Pfister quite rightly also notes that this primary truth about dramatic texts often goes unacknowledged; even Aristotelian poetics obscures it by focusing instead on abstractions such as "the plot." The question Pfister leaves unanswered, and unasked, is: *Why* does discourse in drama consist mainly of direct dialogical debate?

We have begun to see how writing would have played a part in making obsolete the mediating voice of the narrator, or bard, whose function before writing was to remember and with his own voice report what all the characters said and did. But the emergence of this characteristically dramatic "verbal matrix," this direct dialogical speech, may have been equally beholden to the agonistic free-for-all of Athenian jurisprudence. In the absence of an authoritative judge in the legal sphere, human disputes became precisely what we see in drama: direct dialogical speech without interruption, without narrative manipulation, and with judgment passed only by an ordinary listening audience at the end of the performance.[46] In our time, on the contrary, even jury trials are regulated by an authoritative judge, whose specialist knowledge and impartiality are supposed to ensure that justice is properly administered. In such forensically mediated atmospheres as ours today, it is not surprising that the main storytelling arts of our time are the heavily mediated genres of novel and film. Indeed, it is only in our time that the presence of the guiding hand of some outside authority has come to be expected even in the theatre (i.e., the director).[47] In short, the potentially unmediated verbal agon of all dramatic form may derive from the forensic style of Athens's literate legal system.

It is not, however, only the nature of discourse in drama that is traceable to Athens's literate legal system; the identity of the *speakers* is equally indebted. In the long speech from the *Suppliants* cited earlier, Euripides also equates written law with an expansion, to more types of speakers, of the freedom to speak and give "good advice" to the city. The phrase he uses toward the end of the speech is actually a quotation from ordinary civic proce-

46. The audience at the theatre was judging the performance of a play, whereas the listeners at a trial were supposed to be judging the merits of the case. This might seem to suggest that the type of judging being done was different in each case. As we shall see, however, the difference between the two is not as great as it might appear. As Bettyruth Walter (1988) and Dennis Kurzon (1986) have shown, speakers in legal contexts win the support of their audiences mainly on the basis of their *performances,* which in many cases means that acting coaching is required even by those litigants who are "innocent." *Being* innocent is never enough; one must *appear* to be innocent as well, which sometimes means *acting* innocent.

47. See esp. Pavis 1982 for uncritical acceptance of the mediating role of the director in theatre art, and unexamined assumptions about the existence of such mediators in theatre practice throughout history.

dure. The Athenian Assembly always opened with a herald asking: "What man has good advice to give to the *polis* and wishes to make it known?" (Finley 1983:139). With the existence of the "shield" of written law, not only does the speech of the poor have protection,[48] but so does that of the younger members of the community. Euripides' speaker goes on (after the quoted section) to discuss the plight of the "youthful townsmen," who, like "ears of corn in a spring field," are likely to be cut off by their power-jealous elders (*Suppl.* 291–310). But with the publication of written laws, the legal decision-making process, and speech itself, is "liberat[ed] . . . from its attachment to immediate reality" (Meier 1990:86), and "good advice" can for the first time be judged without reference to or prejudice against the speaker's own identity. As Humphreys puts it, legalized debate meant that those who would not otherwise have been called upon to speak in public found themselves addressing large audiences for the first time, and doing so in a context where attention had to be paid to "the way in which opposing views were argued rather than [to] the status and achievements of the proponents" themselves (1985:317). In the oral world of the epics, as in oral societies generally,[49] we see clearly how the speech of the young is devalued in favor of that of the elders (*Il.* 9.53–54; *Od.* 3.21–24, 125, 362–63; 4.205; 7.155–58). In the tragedies, on the contrary, as Robert Garland (1990) has pointed out, elders are not depicted as having any innate monopoly on wisdom, and have moved mainly to the periphery of the action. In the written world of drama, even youths such as Neoptolemos can speak with more wisdom than their elders, such as Odysseus, and elders are themselves often portrayed as crotchety and conventional in their thinking.[50] The growing power of the younger members of society is amply demonstrated by Aristophanes throughout his oeuvre, especially in the *Knights, Acharnians, Clouds,* and *Wasps.*[51] Martin Ostwald has amassed considerable evidence connecting the increasingly visible presence in public life of the young to use of the law courts (1986:229ff.). For this empowerment of more types of citizens to have their say, Euripides credits writing.

And the theatre, of course, reflects this widened speech community. In marked contrast to the epic, the drama of literate Athens gives power of

48. Solon said that he "stood covering both [rich and poor] with a strong shield, allowing neither to triumph unjustly over the other" (Solon frag. 5.5–6 as cited by Gagarin 1986:138 and Finley 1983:1).

49. Clanchy 1979:150.

50. For example, the chorus of old men in *Agamemnon,* Tiresias in *Oedipus Tyrannos,* and Oedipus and Creon in *Oedipus at Colonus;* see Garland 1990:266–67.

51. *Knights* 225–26, 731; *Acharnians* 676–718; and the whole of *Clouds* and *Wasps.*

public speech to slaves, women, children, cripples, foreigners—even the insane. I have already mentioned some examples of dramatic presentations of the speech of foreigners (*Orestes, Persians*); Aeschylus also put publicly before the ears of the assembled Athenian citizenry the broken Greek of a foreigner in the *Suppliants* (835–950). In the story of Clytaemestra as told by Homer, the woman is peripheral to the story. She is given power neither of action nor of speech (*Od.* 529ff.). By Agamemnon in the *Iliad* she is compared, unfavorably, to his new slave Chryseis (1.111–14); but from neither woman do we hear a thing.[52] The innovations represented by drama are perhaps nowhere more pronounced than here: written drama gave the women of Greek mythology a chance to speak. In delegating the performative power of public speech to female figures, the Suda reports that Phrynicus led the way (Flickinger 1973:4); but Aeschylus was not far behind. In the *Agamemnon,* Clytaemestra has become one of the main actors in the mythological story of Agamemnon's murder; she has joined the lists of verbal combatants, and her entry into the public order of speakers is explicitly recognized: "My lady, no grave man could speak with better grace. I have listened to the proofs of your tale, and I believe" (351–52). The epic singer, by contrast, confined his song largely to the deeds of Achilleus and Odysseus and their fellow warriors.[53] The speechwriters, or *logographoi,* of the theatre wrote instead for Antigone and Clytaemestra and Iphigenia and

52. The justly famous exchange between Hektor and his wife is often cited as evidence of Homeric sympathy for female speakers, and for the importance of their place in the heroic world. The scene itself, however, shows Hektor telling Andromache to go back to her knitting and her womenfolk and not to trouble her head with thoughts about war, which are the business of men (read "loom and distaff" for my knitting: *Il.* 6.486–90). Helen is indeed given "the last word" (nearly) at the end of the *Iliad,* but in proportion to the length of this vast work, that is precisely what she gets: a word. In a work tens of thousands of lines long, Helen's fourteen-line speech in Book 24 (762–75) is negligible, particularly in light of the fact that the war was supposed to have been about her in the first place.

53. Women are not, of course, *absent* from the world of the epics. Odysseus does meet some interesting females on his way home, and Penelope is never long out of his mind, nor ours. But Homer's women are chiefly instruments in plots about men, or reflect the desires, actions, and aspirations of the men who are the real subjects of both stories. As Werner Jaeger has suggested, the virtues of a Penelope, Helen, Arete, or Nausicaa—loyalty, chastity, beauty, and good advice—are enumerated and praised mainly insofar as they reflect well on the men who are associated with them (1960 1:23). Epic women all remain "prizes" on a certain level, and do not pursue their own actions and agendas. On the contrary, a dramatist's treatment of the tale about Odysseus' return home would doubtlessly have cast Penelope as her *own* protector and murderer of the suitors—or of her unfaithful husband! This hypothesis is amply confirmed by Aeschylus' treatment of the homecoming theme: in Homer, it is Aegisthus who slaughters Agamemnon; in Aeschylus, Clytaemestra is clearly the mastermind.

Lysistrata; for Hecuba and Elektra and Medea; for Helen and Andromache and Alcestis; for suppliant women and Trojan women and women of the Assembly.

As in the law courts and Assembly, however, women were not allowed to appear on the stage in person. Their speech could be represented in writing, but not performed in the flesh. Nevertheless, given the ability of writing to outlive the context of its production, these represented discourses could at least survive, perhaps to be more properly incarnated in the future. For this reason, we might add to writing's virtues a certain measure of immunity from the social conventions regulating public speech at a given moment.[54]

Access to public speech was evidently widened in the age of drama, but speech *in propria persona* was still limited, by the Athenian concept of citizenship, to landowning males. And it is here that writing's connection with *isegoria* shows its most interesting face. For while foreigners such as Lysias and women such as Aspasia could not speak publicly themselves, they were enabled, by the existence of written forms of communication, to write speeches for others to deliver.[55] Such writers, or *logographoi,* wrote speeches for others to memorize and deliver in public, guaranteeing that their own voices could, in some manner, be heard. So popular were such written speeches that by the fourth century, "court speeches were—in the company of dramatic texts and mimes, with which they have much in common . . . —the light reading of the period" (Humphreys 1985:318, 320).

Women, foreigners, and slaves did not enjoy the same rights of public speech as landowning males in Athens of the fifth century B.C.E. Neither, of course, were blacks, Indians, and immigrant Chinese allowed to testify as witnesses in court in California as recently as the nineteenth century.[56] The disempowerment of some speakers in public is not, however, just a political issue. Speech contexts often do exclude many potentially wise speakers for technical legal reasons, for example, for lack of proper credentials such as citizenship or membership. But *all* speech contexts disempower *some* members of society "naturally" or inevitably. Isocrates was evidently a case in point in Athens. He had much good advice to give the city, but apparently was not gifted by nature as a pleasing speaker (Rowe 1986:215ff.). There is

54. I do not mean to suggest that the dramatists themselves hoped that women would one day perform their female roles. That writing accumulates meanings and performative possibilities through time which were not intended by the author is a matter to which I shall be turning shortly.

55. Stockton 1990:18; Cole 1981:135.

56. L.-W. Doo cited by Humphreys 1985:356 n. 1.

also a funny story told by Aristophanes about the book-loving Thucydides, who became suddenly tongue-tied, "paralysed in the jaws," when he was called upon to speak in a trial (*Wasps* 945–48). Not all members of a given speech community will be effective speakers, but some may not be able to speak at all. For example, at a moment just before writing had revolutionized the legal sphere in Europe, an unexpected case came before a medieval English court with remarkable results. In a judicial system where testimony and proof still had to be authorized by speech in person, a certain Agnes, a deaf-mute, was denied all legal rights because she could not speak on her own behalf (Clanchy 1979:222). Her case could not be *represented*, either by writing or by someone else's speech, as it could have been in literate Athens: she either spoke for herself or was disqualified from receiving legal redress. Without a technology for representing speech, citizens like this English mute cannot enjoy the rights of *isegoria*, even in places where they do exist.

From Aristophanes in particular we know that playwrights were valued largely for the advice they gave to the city; but not everyone who has a valuable contribution to make is gifted by nature with prizewinning charm. As we see from the inscription on a statue erected in the Theatre of Dionysus, actors won audience favor above all for "the charm of their speech" (Herington 1985:126), and apparently they still do. According to the New York theatre critic John Simon, charm is the one quality an actor cannot do without (1975:216–18). Socrates, who was said to be the ugliest man at Athens, may have lacked this particular quality himself—a detail that might help to explain his sardonic treatment of crowd-pleasers such as Ion. With the existence of writing, however, the public platform is opened up to anyone who merits an audience, regardless of his or her natural physical equipment and prevailing social taboos. Foreigners and women, such as Lysias, Isocrates, and Aspasia, were allowed to have their day in court, so to speak. In a world of speech without writing, the pragmatics of performance will tend to accentuate the speaker's identity and the degree of his personal charm over and above the substantive qualities of his argument. Without the need to appear in person, the dramatic logographer, by the same token, is free to make his or her contribution on paper, and leave the public communication of these ideas to those best suited by nature to win an audience's approval.

Nevertheless, like the switch from oral-intensive instruction to book-based schooling, which we looked at in Chapter 2, the writing down of law has a cost. The loss of their lived, context-bound particularities made disputes into abstract cases rather than contests of identities, which was a decidedly good thing as far as justice and fairness were concerned. But this loss of context, which always accompanies writing to some extent, means a corresponding loss of meaning. Although some degree of interpretation is required even in speech, interpretation takes on a much greater burden in deciphering meaning when communication is done in writing. I spoke earlier of the ease with which alphabetical writing can transcribe speech; but newer technologies of communication, such as film, video, and tape-recorders, have revealed just how much of speech is in fact *not* recorded by writing. In ancient writing up to the invention of the printing press, this was especially true. Since then, we have developed a detailed and more consistently used system of nonverbal signs to take the place, in writing, of the gestures, inflections, tones, pauses, emphases, and so on that organize and give meaning to our verbal utterances in oral delivery. But punctuation, paragraph breaks, italics, and font size can go only so far as substitutes for the sounds and gestures which in oral communication have enormous semantic value even though they have no alphabetical equivalents. It is for this reason that, in literate communication, interpretation comes to the forefront in the search for meaning.

Using Paul Ricoeur's words, we might say that writing can fix only the "noema" of speech, the "saying as said" (1981:203); what the alphabet is not equipped to represent is the "noesis" of a given speech act, the communicative intention in the mind of the speaker. In direct oral interlocution, nonverbal gestures and other bodily signs carry most of the burden of communicating intentions. For words themselves are inherently ambiguous. They possess only more or less strictly delineated *potentialities* for meaning; it is *how* they are used that determines what is meant. And so with written law such questions arise as "What exactly did Solon *mean* when he wrote that 'anyone' can submit a *graphé?*" It is context alone that tells us that when he wrote "anyone," he did *not* mean women and slaves. Meanings such as these, which are more or less directly manifested to listeners located within the historical and psychological context of the utterance, must be actively supplied by readers. For readers are by definition those receivers of verbal message who inhabit contexts separate from those in which the messages are produced. The contextual difference between conditions of production and of reception may be one of space or time, but is usually both.

The difficulty of interpreting such written locutions is often faced directly by our ancient sources. To the Solonian rule about the ability of "anyone" to submit a *graphé* on behalf of an injured party, Demosthenes adds the qualifying "of those Athenians entitled."[57] But the identity of even these "entitled" Athenians was obvious to Demosthenes' contemporaries in a way

57. *Against Meidas* 31–34; 47, as translated by Csapo and Slater 1995:180.

that it is not to readers from other contexts. Lysias also acknowledges the difficulties of interpretation that come with writing when he points out that a legislator who refers in writing to a person who "killed" someone is also intending to refer to a "murderer," even though he may not actually have used that particular word. To eliminate all ambiguity in writing, the legislator would have to accompany each written word with every single one of its synonyms, which would obviously be too much work.[58] Instead, continues Lysias, the legislator assumes that readers will interpret his writing by augmenting what he *says* (the saying, or noema), with what is being "signified" or intended (the noesis).[59]

As a decontextualized communication, writing thus makes the need for interpretation explicit. But interpretation was not unknown before writing. In Homer, for example, we notice that interpretation was widely practiced. Given the naturally decontextualized nature of dreams, omens, oracles, and other ambiguous phenomena, meaning must be actively supplied by anyone interpreting these phenomena if it is to be had at all. The interpretive reading of signs assumed to be significant was described by the verb *hupokrinesthai* (Svenbro 1990:373). In contrast to the *manteis,* whom Plato describes in the *Timaios* as the soothsayers or oracular mediums who themselves *produce* the ambiguous phrases, a *hupokrites* is one who (only) *interprets* such "words and enigmatic signs" (72a–b). Interpretive practices of this kind—be they aimed at the cryptic sayings of a Delphic oracle, the flight of birds, the cracks on heated animal bones, or the entrails of beasts—are widespread in early societies from Newfoundland to China. Judging from the occurrences of references to interpretation in Homer,[60] the meaning of the activity for the ancient Greeks is fairly clear: a *hupokrites* is one who suggests the "real meaning" of a verbal or visual sign. What oracles, entrails, and the flight of birds have in common with writing is that all are experienced as autonomous, meaning-laden sign systems which are cut off from ordinary, explanatory embeddedness in a communicative context.

With the advent of written law, a new kind of decontextualized utterance makes its appearance, and interpreters are required. Accordingly, orators or lawyers quickly come into existence with the advent of written law, joining the ranks of Greek culture's other interpreters. Given their function, it should not be surprising to learn that the Greeks used *hupokrinesthai* and

---

58. Although some legislators do try!
59. *Against Theomnestos,* 1–12, as translated by Csapo and Slater 1995:183.
60. *Il.* 8.407 and 12.228; *Od.* 2.111, 15.170, and 19.535; Hymn to Apollo 171.

related words to describe the public speech of orators (Pickard-Cambridge 1968:127).

Like law, poetry too needs interpreters once it is written down. In conditions of orality, poetry does not exist in a decontextualized state. Poetry is
manifested only in concrete conditions of utterance, where producer and receiver are co-present. When a poetic utterance comes through the mouth of
the bard, jongleur, or griot, there is no textual "locution" to interpret; the
"real meaning" intended by the speaker is present in the context. But once
poetry is composed directly in writing, outside of a physically engaged communication event, interpretation—both the possibility and necessity of it—
is built into poetry from the start. Even the poet must to some extent be the
interpreter of his own work, for production and reception cannot coincide
absolutely. And so, predictably enough, a class of interpreters quickly sprang
up in writing's wake within the sphere of poetry, too, and one that was analogous to that of orators in the legal sphere. And the interpreters of poetic
texts, of course, were those performers called *hupokritai,* "actors." From the
official lists of victors in poetic contests,[61] and from Aristophanes (*Wasps*
1279), we know that *hupokrites* was the proper word to describe the dramatic
actor from at least the fifth century on. Distinguishable from the rhapsode
and from other types of performers through the use of this special name, the
actor for the ancients was first and foremost that performer who, like a
lawyer, *interprets.*

Although theorists of drama today are likely to emphasize the actor's
role-playing capacity[62] or physical presence as the essence of the actor's art,
it must be remembered that these ways of distinguishing actors from other
performing artists would have had no meaning in antiquity. It would have
been meaningless to say that the actor was the one who danced or sang in
person, or impersonated other men, for in the time and place of drama's invention, *all* poetry, not just drama, was performed, sung, and danced and
involved impersonation. As John Herington (1985) has shown at length, epic
and lyric and dramatic poetry were all, equally, arts of musical, corporeal
performance. Plato speaks of both theatrical actors and epic rhapsodes as

---

61. Pickard-Cambridge 1968:132 cites *Inscriptiones Graecae* 2.2.2325.

62. Cf. Svenbro 1990 and Pickard-Cambridge 1962:110 for other interpretations of
hupokrites among moderns (the "answerer," for example, was briefly popular but was discredited by Ingram Bywater and Pickard-Cambridge). I accept H. W. Parke's definition of
the word as "one who suggests a meaning" (1967:17), and I trust it mainly because, as a
scholar writing on a subject other than theatre, Parke can be assumed to be disinterested.

"out of their proper minds" when impersonating mythological characters; and Arthur Pickard-Cambridge provides good evidence that lyric recitation involved impersonation as well (1962:41–43). According to Herington, the main shape of histrionic performance, which came increasingly to be associated with actors, had in fact already been worked out by rhapsodes before the invention of dramatic form proper. Working from his written "reminders" of Homeric texts, the rhapsode was essentially the same kind of performer that the actor became. Differences between rhapsodic and theatrical performance do exist, but they do not pertain to questions of impersonation or corporeal presence.

One of these differences has to do with the nature of their respective texts. Once writing was available for recording Homeric poetry, rhapsodes used written reminders. This determined that their function—like that of the actor—would be "to interpret the meaning of the poet to the audience" (*Ion* 530c3–4). But the rhapsode's script was essentially a record of an oral performance, a written version of a poem that had originally been oral, untouched by writing. In Ricoeur's terms, it was not yet a "text." For Ricoeur, a decisive break is made when writing is not just used to record preexistent spoken utterances in a fixed form, but is chosen from the start, *before* the commencement of spoken communication or *in place* of it. Text takes over from "reminder" when writing ceases recording discourse and starts creating it. The birth of text is what brings the actor as *hupokrites* into existence, for he is the first performer ever who comes *after* a writing, a writing that antedates any corporeal performance of it, and must therefore be interpreted prior even to its first performance. Whereas the rhapsode interprets an oral singer, the actor interprets a *text*.

The actor's performance, like that of the rhapsode or lyricist in so many ways, thus distinguishes itself from theirs insofar as what is performed by the *hupokrites* is already an interpretation of ambiguous signs (as the name suggests). Common parlance even among actors today confirms this interpretive function. In order to understand the meaning of their "words and enigmatic signs," actors must supply the illocutionary and perlocutionary intentions and effects that are missing from the textually fixed locution. They must decide what a given locution "really means" in a given context— which, as we saw earlier, is tantamount to deciding what it *does* in the context of the utterance: issues a threat, makes a promise, changes the subject, and so on. The actor must also decide what perlocutionary effects this illocutionary act is able, or is intended, to achieve: bring the conversation to a halt, attain the interlocutor's trust, and so on. Actors ordinarily speak, in

Stanislavskian terms, of "motivation," "through-line of action," and "objective" instead of illocutionary and perlocutionary acts, but as the foregoing discussion should indicate, these are effectively the same things.

Of course, actors and lawyers are not the only interpreters that writing spawns. Textual scholars and exegetes, literary critics, historians, and theorists of various kinds are also called into being with the separation of utterance from context. What actors and lawyers do at the level of individual sentences (what Medea or article 10 of the Constitution says *here* . . .), textual critics, historians, and theorists do at the level of utterances taken as wholes (what Euripides' works say in their totality; what the law intends or effects generally). As far as theatre and the law are concerned, there appear to be two main consequences of this growing reliance on textual interpretation.

The first is a potential for seeing meaning as static and singular.[63] Partly because, before print, text had to be copied laboriously by hand, word for word, the "truth" of the text could easily be equated with its "literal" accuracy. Furthermore, an assumption that such "literal meaning" is a property of language itself could ensue. An assumption of this kind is what Per Linell has called the "myth" of literal meaning. It is a myth, of course, because "there are no fixed 'literal' meanings which are invariably activated when utterances containing certain specific words are processed, no invariant features constituting the subject matter every time a particular word is used. In each single case different things are, or may be, known and understood" (1988:47). Words themselves are "dynamic, only partly determined"; it is their use in particular contexts that decides what they mean. What Manfred Pfister has said of dramatic utterances is equally true of speech acts of any kind: they do not "just consist in [their] propositional expressive content alone, but also in the way [they are themselves] the execution of an act—whether in the form of a promise, a threat," and so on (1988:6).

Textual interpreters have been known in our tradition to fall into this literate trap of forgetting about the context-bound, action-oriented nature of linguistic utterances. Particularly in interpretive spheres where texts are not integrally attached to action and performance, there is potentially nothing to prevent equations between meaning and "literal" truth. For example, where interpretation is modeled on scribal letter copying, meaning may seem to be decidable only with reference to the exact letters of an "original,"

---

63. I have already referred to the appearance of this literacy effect in Platonic philosophy. Compare also G. S. Kirk's observation that writing will tend to encourage the establishment of a standard authorized version: "With the concept of the fixed text comes the concept of the correct text, and incongruous versions are gradually eroded" (1985:110).

and verifiable only with a textually based true or false. Meaning, in short, can be confused with textual qualities, and be assumed to have the fixed and single form of letters. Nevertheless, those interpreters of texts whose interest is explicitly performative—such as actors and lawyers—know in principle that the letters of a literal locution may reflect very little of the "real meaning" of a given utterance.

A literacy-sponsored belief in the existence of single, "literal" meanings is, however, an extreme case even in modernity and was certainly not typical of fifth-century Greece. Although our culture does know of them, literate activities so divorced from life as to become breeding grounds for such hermeneutical mistakes or "literacy myths" are rare. Even rarefied religious exegesis is on guard against the letter which killeth. A more common and representative effect of textual analysis on language practices is rather the reverse: that writing actively encourages the *multiplication* of meanings.

Meanings are multiplied in two ways. In the first place, it is possible for an utterance on the page to suggest a variety of mutually contradictory referents and connotations. Such overdetermination is possible and to some degree inevitable in writing because written locutions are intentionless, as we have seen. In speech, however, a locution so lacking in intention would be impossible to understand: What is this speaker trying to say? For example, as Howard Felperin (1985) has argued, echoing a sentiment that we might associate with Hazlitt, even a single Shakespearean word such as "virginalling" cannot be delivered orally without the loss of many of the meanings that attach themselves to it as long as it remains written down.[64] Whoever wishes to turn an ambiguous textual locution into meaningful speech simply has no choice but to rule out *some* of its potential meanings in advance.

But in addition to the greater polysemy of written language at a given moment, there is also the fact that texts accumulate meanings over time. As Ricoeur points out, this is the "positive significance" of writing's *Verfremdung* (alienation). For while writing deprives documents of the intentions of their creators, it also releases documents from the *limitations* of those intentions; and meanings that were either not available to writers in their present contexts, or were even expressly foreclosed or "censored" by them, can be discerned and contributed by readers from other temporal contexts. In artificially extending the life of a given utterance, writing thus extends the *range*

---

64. Felperin writes: "The impossibility of rendering theatrically the suggestive force of the word 'virginalling' must stand as a perennial caveat to those who maintain the primacy of performance over text" (1985:7).

of that utterance's meaningfulness, making it available to more receivers in more contexts. And writing extends the *depth* of an utterance's meaningfulness as well, permitting it to be interpreted in light of *previous* readings. To take an example from the legal sphere, the reforms of Solon and Cleisthenes were hardly intended to put political and legal power into the hands of the *demos* (Ostwald 1986:15ff.). *Isegoria* was the eventual result of written law, not its motivation (Gagarin 1986:123–24). The same could be said about the Constitution of the United States when it was drafted. The survival of such locutions in textual form has been accompanied by continued reinterpretation of them, and a gradual accretion around them of additional meanings: that government by "the people" should by right include the enfranchisement of women, naturalized immigrants, and landless citizens; that "equality" among citizens includes equality among races; and that "anyone" means more than landowning males. Equality among the genders or races was always contained in and justified by the concept of equality among citizens, but it was a dormant and invisible meaning which had to await later readings. As Carol G. Thomas puts it, social inequities of these types are brought into consciousness largely on the basis of the decontextualized analysis of terms: "Although written codes were a precondition for the eventual perception of inequities, such a perception was surely the result, not the cause, of the codification" (1977:455). Pressure for concrete social reform may come out of such perceptions (458), and this sometimes in spite of the writer's own intention.

After centuries of interpretation of the Greek plays, there is no doubt that some of the meanings available to us today were scarcely visible to Sophocles' audiences and not intended by Sophocles himself. But that does not mean that they were not there as potentials. In the case of the Greeks and even Shakespeare, a huge time span and great lack of documents would prevent us from even attempting to distinguish "intended" from surplus meanings. For a concrete example of this accretion of meanings around dramatic texts, we might be better off looking closer to home, say, to the nineteenth century. Erckmann-Chatrian's *Le Juif Polonaise* was performed in London in 1871 in a stage adaptation called *The Bells*. It was a big success and consolidated Henry Irving's fame. In its original context, the play's meaning had to do with a greedy father's guilty conscience and the psychology of guilt generally. Interpreted by us today, after ovens actually were used in Europe to dispose of Polish Jews after they had been robbed, the play reads as a much more sinister document and even as a work in some way "about" Auschwitz. This meaning, which is now undoubtedly "in" the play, would obviously not have been available to its first audience or to its author.[65] Some truths, invisible to contemporary speakers, come back to pester later readers.

As Peter Szondi (1986) and Paul Ricoeur (1981) have demonstrated, textual interpretation involves a special kind of analysis, and cannot be thought of as merely a variant of the interpretation of speech. The textual utterance, already decontextualized, provokes readers to different sorts of mental operations, for their understanding needs to be *constructed.* In speech, understanding is guided by the speaker's present intentions. In writing, an experience of authorial intention fades, and the focus shifts to the reader's own internal repertoire of available meanings. Attributing meaning to texts thus inevitably sends readers into a kind of self-reflexive process through which their own world-making and world-imagining apparatus is brought into active operation.[66]

Thus, despite its orality in performance, the language spoken by actors on the stage has been shaped by textual properties and properties of textual interpretation. One of the effects of writing on speech, as I discussed briefly earlier, is the infusion into discourse of an abstract ideological dimension. For conflictual forensic and dramatic speech, this means that spoken debate will take on a "principled" quality. In forensic speech we can see with great clarity how disputes in a literate context have come to be inhabited by larger, more general social and political issues. In marked contrast to pre-legal arbitrations, "the formal hearing of a dispute essentially dramatizes power relations between opposing *groups* within a society" (Humphreys 1985:315; my italics). As we see from the *Wasps* and the *Knights* in particular, public debates in fifth-century Athens took on social dimensions larger than the individualities of the disputants themselves: they were experienced as representative of power struggles between rich and poor, old aristocracy ver-

---

65. The climax of this play is the famous courtroom scene in which the Jew's murderer is tried and found guilty of the crime through verbal cross-examination.

66. Note, however, that I am speaking here about the textual interpretation accomplished by actors, not about the experience of listeners in the audience. Theatre audiences are placed in a position vis-à-vis meaning that is fundamentally different from the position in which actors find themselves. The process of shuttling back and forth internally between intentionless signs and self-supplied interpretations is a hermeneutical process alien to the listener of live speech acts. The listener in the theatre is instead given a continual supply of already constituted verbal meanings and intentions which he or she is, instead, called upon to internalize, let resonate there, and organize into patterns and conclusions. For this reason, it makes no sense to attribute "readerly" responses to theatre audiences, as have so many theorists in our time (esp. Bennett 1987; Cole 1992). The actor, like the lawyer, is a textual interpreter; but listeners, both in the law courts and in the theatre, are subject instead to oral models of interpretation.

sus nouveau riche, young Sophists against old democrats, and so on. In epic speech, by contrast, stories about Agamemnon, Clytaemestra, Orestes, and Antigone are told without reference to generalized ideological conflicts. Epic disputes always seem to be contained comfortably within a unified worldview where heroic and familial or dynastic values are taken sufficiently for granted not to need expression. Eumaios does not tell us how he likes being a faithful servant; Penelope has nothing to say about her position in the heroic society—she goes quietly upstairs when her son tells her to get lost. But these same basic stories, when staged, became the vehicles for exploring power relations between societal groups: Antigone's conflict with Creon is explicitly cast as a "gendered" one (*Antigone* 70–73), and representative of social tensions between the *oikos* and the *polis* in general; the effects of the Trojan War on Clytaemestra are also conceived in terms of the inequities of a gendered social hierarchy (*Agamemnon* 859, 940). The investigation of Orestes' bloodguilt is similarly conceived as a problem of power relations, a contest between fathers and mothers for status under customary justice, and between customary justice and Athene's city court for status as legitimate law. In Homer, on the contrary, Achilleus' wrath runs its course oblivious to underlying social conflicts. The dispute is not, for example, a principled disagreement about whether women are appropriate tokens of status, but only about who gets which one. According to Jack Goody, the kind of ideologized debate that one sees emerging in drama is not "based exclusively on a particular political system, nor upon [a] clash of cultures in a general sense"; rather, it depends "upon the framed opposition of theories set down on paper which permitted a different form of scrutiny, the analysis of text" (1987:77).

In addition to being shaped by this ideologizing tendency, dramatic speech is also characterized by a related literary impulse: the demand for logical proof. In opening up what Roy Harris calls the "autoglottic space" (1989:105) between utterance and sponsor, writing makes abstract, conceptual thinking practicable, as we have seen. But the putting down of ideas on paper leads to a particular form of abstract reasoning, and one that is especially dependent on the visual plane of the textual medium. I am thinking here of the syllogism, the noncontradictory proof. This noncontradictory syllogism—if all men are mortal, and Socrates is a man, . . . —tied by so many scholars to Greek literacy, is the bedrock on which both legal and dramatic thought processes are based.

The indebtedness of legalistic thinking to the syllogism reveals itself with especial clarity in the *Hecatompedon* (485–84 B.C.E.), one of the oldest extant legal texts from the period. This document revolves around the question of whether an offender against the law must have acted knowingly (*eidos*), or should be found guilty even if he acted in ignorance (*agnoia*), or despite himself, without criminal intent (*akon*).[67] The syllogistic problem posed here—"If a man breaks the law, but does so in ignorance, . . ."—is also, of course, an accurate synopsis of the plot of the *Oedipus*. Indeed, the tragedy as a whole is a kind of exercise in abstract, noncontradictory logic: if all men are prohibited from committing incest and parricide, and Oedipus is a man who did both of these things, then Oedipus is therefore a criminal, *despite* who he is in this particular case—a good king with no *mens rea* (criminal intent).

But it is not only the *Oedipus* that exemplifies this autoglottic concern with an abstract truth, demonstrable syllogistically. The organization of incidents in tragedy generally shows a like use of the noncontradictory proof, and could even be said to depend on the syllogism. For dramatic poetry, as Aristotle described it, is not about unrelated or mutually contradictory particulars (as history might be), but is about "demonstrable" truths of probability and necessity (*Poetics* 1451b36ff.). Like the conditional structure of the dramatic utterance as a whole—"if . . ."—the arrangement of incidents within particular plays is generally aimed at the eduction of the third term in a logical demonstration: "If Character X does/did Y, and Y is Z, then X is Z." As Aristotle says of all such tragic syllogisms, their possible outcomes are strictly limited in number by logic: "Besides these there is no other way, for they must either do the deed, or not, either knowingly or unknowingly" (1453b15–16).

Forensic demonstrations of this type, which first come into existence when law is extracted from personality and written down, manifest their connection with dramatic discourse again when literacy has its renaissance in Europe. From the point at which the monastic class begins to dominate our literary records in the Christian era, writing is not often used to record secular civic debate in Europe until around the ninth century.[68] But when secular documents do begin to appear, between the ninth and twelfth centuries, we notice that writing is used earliest for two significant and probably related purposes: for transcripts of juridical proceedings, and for the stage scripts of jongleurs.[69] Why the benefits of writing should be recognized so quickly for these two speech practices is clear: in both cases the exact wording is important to the outcome, as is the order in which the ut-

67. Vernant and Vidal-Naquet 1990:64; Ostwald 1986:23.
68. Clanchy 1979; Elsky 1989; Auerbach 1965.
69. Auerbach 1965:280–91; Clanchy 1979:225.

terances are delivered. Syllogisms about Socrates' mortality or Oedipus' guilt will fail to induce the final term if individual words are changed even slightly. Scripts, "whether for jongleurs or lawyers," enable their readers to see exactly what was said, or how they should speak, and "see the manner directly" (Clanchy 1979:225). And what is true for the jongleurs who learned vernacular romances by heart is even more true for the actors who replaced them after the thirteenth century. An oral bard, working alone and without anything to "prove," can deliver the episodes in nearly any order at all, without consequences for his recitation as a whole. Witness the invocation that starts the *Odyssey:* "Begin it, goddess, at whatever point you will." In the communal production conditions of drama, the order of incidents must on the contrary be known in advance: unexpected departures can result in pandemonium for everyone. But more importantly, if the order of incidents in a dramatic story is not strictly predetermined and adhered to, the syllogism will fall apart, fail to induce any logical conclusion. The same goes for proceedings at the bench: exact verbatim records of the litigants' and witnesses' testimonies are crucial to the outcome. This fact of forensic speech is recognized instantly by Bdelykleon: he writes down the key points in the defendant's argument verbatim (*Wasps* 576–77). Indeed, one could go so far as to assert that one of the earliest secular dramas of the European period was actually a lawyer's handbook, called *The Court Baron* and published in 1265. The lively, vernacular-style[70] forensic dialogue in this practical guide to pleading so closely resembles the speech of Shakespearean characters that one cannot help but appreciate the extent to which legal discourse, even the fictitious legal discourse of *The Court Baron,* provided a ready-made model for dramatic composition. (Asked a simple yes-or-no question by the crown, the naive poacher Walter de la More launches into a lengthy digression about how his wife, off her food for a month, was suddenly taken with a mighty longing to eat a tench—a speech that parallels, in nearly every aspect, Pompey's rambling discourse about Mistress Overdone's sudden "female" cravings for stewed prunes in *Measure for Measure.*)

The "reckoning all together" of syllogistic reasoning depends on an ability to arrange the major and minor premises simultaneously, and to see the relationship between them. For this reason, as Jack Goody has argued, formal operations such as the noncontradictory syllogism cannot be pursued beyond a very rudimentary point in the absence of writing (1987:77). In oral contexts, without the ability to arrange thoughts in simultaneously

---

70. Vernacular-*style* because it was written in French, the written language of the time, but intended as a lifelike representation of regular speech.

co-present configurations, contradictions are difficult to see. Writing for this reason is conducive to the invention of the formal proof; but perhaps even more significantly for science and the humanities, "it also accumulates and records these proofs (and what they prove) for future generations and for further operations" (68). Thus we are not surprised to find that the scientific method and empirical observation begin to replace ritual magic, shamanism, sacrifice, and belief in oracles and other supernatural agents in literate societies. As Goody suggestively describes it, it is only when one keeps a running, systematic record of the relation between one's dreams or horoscope and reality that one begins to discover for certain that the former hardly ever actually "foretells" the latter: "In oral memory the many misses tend to be forgotten in favour of the occasional hits" (69). Writing thus not only makes possible logical demonstrations and proofs, but also produces an atmosphere in which such methods of argument will tend to be expected.[71]

A good example of this expectation of rational argumentation can be found in Jocasta's speech to Oedipus against putting one's trust in oracles. Like any forensic speaker, she is of course partial: she has no desire to lose a loved one *again* to a husband's irrational fear of oracular predictions. But her demonstration nevertheless depends on abstracted, syllogistic reasoning: the future is by definition unknowable; oracles pretend to be able to predict the future; therefore they are necessarily untrustworthy (*Oedipus Tyrannos* 977–84). To say that Euripides was even more famous than Sophocles for such rationalist inquiries would be a serious understatement; as Aristophanes jokes in the *Frogs,* Euripides' characters walk around muttering, "*Is* life life?"[72] Euripides' "bookish" preference for what can be visibly proven true is also accurately reflected in a line from *Wise Melanippe* (frag. 286 Nauck 1964): "Zeus, whoever Zeus is, for I know him only by report."[73]

To be able to induce visible contradictions and logical deductions on papyrus is one thing, however; communicating one's true deductions in public is another thing entirely. The uttering of Euripides' line about Zeus in the theatre is reported to have caused such an explosion of disapproval from the

71. This is not to say that literate Greece did not remain a profoundly superstitious and religious society. People still put their trust in oracles and priests, and remained irrationally terrified of curses, symbolic acts, and religious gestures. But atheists, scientists, and other empirical observers began to appear in increasing numbers, and such "proofs" as the empiricists were developing came to be expected even in other spheres as well. See especially Lloyd 1990, but also Thomas 1992.

72. See Arrowsmith for the Euripidean sources of the joke (1962:97–98 n. 69).

73. See Ostwald for other "atheistic" statements of Euripides (1986:280–81).

audience that Euripides was forced to retract it (Ostwald 1986:281). And so at last we are brought to one of the central issues in our discussion of dramatic logography: What is the relation between the accusation and the public hearing? We have established so far that the former is written, "comes first," and possesses certain qualities, and that the latter is oral, follows it in time, and produces a popular judgment. What are the implications, for speech genres such as drama, of this hybrid use of two separate media, temporally thus configured?

The tragedians Aeschylus and Euripides are shown competing, in the *Frogs*, largely on the basis of what they wrote, for the honor of being judged best civic adviser; but all evidence shows that in the auditorium itself, it is the charming speech of the performers that will tend to carry off the prize. Socrates is reported to have cautioned that charming speech and good advice are two different things, and those blessed by nature with an abundance of the former are not necessarily the same people who have any of the latter to offer (Xenophon *Memorabilia* 3.6). A performer is by definition someone who seeks the spotlight, who desires and often needs recognition for his personal charms. But as Socrates of the *Phaedrus* sensibly warns, if we give our attention to those who *need*, rather than *merit*, our attention, we are putting ourselves into the hands of "not the best people but the most helpless" (233.d.5).[74]

Socrates' warnings about the hazards of trusting good advice to performers deserve our attention. For we have already seen at least one compelling reason why the pragmatics of performance will have a tendency to run counter to the pragmatics of dramatic speech writing, that is, giving good advice to the city: the need for public favor, the need to please and, by pleasing, to win. As Aristophanes warns his potentially "indignant" audience at a performance of the *Acharnians*, "What I say will be shocking but it will be right" (496–509). In other words, the poetic motive to speak about "justice" and what is "right" can be difficult to reconcile with the performative need to please. In fact, it appears that as long as it remains an oral process, the giving of public advice will tend to remain tied to the kind of audience psychology that "blames the messenger."

Herodotus reports that in the summer of 479, a messenger was dispatched to propose a peace settlement to the Athenians on Salamis. Lycides, who stood up before the Assembly and advised that the offer be accepted,

---

74. This suggests that there is good justification for a division of labor among writers and performers. Nevertheless, the existence of actor-playwrights such as Aeschylus, Shakespeare, and Molière suggests that Socrates may have been mistaken in this after all.

was stoned to death by his indignant audience (*History* 9.5.1–3; cf. Ostwald 1986:25). We begin to see what might have been at stake in Ibsen's revocation of his shockingly feminist ending to *A Doll's House* for the first performance Germany. In fact, the retraction of such "shocking" statements as Euripides wrote for the theatre may therefore be an inevitable consequence of arguing cases orally before a democratic, ideologized public. Athenian jurors normally dropped their stones harmlessly into urns rather than hurling them homicidally at the defendants, and the tomatoes we throw at our public speakers today are unlikely to result in mortal injury, but the pragmatics of audience response is the same in all such live speech situations.

According to Aristotle and Aristophanes in particular, public performance, for all its democratizing strengths, will tend to compromise the integrity of public debate in certain ways. Aristotle lamented this development thus: "And just as in drama the actors now count for more than the poets, so it is in the contests of public life, owing to the defects of our political institutions" (*Rhetoric* 3.1.1403b33). What he meant by the "defects in our political institutions" was fully articulated by Aristophanes in the *Wasps* and the *Knights,* both admirably analyzed by Martin Ostwald (1986:219–26). In the *Wasps,* we see how unfettered popular power in the law courts can produce a situation where the class interests of the jurors take precedence over abstract values of juridical fairness. When civic debate is itself ideologized, every case becomes an opportunity for the common man to bring the rich man down, and make him pay, and this regardless of the particulars of the case (*Wasps* 241). An ideologized text is one thing; a live public with an ideological axe to grind is a force not to be messed with. To such an audience, every defendant becomes an "enemy of the people," a "lover of monarchy," a "conspirator," or a "dictator" (463–500). Even wrangles in the marketplace over onions and salt fish are invested with ideological implications (488–99). Furthermore, the omnipresence of such ideological hostilities created a paradise for demagogues, who fanned the flames and, in Aristophanes' view, made the practice of truly blind, impartial justice an impossibility in Athens.

The resulting situation, at least in Aristophanes' view, is one in which the decision-making process is corrupted by the need to "feed" the audience, to bribe it with tasty treats. Successful public speech is thus presented in the *Knights* as a matter of flattering the audience with appeals to its stomach: here a sausage seller is the ideal orator, for he will know the most delicious recipes. He is advised to make his speeches, literally, palatable (*Knights* 214–16). The use of cookery images in Aristophanes' discussions of successful public speech reminds us, of course, of Brecht's warnings about "culinary theatre." The danger of "catering" to audience "tastes" is similarly warned against by Aristophanes in the *Acharnians* (370–74, 634–40). In the legal and political sphere in Athens, this need to flatter the audience in order to get a favorable judgment was epitomized by the sycophants, orators who grew rich by prosecuting wealthy men before hostile juries (Ostwald 1986:219–26).

Such weaknesses of a theatricalized judicial system are still of concern today. In her study of modern forensic speech and its effect on juries, Bettyruth Walter found that juries tend to have a built-in bias in favor of prosecutors (1988:vii), a proclivity that may be a holdover of the democratic ideal expressed earlier by Euripides—that common written law will bring the great man low. Walter calls the lawyer's final summation speech to the jury the "aria" of the performance (225), and concludes that the most successful lawyers are those who are most aware of their histrionic function (vii). Confirming Socratic and Aristophanic fears about the pragmatics of performance, Walter found further, from hundreds of case studies and interviews, that "much of what [lawyers] do and say during the trial, including summation, is directed towards getting the jurors to like them" (221).

And apparently, both today and in ancient Greece, the straightest route to a popular audience's heart is through its stomach, the organ most susceptible to emotion and ideology. What is most intriguing about Walter's findings is that in legal contexts where lawyers are not competing directly for a popular audience's affections—in appellate court, for example—they are less inclined to demagoguery, more inclined to demonstrate expertise in law. When arguing in appellate court before legal colleagues only, lawyers are equally constrained by audience response; but they are constrained in the direction of high (legal) standards and away from what we might call "low" emotional tactics and direct appeals to the audience's ideological sympathies (224). In ancient Greece, however, there was no appellate court, and all public speakers had to cope with the tastes of popular juries. From what we see in Aristophanes and Aristotle, these tastes have not changed. The pressure to appeal as directly as possible to the emotions is hilariously described by Philokleon in the *Wasps* (565–75). As for the need to cater to the audience's ideological sympathies, Aristotle complained in the fourth century that juries care more "for what is to the people's advantage than for what is just" (*Const. Ath.* 1.13). Walter concludes that even seemingly monologic forensic speech is "in fact a two-way communication" (viii), for argument in the presence of a judging audience will always perforce be a "response" to the audience's needs, wishes, tastes, and prejudices.

Theatrical analogues for these pragmatics of performance are not hard to find. Brecht's "culinary theatre" is of course one of them, as are the many hams, schmaltz mongers, and sycophants of stage history. Like Walter's lawyers, performing artists are probably equally likely to find their performances changed by their audience's perceived level of expertise. A Diana Rigg or a Christopher Plummer might think twice about using, before an audience of respected actors, certain histrionic devices which they would use with impunity before a popular audience of nonspecialists. The same could be said about musical performers: a "pops" concert is not above resorting to the kinds of bells and whistles that are thought "too low" to be offered for the delectation of expert musicologists. Like the high/low dynamic which I discussed in Chapter 2, there appears to be a high/low polarity in the cuisine of performance technique as well: one "caters" to expert taste with rarefied specialist knowledge and textual fidelity, and satisfies the lay audience with emotion and ideology. Speaking of the "low" tactics used on stage to win the favor of the mass festival audience, Aristophanes describes plays that feature "slaves scattering nuts from a little basket among the spectators" (*Wasps* 58). Such culinary tactics, although ridiculed as vulgar, were apparently quite common.[75]

There is evidence to be had, particularly from Denys Page's analysis of ancient actors' interpolations, that the pragmatics of performance will tend to have a number of other, related effects. Performers often appear to have "improved" their texts by making them, on the one hand, more conventional and repetitious and, on the other, more gratuitously spectacular and sensational. Tragic endings were often changed to implausibly happy ones, and the addition of redundant virtuosic ornamentation seems to have been common as well (Page 1987:43). There also seems to have been an urge to suit the presentation to the tastes of the audience, which in some cases may have led to the deletion of certain speeches or episodes that were crucial for the coherence of the plot (38–39).

What is perhaps most fascinating about such interpolations is that they appear to characterize oral speech practices generally. In oral speech as in performance, the pragmatics of action and effect on the listener take precedence over the syntactic coherence of what is said. I discussed this earlier with reference to Plato's equation between the oral speaker and the lover in the *Phaedrus*. In that discussion I suggested that, despite its weaknesses, writing does have the virtue of fostering greater disinterestedness and logical consistency. In Rosalind Thomas's study of Athenian family and state history as perpetuated by written and oral means, respectively (1989), we find

75. *Peace* 962; *Wealth* 794–801; and see Sommerstein 1983 4:157.

some interesting corroboration for the Platonic view that speaking in public "means frequently saying good-bye to the truth" (272e).

According to Thomas's findings, an oral version of a given event will tend to take a more "conventional and repetitious form" than will the same material recorded and communicated in writing (214). Furthermore, an oral history quickly becomes ideologically selective as well: historical events (and people) which do not explicitly confirm the basic ideological picture of Athens as a bastion of freedom and justice and a bulwark against enslavement get deleted from the account. Only the written documents retain traces of military defeats, shameful deeds, collusion with tyrants, bribery. The reason for this is clear: a speaker is always dialogically engaged in a concrete communicative context where some kind of real action is taking place. An orator delivering a funeral oration, for example, is not in a position to remind mourners that the battle in which their loved ones lost their lives was a disgraceful defeat, or that victory was gained by morally dubious means. When delivering obsequies, one must perforce be obsequious.

From this we might conclude that the same is likely to go for speakers in other contexts as well: the needs of the listeners and the context will tend to be given precedence over the internal completeness or accuracy of what is said to them. As Roland Barthes has put it, the needs of interlocution tend to "overwhelm" what is said. In speech situations, my body, as speaker, must respond to the needs of your body, as listener. In writing, the listener's body is absent, and so are its needs; in writing, in Barthes's words: "I think less for you, I think more for the 'truth'" (1985:6). Writing at home, Phrynicus must have thought *The Capture of Miletus* a great idea; within the festival context of dramatic performance, it was a disaster. Ditto for Euripides and his skepticism about Zeus, or his praise of money in the *Danae,* which also caused a riot in the theatre.[76] It would appear, then, that written logography and oral performance do seem destined to run at cross-purposes in this respect: truth pursued disinterestedly on the page must somehow be made palatable on the stage.

Not only are speakers likely to have the motive for glossing over certain unpalatable truths in a speech situation, but such is the ephemerality of the spoken word that these omissions and illogicalities will tend not even to be noticed. It is only when one writes down, say, a family genealogy that missing generations and impossible chronologies become obvious and undisguisable. Accordingly, it is only because Page has the text before him, in a written version that can be inspected with the eyes, that he can see that

76. Pickard-Cambridge 1968:274.

something important has dropped out of a plot. Similarly with Aristophanes' jurors and his festival audience: without the aid of some kind of written version of the case being argued, it is hard—if not impossible—to judge the truth of what is being said.

In stage history from antiquity to the present, we can easily find examples of all the types of distortions and falsification which Thomas discerns in oral versions of family and state history: dramatic characters are deleted or merged into composites, incidents are wiped out or get mixed up in performance with other incidents, complexities are simplified, time telescoped. Oral history's tendency to remember defeats as victories has a clear analogue in the stage's proclivity for turning sad endings into happy ones, as so many performers have done with *Romeo and Juliet, Lear,* and other plays. Oral history also has a habit of foregrounding and then remembering only sensational aspects of an event at the expense of its "substance." For example, a political reformer in ancient Greece is remembered not for his role in introducing radical democracy, but for the mysterious circumstances surrounding his death (Thomas 1989:203). Similarly in the modern theatre, a play such as *The Bells* enters stage history not as an alarming symptom of European anti-Semitism, but as a stunning spectacle in which Henry Irving slowly laced up his boots. Just as Thomas has found that the needs of the context of the *epitaphios*—the glorification of Athenian democracy—pragmatically dominated everything said there, so too do the performative choices made throughout theatre history often suggest that the audience's culinary and ideological needs are the altar on which abstract values such as logic, fairness, and truth may be sacrificed.[77]

In the previous chapter we looked at the crucial role played by the student/actor's "gut" reaction in the process of textual interpretation. But as we see from the behavior of Aristophanes' jurors and Athenian audiences alike, such live visceral responses are a mixed blessing: sometimes the one thing an audience cannot "stomach" is the truth. And the same may go for actors. In the final analysis, perhaps the most pertinent question to ask of a theatrical presentation of a written accusation is *not* whether it compromised the truth of the text, but whether it gave the case a fair hearing. And fairness is not

---

77. I do not mean to suggest that sad endings are better than happy ones or that catering to audience taste is necessarily a bad thing. As in other "free market" situations, the need to satisfy public demand creates competition and can produce brilliant and original results. For the other side of the coin—that is, for a more sympathetic account of the role played by performative forces that run counter to the "truths" expressed in texts—see Chapter 2.

easy to achieve through the medium of public speech. Students of linguistics generally claim that writing lags behind speech and tends to conserve outmoded forms. In the realm of public performance, however, where audiences may come to judge a case or a play already convinced about what is right and just and what is not, it is liable to be writing, not speech, that is more open-minded and progressive. Writing is able to imagine new kinds of speech long before they would be applauded in actuality. Not only do the writings of Aspasia and Lysias come to mind, but also those of Maria Stewart in nineteenth-century America. She gave the very first public speech by an American woman, in Boston in 1832. But her oration, about the need for higher education for blacks, particularly black women, met with an audience so hostile that she was forced to give up public speaking within the year (Safire 1992:562). So we cannot but be sympathetic, ultimately, to the actor in Germany who refused to outrage her audience by performing Nora's door-slamming departure at the end of the play. She may simply have known her audience well enough to know that Ibsen's indictment of Nora's marriage would never have received a fair hearing had she left it in. A theatrical audience, like Aristophanes' jurors *Philo*kleon and *Bdely*kleon,[78] often knows what it likes and what it hates—before even hearing the evidence.

The ability of writing to promote types of speech that would be hissed in public is of course witnessed whenever written episodes and sentiments are expurgated in performance for ideological reasons. This same feature of writing can be seen in the many female, "foreign," or otherwise ethnic roles that were written into the theatrical repertory by individual playwrights only to be performed in public for years, sometimes even centuries, by speakers less likely to be pelted with fruit.

As Rosalind Thomas has shown, oral performance tends to perpetuate stereotypes, whereas the greater detail and accuracy of writing tends to expose these stereotypes for what they are. Without the checks to their generalizing, simplifying tendencies provided by such written documents as, say, the written histories of Thucydides, oral accounts can take on "the quality of a timeless catalogue of heroic deeds" (Thomas 1989:232). An example of how dramatic texts may indeed function much like historical documents in recording the more "unsavory" or difficult truths of a given society can be seen if we compare Euripides' *Ion* with oral tradition on the subject of corruption at Delphi. Oral history, as Thomas shows, "forgets" the Alc-

---

78. *Philokleon* means "loving Kleon" and *Bdelykleon* "loathing Kleon."

maeonids' bribery of the oracle and remembers only that they were great enemies of tyranny. The "bookish" Euripides, by contrast, does not hesitate to call the oracle a "Delphian fraud."

Temporarily sheltered from the sting of voting pebbles and rotten vegetables, writers such as Euripides may be slightly freer than speakers of the obligation to cater to ideological stereotype. But they are hardly free of *all* motives, nor lacking in techniques for fulfilling them. Literate decontextualization extends only so far. Even the solitary writer is subject to personal agendas, and if skilled, can devise specious "proofs." As a character in Euripides' *Phoenix* says of this problem of truth and argument: "I've already been chosen to judge many disputes and have heard witnesses competing against each other with opposing accounts of the same event. And like any wise man I work out the truth by looking at a man's nature" (frag. 812 Nauck 1964).[79] In other words, in human conflicts it is sometimes not the written arguments that matter but the disputants' "natures" or intentions. And it is here, of course, that power shifts from the writer to the performer, from the intentionless written accusation to the trial. The arguments are fixed, but performers have considerable leeway when it comes to determining the disputants' natures and intentions. For example, Charles Macklin's decision to perform Shylock as a dignified character altered the nature of this disputant in *Merchant of Venice,* and as a result probably gave the play a fairer hearing in the eighteenth century that it had received formerly. But the controversy that continues to rage around this play, about whether it even deserves to come before the public at all, suggests that performative decisions can go only so far in tipping the scales of justice toward fair trials. Some dramatic accusations may simply be condemned, by history and the accumulation of interpretive readings, to appear irremediably corrupt over time, after which point all the textual tampering in the world is not enough to eliminate a contemporary audience's sense that the playwright has warped the evidence, disadvantaged one of the disputants, or perhaps even charged the wrong man. In such cases, the play in question will tend to fall permanently out of the repertory.

It would not be reasonable to imagine, in other words, that all written accusations, in the law or the theatre, are ideologically innocent or inherently fair or even equally deserving of a public hearing in the first place. But in neither of these two spheres of social life is the text intended to be an end in itself. Rather, legal and dramatic texts are meant to set in motion a dis-

79. See Humphreys 1985:323.

cursive process whose mode is *performance* and whose end is a *decision*.[80] The reliance of law and theatre on performance *can* have deleterious effects on the fairness of a given verdict, as we see both on the stage—when great plays fail, or succeed only through bowdlerization—and in the courts, when juries acquit or condemn defendants on the basis of ideological prejudice rather than legal rules and evidence. But the reliance on performance has its positive function, too, for it is an implicit acknowledgment that the law is meant to serve the actual people living under it, not the other way around, and that even good laws may need revision, while some may deserve to be struck from the books altogether.

A nice example of the positive value of performance, despite the cost, is provided by Aeschylus. After hearing testimony in the interrogation of Orestes' crime in the *Eumenides,* Athene adds her ballot in favor of Orestes' acquittal because, as she says with a feeble attempt at self-justification, she identifies with men rather than women. This is hardly what one would call a reasoned decision. Indeed, the biased nature of Athene's verdict is liable to be so repellent to modern performers and audiences alike that it is hard to imagine the *Eumenides* receiving a fair hearing today. According to Christian Meier (1990), however, there is actually something much bigger at stake in this dramatic moment than the sexist ideology conveyed by Athene's acquittal. Understood in its proper historical and dramatic context, this gesture is less a piece of shameless prejudice than it is an affirmation of the benefits of a public jury system, a celebration of a citizen's authority to make such judgments, be they ever so capricious.[81] The preliterate system of hereditary justice had, after all, guaranteed that bloodguilt be perpetuated ad infinitum; if, in the transition to a properly legal sphere, one man must go unpunished, then this is a compromise whose humanistic benefits for all far outweigh the ideological drawbacks in this one case. As Meier describes it, "what is presented here is, in a nutshell, the 'decisionist' insight" which constitutes one of the main political advances of Athenian democracy. Athene's vote, while poorly justified, is accepted as legitimate because it is a

80. In my comparison between the decision-making process in court and that which takes place in a theatre festival audience, some readers may sense a qualitative difference. They might object that judging the guilt of an accused criminal is fundamentally different from judging the excellence of a play. As the case of David Mamet's *Oleanna* shows clearly, however, audience reaction is intimately tied up with judgments about whether the characters are being justly or unjustly accused. Like the ancient dramas, *Oleanna* is structured as an "indictment" of its characters, and audiences have loved or hated it depending on their "verdicts" about the validity of the playwright's charges.

81. Compare Aeschylus' suppliants, who praise the jury of Argos for siding with them as women rather than identifying with their male cousins.

valid contribution to the public decision-making process. She has heard the evidence, and votes on the basis of who she is at that particular moment, and Aeschylus makes no apology for the blatant partiality of her decision. The point of this scene, for Athenian law no less than for the aesthetic court of the theatre, is that the decision is accepted as valid *despite* its partiality, despite the fact that it "may not necessarily rest on compelling arguments" (107). As a decision taken within the living context of the decision makers' present reality, it may not embody "ultimate truth," but it will at least be an accurate reflection of one real moment in the community's ongoing *search* for it.

In short, the pragmatics of oral performance may produce legal and aesthetic decisions that seem arbitrary and poorly reasoned, especially when compared with the values endorsed by the texts that launched these live speech activities in the first place. The written submission remains, however, long after the ballots have been cast, as a standard against which to review the decisions taken within particular oral-performative contexts. A hearing on the stage, as in the courts, is always subject to appeal.[82] The case may be brought before the public again with different interpreters and different jurors, or perhaps when social conditions are more favorable to a fair hearing. Having read their texts in light of successive readings over time, later performers may be able to see aspects of the case that earlier performers missed, and bring new physical evidence. In performance, low culinary techniques may tend to "cook the books" according to ideological stereotype; but so long as these books *also* survive for reading and interpretation, their high intellectual and professional standards will keep such impulses in check—and vice versa. That is, as long as both written and spoken media are allowed to balance each other's weaknesses, there is a good chance that the decisions made in performance will be able to go on exemplifying democracy in action without straying too far from the abstract call of justice.

What could be said of a society with written laws *and* oral-performative jury courts could be said also of social contexts where written theatre thrives. If the decisions made by interpreters and their audiences in and through performance fall short of the standards set by writing, this shortfall represents less a miscarriage of justice than a guarantee of its responsiveness to the individuals who rely on it. For such decisions can inform the future, without binding it, about the experiential truth of one particular moment in the ongoing dialogue between speakers and their texts. And what is more,

82. Jury trials in fifth-century Athens were not actually open to appeal; but ours are today, of course.

the freedom to make such decisions, as Meier suggests, could even be described as a precondition of any genuinely liberal order, political or aesthetic (108).

When Aeschylus represented Athens's eponymous deity on stage in the *Eumenides,* he envisioned her as a democratic-minded but less than perfectly rational juror casting her vote according to her taste. This image is as fitting a tribute to Athens's populist legal system as it is to the theatrical stage on which it was displayed. Under the protection of a written law code and a city court, free democratized debate could be carried on at Athens—both at law and in the theatre.

Like the jury courts, theatre was a literate civic institution which owed its existence largely to written law and the *isegoria* which it made possible. But writing was responsible for expanding the freedom and mobility of human actors in other ways as well. Not only in legal disputes but in economic exchange, private communication, and in other personal spheres of action too, writing was instrumental in the creation of new types of social intercourse, of all of which theatre was an accurate aesthetic reflection. It is to these that we will be turning now.

CHAPTER 4

Economies of Inscription

Bring out the scales then, if my duty is to judge
two master poets like a grocer selling cheese.
Aristophanes

In death the creature got a voice; in life it had
none.
Sophocles

*T*HE EPIC PLOT OF THE *ODYSSEY* REVOLVES AROUND THE WANDERINGS OF
a husband and father, Odysseus, who has not been heard from in ten
years, and whose absence from home is becoming a serious problem. According to Homer, there is only one way available for Odysseus' news-
starved family to make contact with him: one of its members must step
physically into a ship, set out across the wine-dark sea, and seek out the absent father in the flesh. With a little exaggeration, it could be said that the
whole of the *Odyssey* ultimately boils down to one simple technological
problem: the epic hero's inability to write home.

For in Homer's time, no technology existed for representing human
speech in the absence of speakers: whoever wished to communicate with
someone, to hear or tell a story or news, had to bring himself physically
within earshot of an actual speaker. Before the spread and development of
alphabetical literacy in the seventh and sixth centuries B.C.E., communication was limited to face-to-face exchanges, and stories about such impover-
ished communication conditions—such as the *Odyssey,* in which characters
must physically travel to exchange valuable information—are almost
inevitable.

By the time of the playwrights, however, such stories had been techno-
logically surpassed. As Aristotle was later to observe, the characters invented
during the dramatic age do not need to get into ships to communicate with
absent fathers and friends: unlike their epic embodiments, dramatic characters stay put and simply send letters, write last wills and testaments, pin
suicide notes to their chests. For in the hands of literate playwrights, mytho-

logical figures such as Agamemnon, Iphigenia, Heracles, and Phaedra are writers, and can escape the physical constraints of time and distance by sending written signs as their embassies to others. This new state of affairs, in which disembodied signs can be exchanged in lieu of the things themselves, is clearly reflected in the altered plots of myths as treated by the literate poets of the fifth century; but this literate economy of exchange is reflected also in the institution of the Athenian theatre itself, and helped to bring it into existence.

In *Of Grammatology*, Jacques Derrida makes the following observation about the nature of writing:

> Th[e] movement of analytic abstraction in the circulation of arbitrary signs is quite parallel to that within which money is constituted. Money replaces things by their signs, not only within a society but from one culture to another, or from one economic organization to another. That is why the alphabet is mercantile. It must be understood within the monetary moment of economic rationality. The critical description of money is the faithful reflection of the discourse on writing. In both cases, an anonymous supplement is substituted for the thing. (1976:300) [1]

Derrida's description of the mercantile nature of writing serves usefully to emphasize that texts, like coins, *circulate,* move freely between people in a way that people and things themselves cannot. His conception of the relation between money and writing is also surprisingly identical to the ancients' own view of it: like money, writing is an arbitrary currency, and those who traffic in both are availed of behavioral choices that are denied those who exchange goods and information by more direct and physically embedded means.

Within the world of the epic, for example, there is neither money nor writing, and the behavior of Homer's heroes is constrained accordingly. Like other preliterate milieus, the world of the Homeric epics reflects a "pre-market society" (Donlan 1981:101). As Aristotle was to say later of "barbarian" economies, exchange in the absence of coinage meant the direct barter of "useful objects for other useful objects" (*Politics* 1.9.1257a25). Strabo in his *Geography* similarly spoke of the Albanians as "not like shopkeepers"; they too did not use coins, but rather used "straightforward" barter to exchange

---

1. I have modified Gayatri Spivak's translation very slightly, for she does not use the word "mercantile," which seems a more accurate choice than the two approximate terms she puts together in lieu of Derrida's one.

goods (11.4.4).[2] Aristotle's and Strabo's descriptions of such pre-market systems suggest that while perhaps "barbarous" on one level, these systems were also more "natural" on another. Aristotle associates the use of coinage with "the other art of wealth-getting, namely, retail trade" (1257b). A look at the "natural" economy of the Homeric period shows, however, that the emergence of retail trade out of the barter system meant more than just the emergence of "the art of wealth-getting"; it also meant the growth of a traffic in *theatrical* signs.

We see the barter system at work in the epics when the Achaians obtain wine by exchanging bronze, iron, skins, oxen, and slaves (*Iliad* 7.472–75). But as Walter Donlan has shown in his study of such Homeric transactions, goods given and exchanged were valued *symbolically,* not according to strictly economic principles. Like the aboriginal inhabitants of the Queen Charlotte Islands of British Columbia, for whom the possession of coppers and blankets traditionally secured social prestige,[3] the Homeric society prized commodities in a way that was not commensurate with what we would call their "monetary" value. A cup, tripod, or item of clothing or jewelry, as a "treasured" status symbol or "prize," would not have a direct equivalent in common goods such as animals or other natural produce; hundreds or even thousands of oxen would be needed to make up the perceived value of a single item of "treasure" (Donlan 1981:106). In short, material transactions were stratified into two distinct levels of exchange, the "prestige" economy of "treasure" given and received among the warrior elites, and the substantive economy having to do with livelihood, and in which everyone participated: "Functionally, the social-symbolic sphere of the Homeric economy sustains and perpetuates a graded status-system, enabling those at the top to preserve their positions relative to those below" (109).

It was only by virtue of one's membership in the warrior class that one had access to the items with prestige value, and these were circulated within the elite class according to ritualistic and symbolic rules as opposed to economic ones: as gifts or signs of kingly hospitality. For this reason, Donlan describes the Homeric economy as being directly embedded in the "total social structure," where transactions are carried out according to non-economic motives (101–6). We can see this clearly in the agon between Achilleus and Agamemnon: the allocation of treasure goods is described as symbolic of the relative status of the warriors. And as Donlan explains further, the wealth of objects offered to Achilleus in belated recognition of his

2. As translated in Jones 1993:21.
3. Cole and Lockner 1993:52, 128–29.

status (*Il.* 9.160–61) serves as a "demonstration of the ranking figure's ability to exercise political dominance by controlling the movement of prestige goods" (110). With the adoption of coinage throughout the Greek world in the seventh century (Kraay 1976:25–27), however, the symbolic and socially stratified status system of Homeric exchange was replaced by a liberalized, independent economic sphere. As a result, the circulation within one group of prestige goods was displaced by the economic exchange of natural products between different groups, that is, by trade and commerce (Donlan 1981:110).

Written law, as we saw in the previous chapter, had the effect of replacing aristocratic social values with more democratic ones. In the economic sphere, precisely the same democratizing effect was achieved through the advent of coinage. As the tragedians described written law, so Plato and Aristotle described money: it was a great equalizer. Retail trade, as Plato remarks, had positive social benefits beyond the advent of shopkeepers: "For surely one who makes equal and similar the nature of goods of any kind, when it is dissimilar and unequal, does good; and we must agree that this is what the power of money also achieves" (*Laws* 11.918a–b). Money is an "instrument" (*Politics* 289a–b) which in Aristotle's words makes things equal: "Money is in fact a kind of measure which by making things measurable reduces them to equality" (*Nicomachean Ethics* 5.5.1133a–b). In a free market economy as opposed to a prestige one, exchanges must be able to occur among socially unequal individuals and between one social sphere and another. For in truly reciprocal economic relations, Aristotle writes, it is not always "two doctors [for example] that associate for exchange, but a doctor and a farmer, or in general people who are different and unequal; but these must be equated. This is why all things that are exchanged must be somehow comparable. It is for this end that money has been introduced, and it becomes in a sense an intermediate; for it measures all things . . . [and determines] how many shoes are equal to a house or to a given amount of food" (*Nic. Eth.* 1133a17–21). Money—called *nomisma* because it is a man-made custom or law (*nomos*) rather than a naturally occurring phenomenon—thus makes both goods and the individuals who exchange them commensurate and equal. As an abstract medium for fixing value outside of concrete social relations, *nomisma* gives shoemakers the same economic rights to purchase tripods as kings had monopolized in Homer, just as written *nomoi* had equalized their rights and freedoms in the settling of disputes.

The representational "law" of money was also recognized by the ancients as analogous to the representational structure of writing and language generally. Both are merely customary, have no real meaning or value in themselves, and function by convention in the absence of the thing itself.[4] The writer of the dialogue *Eryxias* (Plato?) wrote at length on the arbitrariness of money: "In Ethiopia they use engraved stones which would be useless to a Spartan"; the Carthaginians tie objects up in leather pouches and the Spartans use "iron weight as a currency." But all these systems are as mutually incomprehensible as foreign languages: "Among us the man who had the most of these would be no richer than if he had a number of pebbles from the mountain" (399e–400c). Like language and writing, which make it possible to discuss things and states of affairs in their absence and even in the absence of (one of) the speakers themselves, so money, by representing absent things arbitrarily, expands people's ability to exchange goods without reference to their own identities or status or to the presence or identity of the things exchanged.

We saw in the case of written law that the first step in the establishment of an independent public legal order was the writing down of ancestral *thesmia* by the *thesmothetai,* the hereditary lawgivers. These laws, although written, were still private property in effect; they had not yet been thoroughly abstracted away from the body of the king. In the history of coinage, we find that a similarly proprietary stage was gone through before money became a genuinely public, city phenomenon. The first issues of Greek coins, which Colin Kraay calls *Wappenmünzen,* or "heraldic coins," were connected with particular ruling families or other individuals who appear to have been personally responsible for minting them (1976:56–57). These coins were stamped with changing imagery (beetle, bull's head, horse, seal, lion, cock, goat, owl); and, like the early coinage of medieval Europe, these heraldic coins with their shifting types seem to have been recognized as valid only for short periods of time each (59). A half-stater from Ephesus, dated before 590 B.C.E.—contemporary with the Solonian law code and predating the first recorded contests in tragedy by several decades—has written upon it: "I am the badge of Phanes" (23). Coins of this kind were associated also with the Peisistratids of Athens, appeared in Ionia and Lydia as well, and functioned, in Kraay's words, as "personal devices of successive rulers or tyrants" (21–23, 25). Although he puts it forward only as a hypothesis, Kraay thinks that the change in types may have had some connection with the Panathenaic festivals.

---

4. Cf. Plato's description of money, where he uses the same terms he uses elsewhere to describe writing (*Republic* 3.416e–417a; also 2.371b); see also Plutarch: "The use of language resembles the exchange of coinage" (*De Pythiae Oraculis* 24.9406b, as translated in Jones 1993:12).

A connection between money and the festival atmosphere within which drama emerged was soon to be palpable, however. By the fifth century, anyway, Aristophanes could speak in the same breath about visitors to the festival and the money they brought with them in the form of tribute: "That is why they will come now from those states bringing you their tribute, eager to see that superb poet who took the risk of talking justice before the Athenians" (*Acharnians* 641–51). Pericles called Athens a "wage-earning city" (Kraay 1976:64); and Isocrates tells how Athens displayed those wages on stage every year at the Great Dionysia as one of the central civic activities of that festival: "They passed a decree to divide the funds derived from the tributes of the allies into talents and to bring it onto the stage, when the theatre was full, at the festival of Dionysus."[5] Theatrical presentations thus shared "top billing" at the festival, shared the stage, with money. What does this tell us about the nature of dramatic performance? The Greeks liked to point out that their theatre festivals had "nothing to do with Dionysus";[6] they clearly had something to do with coins, however. What exactly was the nature of the relationship between money and the theatre?

Sometime after 560, the heraldic coins with shifting pictographic types were replaced by new *fixed* type: the famous Attic owl with a helmeted head of Athena on one side and a standing owl, olive branch in the field, on the other. Most importantly, this coin featured a writing that did not refer to "ownership" by a sponsoring individual such as Phanes. These owls were stamped with an *alpha,* a *theta,* and an *epsilon:* Athens. A coin of this type, clearly marked with the city of its origin rather than the name of an individual patron, is explicitly *international* currency. Unlike the earlier heraldic coins, which have been found by archaeologists only in particular localities (Kraay 1976:58), these "owls from Laurium" (*Birds* 1106–8) circulated widely, ending up in places far away from Athens. Kraay concludes that "all these features suggest a change of function, from a coinage intended for internal needs to one designed for foreign trade" (60).

This new international status of coinage is in keeping with movements elsewhere in Greek social life, during the sixth century, toward greater cosmopolitanism. Many of the first writers of laws for Greek states were also foreigners (Gagarin 1986:60), and nearly *all* of the lyric poets who assembled in Athens around the time of drama's invention were from elsewhere.[7]

---

5. Isocrates *De Pace* 82, as translated by Goldhill 1990:101–4.
6. Flickinger 1973:11; Pickard-Cambridge 1968:131.
7. Pickard-Cambridge 1962:19–58; Herington 1985:61–81.

As I noted in Chapter 2, the poetic heteroglossia that distinguished drama from earlier forms accurately reflected this increased cosmopolitanism. With Athenian coinage now intended for use in foreign markets as well as at home, not only traders but also poets were encouraged to expand their sphere of activities beyond their local markets.

With international currency, economic interactions are extended in two ways at once: spatially and temporally. Plato recognized the first of these when he noted in the *Politics* that with money one can make exchanges indifferently in one's own marketplace at home "or traveling from city to city by land or sea, exchanging money for other things or money for money" (289e–290a). The ability to do so is inherently empowering to the individual: with money as portable as it is, a shoemaker from a land where shoes have no value can travel to a place where shoes are in short supply, trade his shoes for money, and return home to purchase the house that would otherwise have been unattainable.[8] For this reason, Aristotle rightly associated money with the existence of surplus goods (*Politics* 1257a–b) and its workings with the law of supply and demand. But the freedom from *local* conditions of supply and demand that money wins for its users is reinforced by money's abstraction from temporal conditions as well. In Aristotle's words, "money is also a kind of guarantee of *future* exchange," for while money is not always worth the same amount, "its value is more likely to be stable" than that of things themselves (*Nic. Eth.* 1133a–b). This is because a sudden drop in demand can render actual commodities valueless. Unlike money, real objects are subject to decay, damage, and seasonality, physical forces from which a representing medium such as coinage is all but immune.

Just as the Athenian owl represented exchange freed from temporal and spatial constraints, so too did the dramatic text, which came to prominence within the century, signify poetic composition liberated from time and space. With a written text "in his pocket," Aeschylus could restage a play in Sicily which had already been shown at Athens.[9] Aristophanes, too, could give repeat performances of the same play in different years,[10] and revise his texts after their performance,[11] as could Euripides.[12] Unlike the partly improvised recitation of the oral bard, the dramatic text outlives its context,

8. For similar reasons, Shakespeare could travel to London, exchange his talents for money, and return to Stratford to purchase the house that would have remained out of reach had he stayed at home.

9. *Life of Aeschylus* 18; see Csapo and Slater 1995:14, and Podlecki 1966:6.

10. Arrowsmith 1962:98 n. 70.

11. Sommerstein 1982–85 5:xix.

12. Segal 1986:78.

guaranteeing that, like a coin, it retains its value for the future—either for a re-trial at home or a remount abroad. Like city currency, the Athenian play both reflected a local origin and saw itself in cosmopolitan terms, was aware of itself, if you will, as an international commodity.

From this point of view, the presence on stage of foreign monies does seem to tell us something about the type of social institution that the theatre originally was. Perhaps the clearest image of theatre's essentially international, mercantile nature can be had by way of contrast with religious ritual. As Euripides shows in the *Bacchai,* Dionysian rites were explicitly *not* intended for "outside" viewers; like all religious and initiatory rituals, such rites were by nature *local* phenomena (Bynum 1981:142–63). While rituals of propitiation, sacrifice, and fertility and rites of passage are practised around the world, the details of their performance are not universal; on the contrary, rituals are a reflection of prevailing local conditions and do not travel well from one locale to another. Stories, by contrast, have a greater universalist appeal, and the mythological material on which drama was largely based had always had a strong "universalizing tendency" (Herington 1985:59). As songs about the ancestors of a variety of politically and geographically distinct peoples, the epics were not tied to a specific locality as rituals generally are.[13] Sacred aboriginal Canadian songs, for example, are performable in particular localities only; their export to outsiders in the form of a written version is explicitly forbidden (Filewod 1992:26).

The festival context within which drama first made its appearance had also at one time possessed local religious functions and attributes. But during the sixth century, the internationalizing power of money was exploited by tyrants who, according to Eric Csapo and William Slater, entered directly into competition with local aristocrats, re-minting their local, family-run religious activities into secular, centralized, *civic* phenomena (1995:103–4). "The city" thus became the focus of these festivals, which, like the Panathenaia, were reorganized as properly civic institutions in the early sixth century.[14] But the city, the unified political entity whose existence was, from the sixth century, celebrated at festivals such as the City Dionysia, was also that civic entity whose existence was demonstrated on every Athenian coin, whose existence was partly constituted in the first place by the advent of city coinage.

Drama was the sole genre of festival poetry to be invented within this

13. See Kirk 1970; Brask and Morgan 1992.

14. The reorganization of the Panathenaia is conventionally dated to ca. 566 B.C.E. (Thomas 1989:290).

new international money market. Epic recitation, with a long history as an oral form, was already a "festival phenomenon" by this time, involving the performance of acknowledged "classics" (Pfeiffer 1968:8). And lyric, too, was already being practised in the seventh century. Thespis, however, began competing in the musical competitions around 560–34, in what was then a new prize category of tragedy. Competitions in men's and boys' choruses were added to the festive *agones mousikoi* in 509–8 or 502–1, and comedy was added as a prize category in 486.[15] But whereas, for example, the dithyrambic choruses had entered the competitive lists already loaded with distinctly local, tribal associations—having had a long history as a (probably noncompetitive) tribal form[16]—the tragic chorus was a new type of performing group and was free of all such connotations and connections.[17] Both in its (probable) performance by ephebic hoplites and in its militarist dance formations and marching music,[18] the tragic chorus was a competitive art of the Athenian military state and thus had imperial or interstate associations from the start. The tributes of Athens's military allies thus shared the stage with tragic choruses for substantive cultural reasons. The *xenoi,* the strangers and allies who came to the City Dionysia to bring their tribute and watch the show (*Acharnians* 496–509), were by both actions participating, though as "outsiders," in Athens' cultural and military display—and in a sense *paying* for it. One does not perform one's local religious rituals for "wages" paid by foreigners. Yet at mercantile Athens the poets were paid (*Frogs* 367), as were the actors (Dover 1972:15–16), as was "wage-earning" Athens itself in the form of allied tributes. In religious rituals it is local gods, not cosmopolitan citizens, who get paid.

Reflecting its emergence within this mercantilist atmosphere, drama also appears to have been the first genre of Greek poetry to establish this practice of charging money for admission. Unfortunately, the details of the theoric fund are frustratingly vague; the sources say only that a fund was established by the city to help the poorer citizens attend the dramatic contests. Pericles is credited with, or perhaps accused of, instituting the *theorikon* to curry favor with the public, the poorer members of which apparently suffered when citizens of greater means bought up blocks of seats.[19] Evidently paid in cash to citizens whose names were written on citizenship lists, theoric funds were probably used primarily to buy theatre tickets, which are re-

15. Winkler 1990:49; Pickard-Cambridge 1968:82.
16. Csapo and Slater 1995:106.
17. See esp. Gernet 1981:17; Raschke 1988:79.
18. Winkler 1990:20–58.
19. See Pickard-Cambridge 1968:266–68.

ported to have cost two obols individually, or perhaps one drachma for admission to all plays performed over the three days.[20] The precise details and value of the theoric fund are ultimately much less important, however, than the simple fact of its existence, for it represents the first reference in antiquity to the practice of paying for the privilege of hearing a public poetic performance, and paying in a medium that is blind to the identity of the one who pays. As Demosthenes was later to say of the *theorikon,* "the sum of money . . . is small, but the habit of mind that goes with it is important."[21] It was an important "habit of mind" because it reflected a reconceptualization of poetic performance as a properly *economic* commodity to which, at least in theory, everyone had equal access. Not only is drama the first art to have been associated with money in this way, but it is also the first festival phenomenon that we know of to have put local audiences into a "free market" competition for seats,[22] and to have put both locals and visitors on par as ticket holders, and for all we know, ticket scalpers.[23] The religious prohibition against outsiders, with its ritual distinction between here and elsewhere, must be seriously eroded when everyone, both local and alien, has been transformed by money into an anonymous "paying customer."

As Isocrates wrote of the internationalist character of Greek institutions in the fifth century: "Those are called Greeks rather who share in our culture than those who share in our common race."[24] In other words, in this mercantile age of international currency, Athenian culture, too, had separated itself from locality and blood ties to become an international com-

20. Pickard-Cambridge's hypothesis (1968:267).

21. As cited by Pickard-Cambridge 1968:268.

22. The fact that the city eventually stepped in with its subsidy does not alter, and actually reinforces my point, that is, that monetary market forces were allowed to prevail, if only temporarily.

23. The number of seats set aside for foreigners (and women?) seems to have been relatively small, amounting perhaps to two thousand at the most, or two of thirteen wedges of seats (Pickard-Cambridge 1968:269–70). So foreigners were certainly not "on a par" in respect of numerical equality. Rather, foreigners were "equated" with locals in the same way that, according to Aristotle, coinage equated doctors with farmers: all were enabled through money to buy the same things, regardless of their social status.

24. *Or.* 4, *Panegyricus* 50, as cited by Pfeiffer 1968:50. See Jaeger's discussion of Isocrates' internationalist cultural ideals: "The economic exchange of goods by export and import is only the material expression of this spiritual principle. He makes the Piraeus [the port of Athens] the focus of the whole commercial life of Greece. And, similarly, he makes the Attic festivals the great social centre of the Hellenic world. In the immense throngs of strangers and in the many-sided intellectual intercourse which takes place there, both the wealth and the art of Athens and Greece are displayed and harmonized with one another" (1960 3:78).

modity suitable for "export" and expressly directed beyond its point of origin.

The rise in the use of coinage just prior to the appearance of drama helped determine that the theatrical stage was, and remains, a mercantile space. From Sophocles' Theban kings, to Aristophanes' Athenian jurors, to Dekker's and Lillo's London merchants, to Shakespeare's whole cosmopolitan crew and beyond, dramatic characters are forever talking about obols and drachmas and florins and ducats and dollars, and either visibly giving these objects to one another on stage as in *Twelfth Night,* or comparing their value to the worth of actual physical realities as in *The Merchant of Venice* and *Death of a Salesman.* As a perennial stage image the coin represents above all the mobility of signs that Derrida describes in *Of Grammatology,* and one that is integral to the kinds of stories that the Western theatre has told since its beginnings.

By detaching economic value from its former embeddedness in social relations, the coin allowed even Athenian slaves to get rich. Within a decade or so of Aeschylus' death, Pericles instituted pay for public service (Ostwald 1986:223), and his "commodification" of civic life meant that the poor could also take up powerful decision-making positions. As we are led to believe by Aristophanes, jurors were notoriously poor; they took the job mostly for the obols. In a social context not "alienated" by the use of money, only the privileged leisure class can afford to enter public life, which in Athens was almost synonymous with social prestige.

In an oral context, a citizen's perceived social worth will tend to remain tied to hereditary wealth. Homer's heroes are "valued" in precisely this way: a man is judged noble in terms of who his father is. Social worth is measured in vials of noble blood, so to speak. But by Sophocles' and Euripides' time, poetry shows a different sort of economy, and the worth of dramatic figures is measured in such "anonymous" scales as even a shopkeeper might use (Aristophanes accused Euripides of being the son of a greengrocer, but he was apparently just making a joke at the tragedian's expense).[25] In *Elektra,* family prestige is rejected as a reliable indicator of human nobility (367–90), and even the offspring of barbarian slaves will be judged of higher value than swaggering, asinine aristocrats like Agamemnon (*Ajax* 1225–1400). In drama, characters are "written in our hearts" as worthy (*Ajax* 1399) according to calculations other than hereditary lineage. For this we must give at least partial acknowledgment to the revaluation of worth that the anonymous coin effected.

25. *Acharnians* 475–79; see Csapo and Slater 1995:184.

The increasing reliance on such currency in the century before the rise of drama produced a situation in which not only social worth but also debt could be detached from blood-based realities. As a powerful symbol of this freeing up of value judgments, Solon outlawed the securing of loans on the person, probably in the year 594–93 (Ehrenberg 1975:64). In a pre-market economy, debt could be repaid only with a real thing, which, before Solon, often meant the debtor's own body. Victor Ehrenberg believes that many previously free Athenians became slaves as a result of this pre-Solonian equation between debt and actual bodies (62–67). Money, however, made other options possible: a debt could be represented rather than embodied. Where debts were concerned, this principle of representation amounted to a literal liberation of enslaved bodies; but as we saw earlier in the legal sphere, the ability to represent rather than only embody suits meant a comparable expansion of liberty to bodies, as even the grievances of noncitizens and slaves could be represented in court. And in the aesthetic sphere, of course, this literate abandonment of a demand for a thing-to-thing equivalence made it possible for the gods, kings, and heroic legends of mythology to be merely represented, and represented without apology, by ordinary mortals, regular Athenian citizens, young boys, amateurs.

This liberation of exchange from time/space categories, and from determined social relations, has noneconomic corollaries elsewhere in Greek verbal life. Now, dramatic texts, although certainly among the first books that Greek literacy produced, were probably not the very first, that honor apparently going to the works of the pre-Socratic philosophers.[26] But books of any kind are not likely to have been the most common manifestation of literacy at this time. The Greeks wrote on leather, papyrus, and waxed tablets, but samples of such writing could never have come down to us from the sixth century;[27] our sources for these writings are mainly literary and iconographic.[28] The majority of actual samples of writing contemporary with drama's appearance which have survived are inscriptions, both private and public, on the more durable materials of stone, pottery, marble, lead, household objects, and tombs. Let us turn now from coins to the other types of inscribed objects that made up the Greek information economy.

Solon described his written law code as a "shield." In a society where war is as common an occurrence as it was in Greece, a shield is bound to be a

---

26. Harvey 1966:587; Turner 1951, 1971; Burns 1981.

27. An actual sample of a waxed writing tablet has, however, survived from very early seventh-century northern Etruria, with an alphabet inscribed along the top, presumably as a prototype. Reproduced in Powell 1991:155 fig. 55.

28. See, for example, Herodotus 5.58–59; Burns 1981:374.

loaded image. In Book 18 of the *Iliad,* almost two hundred lines are devoted to the famous description of Achilleus' shield. Made by Hephaistos, this shield depicts scenes from the cosmic, natural, and social realms. Central among these painterly vignettes is a description of the workings of preliterate justice, where the blood feud between two men is arbitrated by the elders of the tribe. In *Seven Against Thebes,* Aeschylus takes up the Homeric image of the shield, but subjects it to a typically dramatic revision. In devoting an entire poetic work to verbal descriptions of the shields of Thebes' assailants, Aeschylus is harking loudly back to Homeric practice, to be sure.[29] But the shields of the Seven are not "epic," not image-laden tapestries or colorful murals of the sights and sounds of life, as Achilleus' was. Rather, they are modeled on Solonian literate practice, for they are shields of *writing.*[30]

The play is fairly static in terms of action, but it is nonetheless tightly wound around a central opposition from which it gains great tension. That opposition is between the written proclamations of the shield bearers who aim to sack the city, and the battle as it unfolds in actuality. No distinction is made here between the aggressors' writing and their speech: the written sayings on their shields are descried as "shouts" or "loud cries" (476–78) and "boasts" (437); the letters "declare" (434), are "threats" (436); the characters on the shields are even granted the power to "babble" (661) and utter "dreadful sayings" (678–79). These written sayings are in essence threats, or rather promises and predictions, about the impending destruction of Thebes. One forecasts, "I'll burn the city" (434); one promises that "Ares himself shall not cast me from the tower" (470); the last depicts Justice, personified as a woman, saying, "I will bring him home and he shall have his city and shall walk in his ancestral house" (647–49). Triumphant destruction is what these writings vaunt.[31] But the battle itself proves them false; the attack is repulsed and the city saved. Because we do not meet the war-

29. See Garner 1990:179–83 for other interpretive allusions to Homer in the tragedies.

30. It is worth mentioning here that what Barry Powell has described as the "first literary allusion" of the Western tradition, the poetry inscribed on "Nestor's Cup" (ca. 735–20 B.C.E. and still extant), presents us with another clear image of the changes that were made to Homeric practice under the impact of literacy. For whereas the famous Bronze Age cup of Nestor in the *Iliad* (2.632–37) is decorated with the forms of doves and with golden nails, a cup made in the late eighth century, and meant to refer to Homer's, is conspicuously inscribed with alphabetic writing, complete with punctuation for word, phrase, and line divisions (Powell 1991:163).

31. And, as Derrick de Kerckhove has rightly observed, each boast is an individualized utterance with its own attitude and point of view. By contrast, warriors subjected to epic treatment are typically given nonparticularized formulaic utterances, regardless of their personalities.

riors behind the shields, their writings become a kind of "character" in the play. The contest acted out within the drama becomes one between the promises of inscription and the temporal unfolding of real events.

Shoshana Felman (1983) and George Steiner (1977), following Nietzsche, have written about the paradoxical nature of promises of any kind, written and spoken. How can a physical entity such as a mortal person even make a promise at all? A promise implies a knowledge of the future, which no speaker has; or, let alone *knowledge* about the future, it assumes the mere existence of a future which the promiser may not even live into. That contingent, present-bound creatures such as men and women even dare to make promises at all strikes these two writers as perhaps a "scandal" in itself. But what is merely scandalous about the promises of speaking bodies becomes a kind of ontological emergency in their writing. For what *The Seven* suggests about Polyneices' writing is applicable to *all writing*. To write means to fracture a given act of communication into two or more temporal compartments, each of which is sealed off from the others to some extent. I write in *my* temporal present, a writing that will be read in *your* temporal future. When in that unpredictable future you read what I have written, it will speak to you from the past, since that is where it was written; but it will speak to you in a present which I as writer will not share, and of which I can know nothing. What is noticeably scandalous about oral promises is therefore even more pressingly the scandal of writing, for every writing is directed at the future, yet cannot respond to the changes reality is sure to undergo on the way there.

The inscriptions on the Seven's shields, no less than the inscription of laws on stelae or plays on papyrus, stand as implicit contracts or covenants between temporal contexts. In general, they intend control over the future—"All men shall . . ."; "Thou shalt not . . ."; "He shall have his city . . ."; "Ares shall not . . ."; "I will burn . . ."—and into whatever contexts they enter, they bring the future-controlling echoes of the past in which they were authored.

For an art form such as theatre, this "promissory" structure of writing—what Aristotle called money's "guarantee of future exchange"—has important theoretical implications. It suggests that theorists such as Peter Szondi (1987), who speak of drama as the genre of the "absolute present," are telling only a small slice of the tale. Using Bakhtin's category of the chronotope, we might agree that drama's *internal* representation of time is oriented toward and in favor of the present. Radically departing from epic speech in this respect, which always speaks of events that took place in the distant past, dramatic discourse inhabits the same temporal context as the story it speaks about. What in the epic is presented as legendary material, cut off from any experiential contact with the singer and his audience, is represented in drama as a contemporary event, unfolding in the same temporal context which the actors and audience themselves inhabit. As Bakhtin has persuasively argued, a discursive shift into the present and away from an illustrious but inaccessible past is loaded with political and ideological significance. The implicit message that epic speech sends to its audiences is, in effect: "Everything is already over and done with. Nothing is happening now; yours is just to marvel as a descendant." But by telling of tragic and comic events that are unfolding now, before the audience's very eyes, drama for its part acts as a kind of validation of the present. Contrary to epic speech, it says, in effect: "The great decisions are being made *now*, in your lifetime. This world is *your* world, these figures are your contemporaries, and these problems belong to you, to us." Or as Goethe noted in his 1797 essay on epic and drama (1986:192–94), "The epic poet describes an action as being altogether past and completed"; he speaks as one recollecting things that have happened, and that "belong absolutely to the past." The voice of the epic poet is "the voice of the muses in general." Against the epic word, Goethe contrasts the explicitly anti-transcendent, living contemporaneity of dramatic presentation: "With the stage player on the other hand, the position is exactly reversed. He comes before us as a distinct and determined individual. He wants to interest ourselves in him and his immediate surroundings." Even when the subject of a play is taken from the past, as the ancient dramas often were, it is still presented from the point of view of the still-evolving historical present being jointly lived by the actor and his audience, within the concrete present of the theatrical event. So Szondi is at least partly right to stress the "presentness" of drama in comparison to other modes.

But only partly right, since the structure of the written word has determined that this *internally represented* present, this dramatic chronotope, is already inhabited by the past—the past of the author's inscription. Because written works outlive this past, in performance they rather open up an intercourse between past and present which is infinitely renewable. And because they position themselves for unlimited future readings as well, the "present" of each performance is in fact merely a single juncture of temporalities in a potentially infinite series aimed toward the future. Anything written both comes from the past and positions itself as kind of promise toward the future.

This polytemporality of the dramatic text gives it the structure of a legal utterance, as I noted earlier. But it also reflects a feature of all linguistic communication that is not normally apparent in speech. What is rarely tangible to speakers is that even regular speech situations are inhabited by a complex of temporalities. Every here-and-now, in life as on stage, both is inhabited by the past and projects itself into the future. The thought of writing's "pastness" has been known to offend theatre theorists since at least Artaud, who called for the speedy destruction of texts after their first use. Insofar as Artaud was not talking nonsense, his view has the virtue of reminding us that writing cannot help but offend our purest notions about human communication: that it should remain fully alive and attuned to the present moment, be free of anything ossified, worn-out, stale. Living speech should not, like Polyneices' text, be so fixed and finished that it is unable to respond to changing realities as they unfold in present time. From an Artaudian perspective, the flaw in the assailants' inscriptions is the flaw of all writing: it dies as soon as it is inscribed, and tells lies thereafter.

By the same logic, however, even speech is guilty of importing dead forms into the present. For it is not only written words but all words which are already old when we use them. We are not, as Bakhtin wrote, Adams and Eves uttering the first words of speech. Even if each of us were able to freshly fabricate a brand new language for every new moment of our experience, we would still be the inheritors of thousands of years of meaningful verbal communication and all the established semantic and syntactical habits and patterns that have grown out of it. We are rather scavengers, taking words from wherever we find them—from previous contexts, past experiences, other people's mouths. Any act of speech requires that we breathe our own breath into these *mots trouvés,* that we make them adequate to our needs in a given context, that we make them *live* for us, and for our interlocutors. Like the dramatic actor who must take locutions from a text and new-fashion them into personal, living acts of speech, so too must every speaker off the stage work at bringing old language into the present, and into life. The difference between speaking a line of written text and making a "spontaneous" oral utterance is therefore *in principle* not as great as is sometimes imagined. Every word we use in speech is already a linguistic quotation from elsewhere, and thus even in its natural, spoken form, language possesses some of the scandalously ossified properties that we might more readily associate with writing.

Once having taken up a word for use, even speakers enter into a pact with the future. To speak at all is to promise implicitly that one's words will "hold," that they will remain adequate to one's intentions during the time it takes for them to travel to the other's ear, and on the following day as well.

Language itself has this structure of a promissory note; writing simply makes our verbal contracts with the future explicit.

The issue for the theatre, then, is not how written exchange may or may not sin against some illusory ideal of perfect presence—for not even speech achieves this[32]—but rather what it makes possible, given the inevitable polytemporality of all linguistic experience. As Derrida has argued throughout his work, human consciousness is always inescapably putting its faith in the mental signs, words, and images that extend consciousness beyond itself, into the future, merely as a function of its self-preservation. To write may perhaps simply be to have greater faith in the ability of meaning to survive the vagaries of this temporal slippage. But from the *Seven Against Thebes,* we can glimpse one thing that writing can do that speech cannot.

As we saw in Chapter 3, live speech situations in the present are hampered in ways from which writing is comparatively free. Being in the present means being subject to the needs of the present, the ideological blindnesses of the present, and so on. Because the present cannot, at any given point in history, accommodate all truths, writing, precisely because it is *not* contextually embedded in any given point in present time and space, can go on insisting on those ideas that present contexts have disowned or failed to hear. Like the inscription on Polyneices' shield, writing can uphold the rights of the losers, whose speech is silenced altogether in the decisions of real events. To the Theban hearers of Polyneices' sayings, his words were foolish "babblings"; and the fact that Thebes won the day confirmed them in this view. But were they really babblings just because present reality nullified them? Polyneices did have some rights to the Theban throne, after all. In writing about the justice of his claim rather than just speaking about it, Polyneices makes reality accountable for the partiality, one-sidedness, and occasionally arbitrary nature of its decisions.

An example from Aeschylus' own temporal context is illuminating here. In the 470s, coincident with the appearance of *The Persians,* the institution of the public funeral oration was established at Athens. So intent were the Athenians of the time on dismantling the old aristocracy and establishing in its place a "de-tribalized" democratic polis that legislation was passed prohibiting the singling out of individuals for praise (Nagy 1986:95). Speech at the public funerals of war dead had to confine itself to praise for the polis as a whole. Soldiers and generals alike were to be lauded simply as citizens who had communally, not individually, contributed to the glory and triumph of

32. See Derrida 1973.

Athenian democracy. After centuries of Homeric-style emphasis on ancestors and noble lineages, it became "politically incorrect" to refer to such
things. Gregory Nagy has suggested that these legislated restrictions against
a certain kind of speech may have led directly to the invention of a new
written genre, the poetic epigram (1986:95). If so, this might provide a good
illustration of the remedy that decontextualized, "non-present" writing can
provide to speakers in literate milieus. Like written law, which traffics in hypothetical futures in order to better protect the liberties of those living
under it in the present, the dramatic text stands also like a shield over performance, guaranteeing that what sounds like babblings to an audience
today may be given a fairer hearing tomorrow.

Laws, coins, and written promises, like dramatic texts, are thus all
covenants between temporal contexts. Like the written contract described
by Euripides in the *Palamedes,* they are "medicine against forgetting" (frag.
572 Nauck 1964).[33] In this fragment Euripides praises writing for protecting
truth as it travels into the future: "The tablet . . . does not allow lies." We
will look shortly at the *Hippolytos,* which shows that things are not quite so
simple: writing can preserve lies as well. For the moment, however, let us see
what other insights for dramatic texts we can wrest from the structure of an
inscription.

The next thing we find, unexpectedly, is that the earliest alphabetical
inscriptions found so far in Greece by archaeologists are not public but private and fairly personal in nature. The thousands of clay tablets that have
come down to us from the brilliant Mycenaean palace cultures of Knossos
and Pylos, written by a handful of official scribes in Linear A and B, are generally palace inventories.[34] No private correspondence, poetry, or laws have
been found in this writing. When alphabetical writing begins to appear in
the eighth century, however, we find writing first put to rather different
ends.

In the earliest alphabetical inscriptions now extant, writing is used to
make objects speak. The objects in question are jugs, cups, vases, statues,
and tombstones, and the speech is in verse, sometimes with punctuation included. An eighth-century cup, in dactylic hexameters, says: "I am the delicious drinking cup of Nestor. Whoever drinks from this cup, swiftly will the
desire of fair-crowned Aphrodite seize him" (Stroud 1989:111–12). A seventh-
century marble statue says, in three hexameters, "Nikandra, daughter of
Deinodikes the Naxian, a maid beyond compare, sister of Deinomenes, now

33. Translated by Burns 1981:377.
34. Stroud 1989:108; Finley 1968:7–23.

wife of Phraxos, dedicated me to the far-darting goddess who delights in arrows" (112). A final example, analyzed most provocatively by Jesper Svenbro (1990), is most stunning in its relevance to theatrical practice: "I explain [*hupokrinomai*] the same thing to all men, whoever asks me, namely, that Andron son of Antiphanes dedicated me as his tithe."[35] This example is so provocative, of course, because *hupokrinomai,* "I interpret/expound/answer/speak dialogue/reply," belongs to the word family used by the Greeks to describe their actors as well, who were *hupokritai.* This speaking object, in Svenbro's view, shows how, in sixth-century Greece, "the written word and the actor [were] analogous, interchangeable" (374). Andron's statue describes itself as a *hupokrites* whose textual message says the same thing to all men. And as Svenbro points out, this interchangeability of writing and acting becomes explicit in Plato, who criticizes *both* writing and acting on precisely these grounds—that they both "always signify the same thing" (378; *Phaedrus* 275d; *Ion* 532d). Both inscribed statue and actor are the agents for the transmission of someone else's textual message; both communicate a fixed message to all men indiscriminately. There are a few things about this use of writing that deserve attention.

In the first place, the inscriptions on these "speaking objects" mark what Paul Ricoeur might call the birth of "text," the birth of writing as an autonomous form of verbal communication.[36] Because jugs and statues do not actually speak, the utterances inscribed on them are not *records* of speech. They are not even really representations of it, for there is no conceivable model on which such a representation could be based. Writing here is not so much representational as it is *authorial.* This is someone writing, someone initiating communication through inscription as an alternative to speech rather than as an echo of it. A palace inventory in Linear B, on the contrary, was probably not experienced as autonomously communicating with its readers. Its contents were likely thought of as a mere potential to be actualized by the reader's voice.[37] But the inscriptions on the speaking objects are in the first-person singular; they present themselves as an "I" who

35. The verb *hupokrinesthai* in Homer denotes a spoken reply in the form of an interpretation (see Svenbro 1990:373). Svenbro translates it here as "answer" for convenience, but rejects "answer" as an unacceptable English equivalent for *hupokrinomai* in this context. As Svenbro does not himself supply a better alternative, I take the liberty of suggesting "explain."

36. Speaking of fifth-century funerary inscriptions, to which we will be turning momentarily, William Harris makes a similar point: writing of this kind clearly went beyond the function of transcribing a spoken message (1989:83–84); such writing is text rather than recorded speech.

37. See Svenbro 1990 on reading before *silent* reading.

speaks by itself. On the speaking objects, then, writing has the power to speak, or rather to communicate by itself *instead* of speech.

The speaking objects are also significant insofar as they represent the earliest extant use of writing for Greek poetic composition. Because pre-alphabetic Greek script seems not to have been used for poetry, these alphabetical inscriptions mark the detachment of poetry from the human mouth in ancient Greece. In their use of the personal pronoun, they anticipate the lyric practice of poets such as Archilochus, who for his unprecedented emphasis on the "I" in poetry has been described as "the first Western man whom we know as a personality" (Barnstone and McCulloch 1962:2). But there is a peculiarity of the use of the "I" on the speaking objects which brings it closer to dramatic practice than lyric. For the lyric poet generally speaks *for* himself in his poems; he uses the "I" with reference to his own identity, as does the epic singer occasionally.[38] The inscriber of the speaking object, however, uses the "I" without reference to himself or herself. It is the jug or statue to which the "I" refers, not the one writing. What this does, in a sense, is to create a hypothetical identity, the use of which declares: "*If* this cup could speak, this is what it would say." The relationship between inscribed speech and authorship in drama is the same. The "I" in dramatic speech refers not to the author, the one writing, but to hypothesized identities: "If the mythological figures of Homer could speak to us today, this is what they would say." For this reason, the inscribing of speech on these *oggetti parlanti* is already *dramatic* composition in the profoundest sense (Svenbro 1990:366–84).

Both dramatic texts and speaking objects are inscriptions of direct first-person speech which is unmediated, unmotivated, and decontextualized: unmediated because the writer is not "quoting" the speech within his own utterance, as an epic singer or novelist might; unmotivated because the "I" does not refer to the one writing; and unusually decontextualized because it is neither grounded in a concrete speech situation (an epic bard singing to an audience) nor constitutive of a real first-person address (what happens when a lyric "I" speaks/writes to a hearer/reader).

This use of writing, as mentioned earlier, is what Manfred Pfister has

---

38. The epic singer also uses the "I" in passages that quote the represented figures' speech, but he is always, in effect, telling us in his own discourse what "they" said. Such first-person speech in epic storytelling is never detached enough from the singer's own identity, as deictically grounded spokesman for the Muse, to become autonomous first-person speech. The "I" in epic, as I discussed in Chapter 3, is the bard; the "you" is the remembering Muse, a character, or the listening audience. The speaking figures represented in epic normally remain at a third-person remove of "they."

called the predominant verbal matrix of the dramatic text. For the phenomenology of theatrical performance, writing of this kind has special consequences. As Pfister notes, it makes the story temporally immediate, which in turn allows for its physical enactment. Following Thornton Wilder, whom he quotes, Pfister notes that the dramatic story unfolds simultaneously with its telling (1988:274). The writer interrupts the story neither with his own "I" nor with any other temporally disjunct material, which means that the story orients itself naturally to translation into real speech in the here and now (performance) and does not need the teller/author at all. But there is an additional consequence.

The direct first-person address inscribed on the speaking object "speaks for itself." Not completely by itself, of course; it needs a reader. But that is explicitly what it needs most. The voice of the performing poet, who used to speak to the listener in his own voice, his own present "I," is not necessary in the presence of a speaking object. According to M. T. Clanchy (1979), Martin Elsky (1989), and Svenbro (1990), writing did not always appear to speak directly to readers in this way. Medieval manuscripts were assumed to need the voice of a living speaker; the idea of silent reading was practically unknown (Elsky 1989:115). The same could be said of writing in Greece before speaking objects (Svenbro 1990:370). But here, as in the dramatic texts that were shortly to follow, the written "I" addresses its recipient directly, regardless of whether it is performed out loud or read silently. This is a feature of the dramatic text which is worth lingering on for a moment, for while fairly self-evident, it argues strongly against Hegelian notions that drama comes into "contradiction" with itself unless performed. Speaking objects do not need to be performed to be understood, even though they are inherently performable. So I agree with Pfister that the unmediated speech that makes up the dramatic text accounts for its performability; but it *also* accounts for its mere readability, and no less essentially—a fact of which Dionysus of the *Frogs* might have reminded us himself, reading from the *Andromeda* by himself on a ship, far away from all possible performers.

Recognition of the directness of first-person speech as represented in drama actually takes us a bit further, toward a realization that the dramatic text addresses itself to any and all readers, to textual interpreters generally. This would seem to go without saying, but it does not, to judge from a persistent trend in theory away from the notion that what the dramatic text intends, as preface to performance, is a *reading* experience. Hegel stands as a precursor to this trend, by way of his proclamation that dramatic texts are not for reading, period. More recently, J. R. Searle's Austin-inspired analysis of the dramatic text stipulates that a dramatic text is like a recipe for baking a cake: "It is a set of instructions for how to do something, namely, how to perform the play" (1975:328). David Cole similarly describes the dramatic text as a "blueprint" (1992:215). Because "there are no general readers of blueprints," Cole extends the logic to the dramatic text, concluding that actors are the only intended readers of plays: "Theirs alone is the kind of reading invited and legitimized by dramatic texts" (215). That the dramatic text is neither a recipe nor a blueprint can be seen clearly from the Andron statue, which says the same thing to all readers, without discrimination.

A recipe tells one how to do something. From our previous look at what written speech does and does not contain, it is clear that the act, the "doing" part of speech, is precisely what the text leaves out. A given line of text can be "done," that is, performed, in any number of ways: it can be mumbled, sneered, shouted, sobbed; said quickly while knitting, drawn out slowly throughout the duration of a sword fight; it can be spoken as an aside to oneself, shared confidentially with the audience, laughed in the face of another actor, or "thrown away" into the wings as the set changes and another part of the forest is revealed. In short, the one thing a dramatic text *does not* tell its readers is "how to perform it." So it is clearly not anything like a recipe. A recipe in which action remained so completely undetermined would not be a recipe at all; it would produce a cake one day and a Waldorf salad the next, depending on who was following it. Actors, in any case, are not objects like the eggs, flour, and sugar which are combined according to the instructions of recipes. A text of written speech simply does not give instructions for action; it prescribes only that it be read, and if read by actors who intend to perform it, that it be memorized and spoken out loud by them.[39]

Searle is not primarily a theorist of drama, of course, and his view of a play as a recipe is not likely to be shared by anyone who has ever worked in the theatre. Nevertheless, proper theatre historians often make the same mistake. As Michael Kobialka (1988) has shown, the still-popular view that medieval drama "began" with the *Quem Quaeritis* trope is based precisely on this assumption: that theatre appears when action is prescribed. When put back in context within the *Regularis Concordia*, as Kobialka has done, however, the text of the *Quem Quaeritis* proves to be not a "play" complete with "stage directions," but simply a description of proper monastic practice—indeed, a recipe. For the *Regularis Concordia* is itself, first and foremost, a

---

39. Writing much more sensibly than Searle about the logical status of performative texts, Thomas stresses that the texts of archaic poetry demanded only that they be read and "learnt by heart as soon as possible" (1992:119). They did not, in other words, prescribe anything specific as far as *performance* is concerned.

rule book specifying how and when the monks should perform the actions of their daily duties: how and when to shave, change clothes, conduct church services. Because some of these concrete actions were properly executed in front of other people (i.e., during religious worship), "authorities" in theatre history call such actions "theatrical" and the texts regulating them "plays." Rather, they were codes of conduct, "recipes," instructions for monastic practice. Like all ritualistic documents, what they prescribe and regulate is, precisely, action, deeds, doings. The first-person direct speech of the dramatic text, on the contrary, does *not* say what to do.[40] For this reason, we can look neither to the *Quem Quaeritis* trope nor to any other set of ritual rules for the beginnings, or even a manifestation, of drama. Not only is there a paucity of instructions for *how* to do things in dramatic texts, but also there is a built-in preference in theatrical activities for doing them differently every time. If Mrs. X delivers a given line while lacing up her corset, Mrs. Y is obliged to give the speech while taking the corset off; and Mrs. Z, if she comes so late, has our sympathies, for she must come up with something altogether new. As Oliver Taplin has observed, ritual performances work in the opposite way: "The whole point about ritual is that it should always be the *same:* it is the aim of its performers to repeat the rigmarole as perfectly, as identically as possible."[41] In theatre, it is not continuity but invention and novelty that guide action: Hamlet on the beach, in the kitchen, in white, in black, with a dagger, with a rapier, in a Nazi uniform, in a skirt.[42]

Cole's blueprint idea is not much better than Searle's recipe. Aris-

40. In recognition of this cardinal rule of the theatrical text, Pavis (1982) goes so far as to claim that stage directions are not really part of the dramatic text at all. His view is that only what is pronounced by the actors on the stage is the dramatic text proper. This extreme position accurately reflects the fact that many dramatic texts have no stage directions, and all can do without them, since they tend to be ignored in practice anyway. I think this takes things too far. The representation of speech in such modern drama as that of Ibsen, Chekhov, and Shaw has focused on very subtle psychological nuances. The "written accusations" of modernity often indict stage figures with inner rather than outer crimes—crimes of thought and motive rather than of deed. With verbal conflict increasingly interiorized, stage directions must carry a larger burden, providing as they do useful aids in a sometimes baffling interpretation process. Statements made by Chekhov's characters, for example, are often so perfectly banal on the surface that extraverbal clues—for instance, that a character speaks while looking out a window at migrating birds—can be a decided help. Even where the author did not himself write them, stage directions are still part of the dramatic text—which is to say that like everything else in the play, they are fair game for the whims of performance.

41. Taplin 1978:161; see also Vickers 1973.

42. That this theatrical impulse toward novelty in performance is not a development of modernity or "postmodernism," but goes back to the ancients themselves, should be clear from my discussion in Chapter 2.

tophanes joked that everyone in the audience has his own *biblion,* which should serve to remind us that it is not by some antitheatrical error of modernity that plays are enjoyed by readers. Indeed, plays are naturally directed even toward *nonspecialist* readers: as the Andron statue remarks, direct written speech says the same thing to *all* men. All men who can read, of course; but they needn't know any arcane codes, as architects must, nor even be performers themselves. This is a key feature, since, as we saw earlier, the first actors were not professionals.[43] Unlike ritualistic and otherwise specialized documents which are meant for or are comprehensible only to the specially trained—blueprints, instructions for surgery, choreographic notation, and so on—dramatic texts are addressed to anyone who can read: military trainees, students, bellows menders. *A Midsummer Night's Dream* points this fact up nicely: even tradesmen with no specialized knowledge of theatrical conventions can respond immediately to the direct speech of their dramatic text just by reading it. And as their bizarre, albeit strangely affecting performance shows, their script does *not* provide instructions for *how* to perform it!

There is another set of speaking objects which sheds some light on this. These are the inscribed tombstones, of which there are numerous samples that predate drama by about a century. These show clearly how, when it comes to written speech, it is not a question of the loss or return of orality, but merely a matter of the fact that writing was chosen from the start *instead* of oral speech. One inscription reads: "Stranger, go back to Sparta and tell our people that we who were slain obeyed the code" (Barnstone and McCulloch 1962:136). This is not the hypothetical speech of a drinking cup but the hypothetical speech of dead people. Like the speech of an inanimate object or fictional character, this written speech cannot be referred back to an "earlier" occurrence of "situational discourse," for this utterance presents itself as the speech of people who are already dead. To communicate information to a living person from beyond the grave is a verbal act that *must* take written form, that can only ever be a written communication.

The advantages of this overtly textual form of verbal communication were as obvious in antiquity as they are today. Writing is especially valuable for recording wills, contracts, and any other vital information that may be in the private possession of one individual and therefore vulnerable to irreplaceable loss in case of death. Euripides celebrated these benefits in the *Palamedes:* "A man dying may write the measure of his possessions and tell his children, and he who receives may know" (frag. 572 Nauck 1964).[44]

---

43. See esp. Winkler 1990 and Slater 1990.
44. Translated by Burns 1981:376–77.

Sophocles explores the phenomenology of the written will in more detail in *The Women of Trachis.*

Deianira opens this play with the observation that "you cannot know a man's life before the man has died," a typically Attic sentiment which proves to have some relevance to writing. The play explores, among other things, the difference between knowledge available before and after Heracles' death, and does so partly through the agency of the writing he left his wife before he set out on his final labors. During more than a year there has been "no word" from him—no spoken word, that is: in his absence, his writing spoke to her instead. The tablet he left is both an oracle and a last will and testament, but it begins to function as a private letter might, communicating directly to one person in the physical absence of the speaker. In the quoted passage from *Palamedes,* Euripides names the letter along with the will as a written remedy for physical absence: "that one not present across the expanse of the sea may know how everything is at home." Deianira says of her absent husband that he sounds, in print, "as though he were no longer living" (161). Because the tablet contains instructions about what should be done with his property after his death, there is no surprise in finding that Heracles sounds "as though he were no longer living."

Deianira's remarks can be taken further, however. To engage in other kinds of writing is also to invoke one's death, structurally, since it is a peculiarity of written communication that it can continue to function and deliver its message in the absence, and even after the death, of the sender. In an oral speech situation there is, if not the illusion of immortality, at least the probability that one will live through the conversation, or expects to do so. Oral speech acts could even be said to be life-giving; at least this is suggested by the many stories performers know of the power of performance to keep illness and death at bay until the curtain falls. In common parlance, "curtains" means death; but until they fall, the actor lives and speaks. It is probably very rare that one of the interlocutors in any type of speech situation dies before the end of the exchange. If they entered the ongoing present of a speech act alive, chances are they both expect to leave it in the same state.

But it is when one thinks of death that writing suggests itself, and vice versa. The possibility that his death might be imminent sent Heracles for his writing instruments, not to his wife's ear. Wills can of course be delivered orally, as King Lear tries to do. But as Shakespeare shows in his play about a will, the oral register is incapable of handling such verbal content without disaster. Instead of signing and sealing his last testament in a decontextualized writing situation, as he might have done, Lear makes his beneficiaries perform for it. And by insisting on delivering his will in a situational present—rather than writing it up for posterity—Lear gives his heirs a cruelly mixed message. He speaks of death, but implies through his use of living speech that he is by no means resigned to its inevitability. Like all of Shakespeare's plays, *King Lear* abounds with scenes featuring the use of writing for communication, and can in fact be read as a sustained exploration of the contrasting characteristics of oral and written modes and the way they interact with one another.

Writing brings a whiff of death not only because much of the writing available to literates was written by people who have since died, but also because, for all a writer ever knows, his or her words may reach their very first reader only posthumously. To write is to defer the presentation of one's words or thoughts to a future date, and the ever-present risk is that one may not live to see it.

This connection between writing and death becomes especially pressing in Euripides, the most "bookish" of tragedians, and one who is rivaled only by Plato for the amount of thought he devotes to the impact of literacy. Three of his plays, *Hippolytos, Iphigenia among the Taurians,* and *Iphigenia in Aulis,* feature letters prominently in the action.[45] As in Sophocles' play about a will, the written messages sent within Euripides' families are all bound up with death in some way. In *The Women of Trachis,* Heracles writes to his wife out of fear that his death may be nigh; Phaedra writes to her husband as a direct result of her decision to commit suicide; Agamemnon writes to lure his daughter to a sacrificial death; and Iphigenia sends a letter to Orestes, written by a dead scribe, to "save [her] from dying" in foreign obscurity. Describing his daughter in death, Agamemnon uses the same phrase Plato would later use to describe a piece of writing: both types of offspring are "cut off and quite separated" from their respective parents (*Iphigenia in Aulis* 669; *Phaedrus* 275d–e).

I have already suggested some of the advantages of this cutting-off: escape from time and space restraints, and freedom from the adverse pragmatics of certain kinds of performances. For Plato, however, the decontextualized or orphaned status of writing is also a weakness. Separated from the explaining, self-justifying presence of its "father," a text can too easily be

---

45. See especially William Harris (1989) for the archaeological proof for the use of writing for such private communication over long distances. One particularly relevant artifact is the lead letter, found in the Black Sea area, and written at the end of the sixth century from a Greek colony of the period. Much like Iphigenia's letter in Euripides, it was written by someone in present danger of enslavement, and is a letter home for help (56). Harris takes Herodotus' mention of Polycrates' letters (520s B.C.E; 3:40–43) as the first existing evidence for letter writing; see also 57 n. 55).

"ill-treated and unjustly abused." It can be misunderstood, and perhaps even more dangerously, fall into the wrong hands. This is exactly what happens in *Iphigenia in Aulis,* when a letter meant for Clytaemestra is hijacked by Menelaus and read by him—an invasion of privacy which Agamemnon describes as "a thing which goes against all conscience" (304ff.). Like the speaking objects and tombstones, the letter is a message that communicates indiscriminately with everyone. For regardless of the intentions of the writer, whoever reads a letter becomes its receiver.

Speech, by contrast, can choose its hearers; it can also rule certain hearers out. This suggests that even private writings such as letters have something of a public character about them, which is paradoxical given the seemingly more private nature of the activity of writing. In *Iphigenia in Aulis,* a private message between husband and wife becomes news for the whole army. While writing's "promiscuity" with respect to its potential readers greatly alarms Plato, it is given a more balanced hearing by Euripides. The interception of the letter is unquestionably a bad thing for Agamemnon and family, but it is a clear boon for the stalled expedition. The inability of writing to control the circumstances of its reception can thus be viewed as either a detriment or a strength, depending on one's politics. To those, like Plato, who value the author's own intention above all, the fatherlessness of writing must weaken and even damn it to some extent; but to those who value the rights of the many potential receivers over and above the authorizing privilege of the sender, writing's orphaned state will be seen rather as one of its greatest strengths. (Given the communal nature of theatrical production, it can be assumed that the performers of plays will most often subscribe to the latter view.)

In *Iphigenia in Aulis,* Agamemnon's first letter has the power to transport his daughter to the sacrificial altar;[46] his second letter proves powerless to avert her transport to death. This theme of death and transportation is a common one in Euripides, appearing also in the *Ion, Helen,* and *Iphigenia among the Taurians* (Lattimore 1964:344). In the two Iphigenia plays, the theme is connected with the potentialities of writing. Because of its ability to transcend her physical conditions in Taurus and communicate with receivers in another time and place, Iphigenia's letter has the power to "save [her] from dying." In an oral context, such immorality can also be attained through the song of the epic bard and the muse of memory. But to achieve acoustic renown (*kleos*), and the immortality that it confers, in the absence

---

46. See Powell's discussion of the "fatal letter" theme (1991:199); see also Thomas for other evidence for the general Greek "distrust of writing" (1992:130).

of writing, one's deeds must already be known, must already have had their public impact. In *Iphigenia among the Taureans,* the writer is living in foreign obscurity, beyond the reach of *kleos,* and is believed dead. To read Iphigenia's letter will be, in her words, to "listen through my opening grave / And hear my living lips cry out" (641–42). Iphigenia's situation thus reminds us of the exiled, expatriate, or otherwise silenced writer—examples of which were as plentiful in antiquity as they are today.[47] Through her letter, as through texts generally, a message may still reach the ears of the community, if only posthumously. Iphigenia also evokes the situation of *receivers* of such written messages: like the many actors who were to speak Euripides' words after his death, she is aware that "[her] words were written down by one who died" (584).

And so the paradoxical nature of texts: at once more private *and* more public than speech, on one hand they imply the death of their authors, and on the other extend their lives almost indefinitely. In *Iphigenia among the Taureans,* writing proves doubly paradoxical in its effects. As long as they confined themselves to oral speech, brother and sister failed to recognize each other. Both believed the other to be dead, and this foreknowledge—or deception, as it turned out—determined that each perceived the other as a stranger. It is only when Iphigenia reads her letter out, verbatim (785), that the truth of their identities is revealed. Their co-presence in a phenomenally real context deceives them and blinds them to a truth only revealed in writing. That writing has the power to manifest a truth which a situational presence obscures is an idea that goes very much against the grain of one of the central myths of modern performance theory. But what this scene demonstrates is that phenomenal perception is never "naive," and the senses are not a tabula rasa on which the pure essences of things imprint themselves. According to Heidegger perception is, "in itself, something which already . . . interprets" (1962:189–90). Merely seeing an object is a presentation to oneself of "something *as* something" (207). Iphigenia presents Orestes to herself "as" a Greek stranger and sacrificial victim; Orestes presents the phenomenal being before his eyes to himself "as" Thoas' priestess. This scene must present audiences with a graphic account of the ineluctable interpenetration of "real" perceptions with the representing "foreknowledge" that structures and interprets them. As in the countless dramas in the repertoire which similarly traffic in stories of disguise, deception, last-minute reversals, and revelations, *Iphigenia among the Taurians* shows how internal cognitive processes can shape even our real perception of phenomenally present realities.

47. See note 45.

But once the writing in Iphigenia's letter has remapped the "as-structure" of her and Orestes' perceptions, the representation is rejected as a poor substitute for the reality it has revealed. The "dead" letters, written by a dead man on behalf of a woman believed dead, have paradoxically succeeded in revealing the living to the living. Speech unaided by writing could not have done this, for perception is ruled by the perceivers' assumptions about what they see and hear. But once a perceptual revolution is accomplished by the letter, the ecstasy of sensual contact follows:

> How can I look at letters! Let me look—
> Oh let me stare at you . . .
> Oh let me touch you with my hands and prove
> That you are real and hold you close, close! (793–96)

Writing can reveal new realities for perception, but the goal of such revelations remains bodily engagement. Writing, in this recognition scene, is shown to be an enabling device, not an end in itself. This goal—of real sensuous contact—is, however, shown to depend on a rerouting of the semiotic circuit within the bodies of the perceivers. This perceptual restructuring, at least as Euripides has it, could only be achieved by bypassing reality and intervening directly in the representational structures themselves (i.e., through abstract text). To use a Nietzschean image, we might say on the basis of Euripidean dramaturgy that the physical co-presence of man to man may not itself be sufficient to break down the dikes that separate them if each perceives the other "as" the enemy. Iphigenia and Orestes would not have embraced but for the ability of writing to remake their world in another image.

Like the coin, the letter is an object of exchange which had transformed human behavior in Greece just prior to the appearance of drama, and which continues to define the concerns of the genre. When Menelaus demands his purloined letter back in *Iphigenia in Aulis* ("give me the letter"), he may be the first speaker to be represented in verbal art as making such a request, but he is by no means the last (cf. *Lear* 1.2.41, for example). In fact, the number of extended incidents involving letters in the Shakespearean corpus alone rises to nearly forty. The very persistence of the image in Western theatre from its beginnings suggests that it is an essentially theatrical image, not just a convention of this or that particular stage.

In some cases, the "fatherlessness" of written messages is exploited by its users for the purpose of deception (Agamemnon's first letter, and those of Phaedra in *Hippolytos*, Edmund in *Lear*, and Maria and company in *Twelfth Night*). However, letters are used in equal numbers to communicate a truth whose utterance a hostile speech context prevents: Agamemnon's second letter, Iphigenia's, and those of Friar Lawrence and Romeo, of Malvolio, and nearly all of Shakespeare's comedic lovers, particularly Beatrice and Benedick, who are forced by the written evidence of their own hands to acknowledge a truth they would deny in speech. Not only are letters used for deception as often as for the revelation of truth, but speech is shown throughout the repertoire to be as effective in spreading falsehood as writing is. There are many Greek characters who, like Clytaemestra, Phaedra's maid, Hippolytos, Orestes, and Odysseus, pledge with their mouths while keeping their hearts unpledged; just as, on Shakespeare's stage, speakers may smile and speak fair while remaining villains. Speech, too, can obscure. If the persistence of images of letters on the stage tells us anything, it is that speech and writing are equally at home there. In literate contexts, speech and writing are, equally, modes through which individuals represent the world to one another; and as Iphigenia says of writing and speech in *Iphigenia among the Taurians,* "In any plan, two ways improve upon one" (759).

There is a final use of inscription at Athens that has bearing on theatrical practice. This is the writing or scratching of an individual's name on a piece of broken pottery, known as an ostrakon. The institution of the ostracism is believed to have been established by Cleisthenes, sometime between the end of the sixth and the beginning of the fifth centuries—that is, a decade or more before Aeschylus' first recorded win at the festival. The purpose of the ostracism—which was held yearly if the citizens voted in favor of holding one—was to rid the city for ten years of the one man whom most citizens wanted to be rid of. Scholars today describe the ostracism as a politically expedient, inverse substitute for voting, since Athenians did not elect many of their civic officials but drew names randomly by lot.[48] Over five thousand ostraka have been dug up by archaeologists—a drop in the bucket, since at least six thousand ostraka had to be submitted each year for the ostracism to go ahead.

The ostrakon functions like a secret ballot. The individual whose name is written most often by the voters wins—not a prize, as in the case of the *agones* of the theatre festival, but exile for ten years. The literate practice of voting by inscribing a name on some surface or other was a common one at this time in Greece: priestesses at the oracles recommended courses of action by scratching names on beans (Parke 1967:87), and theatrical judges wrote the contestants' names as a way of selecting the winner.[49]

---

48. Ostwald 1986:27, 118, 177; Vanderpool 1970.
49. See Csapo and Slater 1996:160, and Dover 1972:16.

To write a name on an ostrakon was to express one's opinion in public without having to answer for it personally, a practice that would have mixed consequences. On the one hand, it would protect genuine, honest desires that might otherwise shrivel into passivity (I might be afraid to ostracize Themistocles or vote for Euripides if I had to do it face-to-face). On the other hand, it could encourage an abdication of responsibility and poorly thought-out decisions. As Plato might ask of such anonymous written practices, from whence comes the writer's authority to vote for Themistocles? Can he defend his scrawl, or is what he wrote the extent of his knowledge? In protecting the writer's anonymity, the ballot may be protecting his ignorance; but it may by the same token be protecting the freedom of his speech. Aristophanes apparently submitted his first plays without revealing his identity (Dover 1972:15), and the option that he exercised in so doing, of making a public contribution anonymously, existed thanks to writing.

Not only did the selection of the winner in the theatrical contests depend on this literate practice, but also playwriting itself was a kind of aesthetic reflection of the institution of the ostracism.[50] In both cases a public event is going to take place; it is already scheduled. The ostracism has been voted upon and is imminent; similarly, the theatre festival is an annual occurrence whose date is set and known in advance. Both civic institutions represent for the individual citizen an *opportunity*, an opportunity to contribute something in writing. For both types of citizens, playwrights and ostracizers alike, writing is a mode of public participation. Although both types of written contribution concern, are in a sense addressed to, the citizen body at large, the immediate context of inscription is largely private, not public. One could always fill out ostraka in groups, of course,[51] and Sophocles, at least, is said to have taken the "natures" of his actors into consideration in writing for them.[52] Nevertheless, there are limits on the extent to which writing can ever be a social act. It takes only one hand to hold a writing instrument, whereas two people at least must be present for a conversation to take place.

The similarity between these two literacy events is evident also after writing's entry into the public sphere. For in both cases the bids for public

50. Humphreys thinks that the establishment of the ostracism coincided with the addition of comedy to the theatre festival, and that both institutions provided citizens with "an opportunity for the expression of public suspicions without formal trial or the possibility of defence" (1978:229).

51. See Vanderpool 1970:11–16.

52. See also Aristotle, who says that dramatists may write to please the actors (*Poetics* 1451b11f.) and/or the spectators (1453a12f.).

participation may amount to nothing, or to something other than was hoped for by the writer. One's inscription of the name of Pericles on an ostrakon may prove to be an isolated gesture, and Themistocles may be banished after all. Or one's inscription of a play about Heracles may be rejected by the archon and one about Oedipus performed instead. After his death, the name of Aeschylus on a submission was enough to guarantee that a chorus would be granted and the play produced. But otherwise, the plays submitted for performance might not reach the public at all (Dover 1972:15).

Now, the performance of a fictional play about a mythic personage such as Heracles may appear only superficially related to the banishment of a living contemporary citizen such as Pericles. But the two activities are in fact related. Tragedy, as we remember, was believed by the ancients to have been invented when a poet named Arion began to write choral compositions based on a *named subject.*[53] The act of *naming* is, of course, the essence of the ostrakon, as it is of the ballot generally. In filling out an ostrakon or ballot, the citizen must survey the whole social scene of competing interests and individuals; he must consider multiple scenarios and zero in on that single name which represents to him all that is rotten about the life of the city at that moment. Similarly, in writing their plays, the first Greek playwrights surveyed the great mass of mythological material and zeroed in on that single character whose story they felt was most germane to the current social scene. From the political relevance and topicality of subjects in tragedy and comedy alike, it is clear that the playwright's choice of a name was, in essence, his answer to a very specific question: Given the current state of Athenian life, a public hearing of whose case would be most pressing and apt at this year's festival?

For example, Aeschylus wrote about the bloodguilt of Agamemnon, Clytaemestra, and Orestes in the immediate aftermath of the Ephialtic reforms, which deprived the Areopagus of "all those accretions by virtue of which it exercised guardianship over the state" (*Constitution of Athens* 25.2; Ostwald 1986:203). The pacification of the Eumenides, about which Aeschylus could write in naming Orestes, had its direct civic correlative in the denuding of the Areopagus of all but one of its hereditary rights as law court, and in the empowerment of the popular city jury in its place. Plutarch has preserved a story which suggests that the topicality of Aeschylus' choice of names in the *Oresteia* was typical of his playwriting practice in general: "And so it befell, as the story goes, that when the verses composed

53. According to Solon in his *Elegies,* the Suda and John the Deacon's commentary on Hermogenes; see Csapo and Slater 1995:100–101; Flickinger 1973:8–9.

by Aeschylus upon Amphiaraus were recited in the theatre [he cites lines 952–54 of the *Seven Against Thebes* here] all the spectators turned their eyes on Aristides" (*Life of Aristides* 3.4–5).[54] At a time when Aristides was up for trial on bribery charges, Aeschylus' portrayal of the mythological Amphiaraus turned the spectators' thoughts to a contemporary citizen similarly fallen in with bad company (Podlecki 1966:39). Here, a mythological name is but a front for the name of a contemporary citizen. Scholars believe that Sophocles' Neoptolemos was meant to evoke thoughts of the young Pericles (Ostwald 1986:413 n. 4), and Anthony Podlecki provides evidence for the topicality of other character names in Aeschylus' tragedies as well.

The topicality of dramatic names is much more readily apparent in early comedy, of course. In his plays, Aristophanes names Kleon, Laches, Euripides, and Socrates directly; Eupolis named Alcibiades in the *Dippers,* and apparently got "dipped" in the sea by Alcibiades in return for this theatrical dipping.[55] Eventually, perhaps in the aftermath of Aristophanes' prosecution by Kleon, a law was passed against naming citizens directly in the plays inspired by them, and comic poets thereafter had to ridicule individuals "figuratively," through symbolism.[56] But before the advent of these slander laws, citizens were as vulnerable to being named by the dramatists of Athens as they were to being singled out by the inscribers of ostraka.

A closer look at the ostraka themselves shows additional similarities with playwriting. On many ostraka, it is true, there is nothing but a name, a fact which might seem to suggest that the comparison cannot be taken too far. Writing a play, which involves plot, characterization, and poetic and musical invention, is obviously a far more involved and exacting undertaking than the writing of a bare name. But some of the ostraka that have survived actually resemble artistic character sketches in miniature. In making their written contributions to the life of the city, some citizens expressed themselves by drawing caricatures of their named choices; some added insults and curses, and one, who submitted an ostrakon against Pericles' father in 484 B.C.E., wrote his accusation in the form of a little poem (Vanderpool 1970:15, 9). When we bear this in mind, the writing of plays and the writing of ostraka begin to seem surprisingly similar.

The *Iliad* and the *Odyssey,* which largely made up that Homeric "banquet" from which the tragedians selected their names,[57] were by nature *com-*

---

54. Translated by Podlecki 1966:37.

55. Scholion to Aelius Aristides *Orations,* 3.8, as translated by Csapo and Slater 1995:178.

56. Iohannes Tzetzes *Prooemium* 1.87–97, as translated by Csapo and Slater 1995:179.

57. Athenaeus *Deipnosophists* 8.347e.

posites of stories, catalogues of sailors' or warriors' tales which were built up through inclusion, accumulation. Dramatic plots, however, both comic and tragic, tend to move in the opposite direction, by exclusion. In writing a play about Socrates, for example, Aristophanes was in effect singling out the individual he thought was most blameworthy in Athenian political life at the time of the festival. Not all plays are about individuals, of course; some are about groups such as the women of Troy or the children of Heracles. But even a play about the daughters of Danaus has singled them out from a larger mythological scene. And as Geoffrey Bakewell (1997a) has demonstrated so convincingly, Aeschylus named the Danaids in response to current political events. In writing a play about the Danaids, Aeschylus had chosen the names that would enable him to address such topical issues as the status of metics at Athens and the logistics of housing them. Kratinos named Pericles in a comedy for similar reasons: this "squill-headed Zeus," this builder of the Odeion may have escaped ostracism, but he could still be named and criticized for his Olympian pretensions by a playwright in the theatre (Kratinos frag. 71 cited by Humphreys 1978:229).

In performing this kind of selective naming operation upon the narrative material available to them, the dramatists, as participating citizens, apparently chose their names for the festival each year in response to the same kinds of civic concerns that would have moved other citizens to fill out ostraka. Like the regular citizen who wrote a poem about Xanthippos, son of Arriphron, for submission to the ostracism, playwrights chose a name by way of making a written contribution to an upcoming civic event. And so we should not be surprised to find that while ancient papyri manuscripts lack many of the extraverbal markers we associate with writing, they do include character names.[58] A written composition about Iphigenia or Prometheus may not have included punctuation, word separations, or paragraph breaks, but it would *name names*.[59] The ability to write a name, and a colloquial or poetic comment, was apparently one literate skill that even the most backward hayseed was liable to have possessed at the beginning of the fifth century (Vanderpool 1970:9): and it was a skill on which the ostracism, no less than the theatre festival, depended.

This ability to write a single name, but also a list of names, is a literary practice on which the theatre depends for a number of reasons. Athenians often wrote lists of names: archon lists, victors lists, casualty lists, lists of cit-

58. This is a complex issue. The papyrus manuscripts are late copies, and often character names were abbreviated. But the fact that some character names were written is sufficient for our purposes here. See Dover 1972:10.

59. See Page 1962:74, 106, 169, and passim.

izens, of jurors, of assemblymen. Now, as I noted earlier, the recital of ancestry lists is a common feature of oral culture, amounting to a distinct poetic genre in some oral milieus.[60] But as Jack Goody (1987) observes with respect to emergent African literacy in the twentieth century, to write a list whose items one can *see* is a very different thing from an oral recitation of an acoustic series. The purpose of an oral list is to *remember* the series. Poetic meter and formulas are used to help the items stay glued in sequence, and the sequence must go on; to stop in the middle is to risk losing one's place. For this reason, the only types of relationships between terms that can emerge are those of sound and sequence. To alter the chronological sequence is tantamount to defeating the purpose of the list.

When the terms in a list are visibly co-present in space, however, they can admit of operations upon them which are neither acoustic nor chronological but abstract and conceptual. As Goody's case study among the Vai shows, people who have learned to make written lists soon begin to manipulate their contents along logical, categorical lines. To cite just some of Goody's examples, to write a list of fruit names is to begin to see the boundaries of abstract categories: Is tomato a fruit? Where do fruits end and vegetables begin? To write a list of supplies is to begin to wonder whether chicken belongs in the meat category: On what basis does one decide whether two items are of the same type? Similarly, a list of expenditures begins to suggest and allow a division into *types* of purchases, rather than just a temporal segmentation into *when* they were made. Goody found as well that a chronological ordering principle for names tended to be abandoned in favor of more useful organizing principles such as age, sex, initial syllable, and so on (213ff.).

In ancient Greece, as it happens, the use of the written list in the sixth century B.C.E. did have revolutionary results of precisely this kind. The citizen body was reconceptualized on paper. Whereas blood and ancient cult ties had traditionally been used as the organizing principle for individuals' names, these customary and naturally occurring categories were replaced by abstract conceptual ones. Ten new tribes (*phylai*) were artificially created, and individual citizens' names were inscribed under the new tribal list headings not according to ancestry (i.e., not according to a hereditary chronology), but according to domicile. By pushing names around on paper, Cleisthenes created new conceptual units, and new relationships between items were revealed. Whereas, for example, "Boutad" had formerly referred only to descendants of the noble Boutes, it became the name "of any per-

60. Halpern 1990:301–21.

son, however humble, who resided in the deme of that name" (Ostwald 1986:20). Accordingly, citizens' names begin to appear on ostraka without their patronymic, and modified by their demotics instead (Vanderpool 1970:6–8).

Not only were individuals reconceptualized and categorized according to deme rather than Dad, but the tribes, which had once been similarly organized according to blood ties, were reconceptualized as well, transformed into what Eric Csapo and William Slater have called "purely administrative units" (1995:107). Whereas tribes had formerly been dominated by a few powerful families with ancient religious affiliations, the tribe was reconstituted in writing according to an abstract principle, in this case the idea of "fair representation." Henceforward, each tribe consisted of inhabitants of spatially disjunct demes, which meant that for the first time, tribe affiliation was an abstraction without "natural," blood-based associations (Ostwald 1986:21). Whereas individuals used to belong to the collectivity—or be excluded from it—on the basis of their membership in hereditary brotherhoods, they were now free-floating items in a written list which could be moved around at will.

The consequences of these paper-based reconceptualizations for Athenian politics were huge, as David Stockton (1990), Martin Ostwald (1986), and Christian Meier (1990) have shown. By creating categories that existed only on paper, Cleisthenes broke up local connections based on religious cults, and for the first time established *citizenship* as the sole organizing principle for items in the community lists (Meir 1990:61, 60). Even the names assigned to the new tribes were arbitrary and detached from traditional connections. A list of one hundred hero names was submitted to the Delphic oracle, and a selection of winning names was made by the priestess in writing (60).

In a corresponding fashion, a poet to whom a list of mythological names is available is capable of performing different operations with and upon them than is a poet confined to the world of sound. In an oral context it is undoubtedly possible to "think" Odysseus separately from the stories told about him. But it is only through the agency of literate practices such as the list that a name like Odysseus will become an object for abstract, decontextualized contemplation (*theasthai*). To write a list of the Homeric hero names is to shake them loose from epic embeddedness in traditional songs—loose, that is, from the singers' traditional treatment of them. It is to be able to contemplate them with less semantic predetermination. Detached from their inherited oral-acoustic chains, character names were allowed to enter into new cognitive configurations. Anything put in a written list is given a new lease on life, as it were. Just as Cleisthenes was able to reconceptualize citizens on the basis of where they lived rather than, as formerly, on the basis of who their ancestors were, so too were the literate poets of the dramatic age able to rethink narrative figures along lines other than those established by traditional stories alone. In making use of epic tradition, as Aristotle advises, the dramatist "must show invention" (*Poetics* 1453b11). Before new interpretations of Odysseus can be imagined, however, his name must be abstracted away from the customary view of him as a many-wiled and always resourceful husband and fighter. Accordingly, in drama he has become a slippery smooth talker, a shameless manipulator, a politician.

The phenomenology of the dramatic text is most illuminating here. What we see when we look at a play today is unique in the verbal arts. At the beginning is often a name: Elektra, King Lear, Minna von Barnhelm, Uncle Vanya, Candida, Amadeus. Works from the other genres are often titled by names as well, of course. But in the dramatic text, the name or title is followed by another written element which is not technically speaking part of the story being told: a list of other names. Now, there is no way of knowing whether the ancient playwrights headed their plays with lists of characters as playwrights do today. Regardless, though, of *when* the practice of writing out a list of character names attached itself to playwriting, it became and remains one of the key distinguishing features of the dramatic text.

The significance of this phenomenological feature of the dramatic text for theatrical performance is enormous. The writing of character names *outside* the storytelling discourse signifies nothing less than the liberation of the mythological figures from their containment within the Muse's monologue. In epic storytelling there is only one speaker. The *aoidos* or rhapsode alone has the power of speech in performing the story, even though there is no limit to the number of characters who can be *spoken for.* This feature of epic speech—that all speech represented in the story is subsumed under and within the single voice of the speaker and the Muse of memory who inspires him—is fundamental to the genre. It is also a defining characteristic of (nonchoral) lyric and novelistic speech as well. When Thetis or Hephaestos, Penelope or Odysseus, Leopold or Molly or any other novelistic character speaks, his or her speech remains an utterance of a single controlling linguistic consciousness, that of the author, *aoidos,* or rhapsode. In drama, by contrast, the names of speakers signify the existence of x-number of autonomous speech positions, actual speakers (actors). The writing of character names in the dramatic text, whether in the list at the beginning or before each bit of speech, is therefore symbolic of narrative exotopy: these written elements remain perpetually outside of the story, just as the actors who stand in for these names remain outside the speech act of the storyteller (the playwright).[61]

The decontextualized list of character names thus stands at the entrance of the dramatic text like an engraved Delphic motto on the architrave above the gates: Speak for Thyself. Before the dramatist can delegate this power of speech to "outside" individuals as the genre demands, however, he must first determine who these individuals are. For nothing happens in drama until the speakers or their names are chosen (see the very start of rehearsals for the play-within-a-play in *Midsummer Night's Dream:* "Here is the scroll of every man's name" 1.2.4). Unlike epic and novelistic storytelling, which can get under way simply on the basis of an impulse to tell a story—"Once upon a time . . ."—the dramatic text *has no story* outside of the speech of its separate characters. Regardless of what stories it is based on or inspired by—and a very large percentage of dramas are based on preexistent stories—the text itself, phenomenologically speaking, consists almost exclusively of names and speech.[62] With the exception of the occasional stage direction,[63] the dramatic text contains the names of characters and what they say. Speaker and spoken, sayer and said: these are the materials out of which the dramatist makes his story.

This use of the speech of named figures to tell a story requires that the single beam of narrative discourse that was the bard's or novelist's be sent through a kind of prism, a prism that fractures it into the separate speech positions which are the separate characters and, ultimately, the actors who will perform them. The list of the dramatis personae is the basic expression of this fracturing, a kind of spectrogram or image of it. Or rather, the list of names may function in the first place as a spectrograph, an instrument for obtaining the kind of atomized image of speech that drama makes out of narrative material.

The visual orientation of this analogy of the spectrograph is apt, since ancient audiences of the first dramas appear to have been struck most by drama's making visible what was formerly only described by the voice of the

---

61. This point is an important one for theory, since it shows that the dramatic text is composed of non-spoken elements which are still integral to performance. See Pavis 1982, who says that the dramatic text must be defined as including only those elements that are actually pronounced by the actors.

62. See Pfister 1988:163ff. on the "limitation" of dramatic storytelling, that is, that figures appear only insofar as they speak, or fail to speak.

63. K. J. Dover thinks that some stage directions in ancient tragedy and comedy "go back to the author's own day" (1972:10).

rhapsode.[64] To liberate mythological characters from their containment in the Muse's song, and to allow them to step forward into the light of embodied day, amounts to a translation into visible space of what was formerly heard. But what is made visible is constructed as a speech spectrograph: the story is broken down into the speech of Antigone, of Ismene, of Creon, Haemon, Eurydice, the Elders of Thebes, and so on. With the whole burden of storytelling, or world-making, now devolved upon the speech of named subjects, a character's speech is no longer just one element in the story—as dispensable as, say, a description of the sunset—as was the case in epic speech. In oral tradition, the basic principles of variability and multiformity which we looked at earlier have been observed to extend even to the story's character names (Lord 1986:20). In the oral mode of storytelling, who says what is not important, nor is the name given to a particular character; in different versions of the "same" oral story, character names may change as well. The structure of drama, with its division of the world into specific speech positions, has determined on the contrary that only Hamlet can say "To be or not to be"; only Jocasta can say "God keep you from the knowledge of who you are."

To write a story based on a list of speakers means to divide the world up into speech positions. And just as one begins to see relations among colors in a spectrogram, or among items in a written list, so too will the relations among speech positions become manifest in a dramatic writing of mythic material. Where does Antigone's speech end and Ismene's begin? What determines which aspects of a story are given to one character for utterance rather than to another? This problem of who says what is for the playwright not just a logistical one. To decide, for example, whether chicken goes in the meat category involves asking questions about the essence of the abstraction "meat," and examining abstract relations among types of animals, methods of husbandry, of food preparation, and so on. Similarly, when the names Antigone and Ismene enter the lists, they can begin to be conceptualized in ways that make their relationship to each other visible. They are sisters: How do sisters speak to one another? To what extent do they speak the same language? To what extent will their age difference manifest itself in linguistic differences? In different values and outlook? And so on. Dramatic writing

64. See esp. de Kerckhove 1979, 1981, 1983; Segal 1986:75–86; Vernant and Vidal-Naquet 1990:185–86, 243. As Herington puts it: "For the contemporaries it must have been dazzling enough, especially in the early years, when each Dionysia might reveal to the audience for the first time ever an Orestes, say, or a Memnon, or a Niobe, or an Oedipus, who was no longer a mere mechanical component of a famous story, but who breathed, walked, and, above all, spoke for himself" (1985:136).

thus involves conceiving of individuals as loci of speech (or silence, as the case may be), and thinking of the world of actions and events in terms of verbal correlatives. In dividing the world up into separate speech positions, the dramatist is thus engaging in a kind of conceptual analysis of the verbal-ideological world.

Like the internal chronotope of the dramatic text, which shifts value from the finished past onto the ongoing present, this spectrographic division of narrative into exotopic speech positions carries social and political implications: characters are subjects who speak for themselves, not "objects" for containment within a single transpersonal discourse of tradition. Just as the institution of the ostracism gave ordinary citizens a voice in public affairs, so too did the shift from epic to dramatic form give the figures of mythology a voice in the telling of their stories. For this reason, dramatic form is democratic and clearly reflects the structure of political institutions such as the ostracism. Without lists of citizens, lists of candidates, and the ability to submit written names anonymously, democratic institutions of this kind cannot function properly, if at all.[65] For similar reasons, the ability to draw up a list of separate speakers and their speech, and to submit it for public hearing and performance by others, is a precondition of dramatic form.

65. See W. Harris 1989:115, 63.

Conclusion: Theatre and Technology

> What should that alphabetical position
> portend?   Twelfth Night

*I*N THE FOREGOING CHAPTERS WE HAVE LOOKED AT VARIOUS WAYS IN which both the dramatic text and the social practice that is theatre were dependent from their beginnings in Greece on the technology of alphabetical literacy. The practice of literary criticism, inaugurated by the writing down of Homer's epics; the decontextualized study of poetry, made possible by the literate classroom; the reconceptualization of conflict initiated by the writing down of law, and the emergence of a literate economy of exchange——all of these literate developments made crucial contributions to the rise of theatre and its displacement of an epic storytelling model.

On the basis of these findings, two things are clear from the outset: that from their inception, theatre and drama were structured according to the same set of social and poetic principles and therefore cannot be described as two separate art forms; and that we can no longer accept those theories which portray literacy and literacy practices as peripheral to, let alone destructive of, the art of the stage. As a genre dependent on the manipulation and exchange of decontextualized, arbitrary signs—in the form of written speech, lists of names, future-oriented contracts and coins, and the documents left by the absent and the dead—theatre is indeed an art of writing.

What these findings suggest for contemporary and future theatrical and dramatic theory still remains to be drawn out. In terms of its historical emergence, theatrical form does appear to be structurally beholden to writing; but in practice, theatrical activities are clearly neither exhausted nor explained by writing to the same degree, or even in the same way, as the other literary genres are. Indeed, the relationship that prevails between theatre practice and the use of texts is unusually complicated, not merely by the standards set up by other textual disciplines, but by any standards. Consequently, and unsurprisingly, no matter where one looks in modern theatrical theory, one finds that discussions of the relationship between writing and the theatre are marked by distrustful uncertainty amounting in some cases to hostile vexation.

The nature of the relationship between writing and the theatrical stage has been illuminated by the evidence from Greece insofar as alphabetical writing preceded the emergence of theatrical form and determined many of its characteristics. Writing introduced the practice of verbatim repetition, which in turn enabled poetry to dispense with the conservatism of previous speech genres, and to develop, both stylistically and functionally, into the actively innovative, critical, and self-consciously fictional art form of drama. The use of the alphabet also shaped theatrical poetry as a highly speech-sensitive genre, a genre of idiosyncratic contemporary speech. The forensic atmosphere created by written law codes shaped theatre in many ways, determining its accusatory civic function, its dialogic structure, and its split orientation toward, on the one hand, abstract textual values, and on the other, popular public judgments. The literacy of the Athenians ensured also that amateurism, internationalism, mercantilism, and ideological competitiveness defined the practice of Western theatre from the very outset.

Literate practices, as we have seen, set off a number of subtle dialectical chain reactions; and theatre, as both an art and a social practice, grew up within this technological force field and contains its tensions on a deep generic level. To reiterate but two of these twists that are sure to be of interest to theatre artists and theorists today, there is the fact that verbatim repetition proves itself, perhaps against expectations, to be a kind of precondition for creative advancements rather than an obstacle to them; there is also the fact that while literacy does tend to cast the body as culturally "low," it also permits readers and writers, through the detachment of meanings from actual contexts, to envision new interpretations of the body which may be more liberal in the long run.

Of all the aspects of theatrical form that have been illuminated by our look at the influence of literate modes, it is perhaps this relationship between texts and bodies which cuts most directly to the heart of theatrical art. As an issue of abiding concern to theorists and practitioners alike, it is unfortunately a theoretical problem that will not easily admit of a simple solution. As we have seen, the relationship between texts and bodies is a complex dialectical one which cannot be solved once and for all: a "final solution" to this most human of dilemmas would be neither possible nor even desirable. Rather, precisely by virtue of its dynamic constitution, the text-body relation is one that needs to be plumbed on an ongoing basis through time and historical change. And this, of course, is where theatre itself comes in. We have already seen some evidence that theatre is ideally constituted as an art form to fulfill this measuring and testing function, so long as there are texts and bodies that use them. Consequently, it is the actual practice of theatre, the concrete use made by real bodies of disembodied texts, that provides the only true theory of drama insofar as the relation of texts to performance is concerned. But because it is not just actors but *all* literates who are afflicted, and blessed, with this text-body dialectic, it would seem that drama's ability, rare among the arts, to stage and interrogate this dialectic should be one in which all members of a literate culture retain a significant intellectual and physical investment.

For theorists of drama, this conclusion—that the text-body relation cannot be theoretically solved once and for all but must rather be tested afresh in every production—may be disappointing. But from the point of view of literate culture generally, and theatre's perennial role within it, this is a conclusion full of optimism and laden with positive implications. Nevertheless, there are a few theoretical issues that remain to be addressed, and the remainder of this chapter will be devoted to them. For modern theatrical theory has tied itself into many unfortunate knots in its efforts to wrestle with this problem of the relation between writing and the theatre, knots which our evidence from ancient Greece has gone some distance toward untying.

Once upon a time, in classical aesthetics, the critical terminology was such that artistic genres as diverse as epic, drama, the novel,[1] and even dance and flute playing could be meaningfully discussed as related activities (*Poetics* 1447a–1448a). What these genres appeared to have in common was the goal of imitative performance. Their formal and substantive differences—the materials they used, the performative means they employed, and the objects they imitated—seemed theoretically insignificant compared with the shared telos which unified them within a single poetic collectivity.

But this theoretical aegis has disappeared over time: Romantic theories of art replaced *mimesis* with *poiesis*,[2] and the history of literacy, with its

---

1. Aristotle speaks about the genre "without a name" which "imitates by language alone" (*Poetics* 1447b). We would call such things novels.

2. Romantic theorists of art such as the Schlegels became disenchanted with the separation between form and content implied by classical *mimesis*. Rather than viewing art as a representation of external nature, they insisted that art should be judged as a made thing, as something that signifies only itself and is therefore creative rather than imitative. See Tzvetan Todorov (1982a:151–76) for a good summary of the shift from *mimesis* to *poiesis*. See also Todorov (1982b:4) for the use of *poiesis* to describe the modern view, and Göran Sörbom (1966:208) for the use of *mimesis*.

"Gutenberg" practices and habits of mind, eliminated performance from many spheres of artistic life. Before writing, of course, all poetry was enjoyed exclusively through the bodily realities of performance; but for literates, verbal art came to mean "literature," things that are *read*. Once capable of contributing effortlessly and usefully to the study of theatre, theories of verbal art, under the impact of technological change, have shriveled into theories of pure textuality, leaving theatre and drama out in the theoretical cold.

In classical theories of poetics, drama—as the genre that incorporates *all* the arts of imitative performance—recommends itself as a kind of sovereign genre; in the *Poetics,* drama assumes a correspondingly central position. But modern poetics, which is concerned mainly with *textual* literature— that is, print-based, nonperformative poetry and prose—either cannot cope with drama at all, or must treat it as an anomaly. Is it a dead historical relic, the literary theorists wonder, an archaeological remnant of our oral past, a merely instrumental stage in the evolution of our supremest, purest literary form, the novel?[3] Drama's multi-medial, performed nature makes it much too expansive a genre to fit under the desk-sized microscope of modern poetics' study of literary art *qua* text. Drama's presence in the discipline is tolerated out of respect for historical ties, but its company is rarely sought. In fact, the dramatic text, always reeking just a bit of real bodies and things, must even represent something of an affront to students of literature raised on Romantic notions about the autonomy of the text. Experienced teachers of literary theory, poetry, novels, and short fiction often avow that it "never occurred" to them to teach plays, or that they feel "uncomfortable" when called upon to do so, for their textual training has ill prepared them to analyze the kind of text that a play is. As a result, drama is often only grudgingly admitted into the republic of literary genres at all, for literature is now expected to be "pure," that is, unsullied by anything "real," meaning nontextual.

We need consult only a few standard reference works for literary theory and criticism in our time to see the uncomfortable position into which drama had been elbowed by post-Gutenberg thinking. In his *History of Modern Criticism* (1981), René Wellek says simply that G. E. Lessing's belief in the centrality of drama within literature is due to a faulty notion of what literature is. Literature, for Wellek and for all the "modern *readers*"[4] on

---

3. See Bakhtin (1981, 1984a, 1986) and Godzich and Kittay (1987) for examples of this view.

4. The italics are mine.

whose behalf he claims to speak, is ideally lyric poetry; if Lessing had not been so blinded by "insensitivity," an outmoded Aristotelianism, and a transparent occupational bias, he would have recognized this too (1981, 1:164). What we find in J. A. Cuddon's *Dictionary of Literary Terms* (1991) is equally telling. Cuddon defines "literature" as the group of "works which belong to the major genres: epic, lyric, drama, novel, short story, ode" (505). When we consult his entries for these genres, we find, however, that the novel receives twenty-two pages of history, theory, and analysis; the epic rates nine and a half pages; both the lyric and the short story merit four pages each; and the ode elicits three and a half pages. Drama is dispensed with in exactly *three sentences,* two of which are not even about drama as a genre. Drama is *named* by Cuddon as one of the "literary genres," but is not treated equally with the others.[5]

Drama's misfit status within modern literary theory is faced more directly by Roman Ingarden in *The Literary Work of Art* (1973), but with equally puzzling results. A more exhaustive and painstaking analysis of "the basic structure and mode of existence of the literary work" (lxxi) could hardly be imagined. Ingarden begins by determining which objects fall under the heading of "the literary work," and although he soon amends the formula to include the "low-brow" genres as well, his definition of the category follows Cuddon's generic approach. Literary works for Ingarden are works from all the "literary genres," and his examples are the *Iliad,* Schiller's dramas, *The Magic Mountain.* Drama, in short, is used along with the other genres to *constitute* the category "literary art." Yet, some three hundred pages of analysis later, drama is found *not* to conform to the very class of objects it helped to define. Ingarden is forced to conclude that a play "is not a *purely* literary work in that entirely new means of representation, precluded by the essential nature of a purely literary work, appear in it: 1) real objects engaged in performing the function of reproduction and representation and 2) aspects appropriately formed and predetermined by the properties of these real objects, in which represented objectivities are to appear" (320). On the one hand, then, drama serves a vital function in defining the category of literature; on the other, it is not really literature at all——it is, in Ingarden's words, "a borderline case" (322).

In response to this marginalization by theorists and critics of literature,

---

5. From biographical information we learn that Cuddon is himself an avid theatre-goer and playwright, so "anti-theatricalism" (see Barish 1981) is clearly not at work here. On the contrary, Cuddon's dictionary elsewhere shows more awareness of theatrical terms than most literary anthologies and surveys. The problem seems to lie rather with the oddness of drama as a literary genre.

twentieth-century theorists of drama and theatre have tended to take up one or the other of two extreme positions. In one particularly striking case both positions were taken up, in succession. I am thinking of David Cole's study *The Theatrical Event* (1975), and his *Acting as Reading* (1992). These two books may not be found on every theorist's bookshelf; but placed side by side, they create an accurate map of the course dramatic theory has charted in our time, from ritual to text.

As Cole himself is aware, these two works make mutually exclusive claims about what theatre is. The first of them, written at the height of the anti-text fever that swept both theory and practice at midcentury, locates theatre "within a pre-literate problematic of tribal ritual," and focuses on shamanism and possession experience (1992:76). The second "presents acting not merely within the framework of literacy and textuality but as, in its inmost essence, a mode of engagement with texts" (76). Although Cole makes a halfhearted attempt to explain away this about-face, his vague tropes about water, depths, oceans, and travels cannot hide the fact that he has, in the space of seventeen years, reversed his position on the relation of writing to theatre and theatre to literacy.

Cole's work does not really deserve to stand as the epitome of the discipline's theoretical confusion. But there is no denying that his wild swing from preliterate ritual to all-encompassing textuality is an accurate reflection of larger theoretical trends. His bibliographies tell the story of twentieth-century dramatic theory at a glance. In the 1970s, Cole's readings in comparative religion, anthropology, and psychology reflected the attempts made by so many Western theorists of drama to explore the extent of theatre's likeness to a variety of nonliterary, non-Western practices: theatre was found to have more in common with shamanism, Haitian voodoo, Tibetan mysticism, Ethiopian religion, and Songhay magic than with European literature. What did it matter that theatre had been deprived of its throne within the commonwealth of literary genres? Theatrical performance was more like religious possession, ritual healing, and psychopathology anyway. By the 1990s, however, Cole's readings in Derrida, Poulet, Iser, Barthes, and Jameson had apparently reglamorized the Western tradition as a source for theatrical theory. The true essence of theatre no longer had to be sought in "primitive" non-Western practices, and the shaman was abandoned in favor of the literary theorist. And so in Cole's more recent book we find that the essence of theatre is now "readerly": acting is reading; being an audience is being read to; and the stage is a site of performance texts, inscriptions, and reader responses. The incompatibility of these two versions of the essence of theatre is obvious. In the first case, theatre is a preliterary religious ritual; in the second case, it is indissolubly dependent on the existence of writing and literacy.

Although the flowering of theatre's romance with ritualism can be dated conveniently to the mid-twentieth century—say, to the 1970s of *The Theatrical Event*—antiliterary sentiments run deep in theatrical theory. Besides Cole's early readings in comparative anthropology, we find the writings of Hegel and Jane Ellen Harrison, both of whom were influential in encouraging modern theorists like Cole to wash their hands of literature altogether. Although not exactly a ritualist, Hegel was one of the earliest aestheticians to attack texts on principle as alien to theatrical performance. In his *Aesthetics,* Hegel argued that drama, being an embodiment of action, comes into contradiction with itself when read.[6] Hegel saw the theatre's only hope in a ban on printing: dramatic texts, to be true to themselves, should be enacted, seen in action, and not read at all (except by actors—and, evidently, by Hegelian philosophers). The impracticality, to say nothing of the arbitrariness, of Hegel's solution can be let pass. Hegel's pronouncement, however, did succeed in bringing into awareness one of the fundamental issues of theatrical theory, an issue that had never before been formulated in so radical a form. Aristotle, for example, seems to take for granted that plays are written, and that they are intended for performance, but he does not explore the theoretical implications of this bi-medial situation. Interested primarily in the plot, Aristotle does not appear to see the medium as affecting the message in any way. A plot heard is the same as a plot seen. If we know better today, and I think we do, we might credit Hegel with making the theatre's "written-ness" into the problem it has remained.[7] Regardless of how it has

---

6. "Drama is concerned to depict an action in all the reality of its actual presence" and "would fall into contradiction with itself if it were forced to remain limited to the means which poetry, simply as such, is in a position to offer" (Hegel 1975:1181). Hegel continues: "Indeed, in my opinion, no play should really be printed" (1184).

7. The history of theatrical theory is of course strongly marked by the debate about the relative merits of performance over the reading of plays. Castelvetro in 1576 was perhaps the first to contradict Aristotle explicitly and stress the primacy of performance: "Aristotle is of the opinion that the delight to be obtained from reading a tragedy is as great as that to be obtained from a performance of it; this I aver to be false" (*Poetica d'Aristotle vulgarizzata e sposta;* trans. and cited in Carlson 1984:48). Lessing has a special place in this history, thanks to his rigorous semiotic analysis of the limits of literary versus plastic media. For Lessing, the materiality of the theatrical sign puts limitations upon it from which literary representations are relatively free (see esp. Wellbery 1984:88). And later Hazlitt, equally sensitive to the phenomenal differences between text and performance, argued for the supremacy of the text: "The representing of the finest of [Shakespeare's plays] on the stage, even by the finest actors, is, we apprehend, an abuse of the genius of the poet, and even in those of a second-rate class, the quantity of sentiment and imagery greatly outweighs the

been solved, the problem of writing and its relation to performance, once revealed, could no longer be ignored, and soon came to occupy the energies of theatre theorists of all kinds, emerging in this century as perhaps *the* issue for theory and practice alike.

What Aristotle skipped lightly past, and Hegel pointed out, twentieth-century theorists began to lose sleep over. The closer they were looked at in theory, the more dissimilar texts and performances appeared. In terms of their sign systems, their phenomena, their temporal structures, in terms of the perceptual apparatus they activate and the social contexts that ground them in practice, texts and performances proved to be incommensurable objects when it came to theoretical analysis.[8] The seeming impossibility of theoretically reconciling theatre's textual and nontextual elements led some theorists to give up the attempt. Jiri Veltrusky (1977), for example, concluded that theatre's literary and nonliterary elements are so opposed in nature that drama and theatre must be viewed as two separate and irreconcilably different art forms. Any actor who has just learned a "drama" by heart in order to perform it in the "theatre" would of course scoff at this suggestion, since theatre and drama, in practice, are simply two different names for a continuous activity. It is only theory that has trouble reconciling them. And so long as texts are conceived according to the standards of post-Gutenberg thinking, the difficulty of reconciling them with performing bodies must seem acute.

With the advent of the ritual hypothesis, however, any perceived need to reconcile text and performance seemed to disappear. For advocates of ritualism such as Jane Ellen Harrison, as for precursors such as Frazer, Freud, and F. Max Müller, the stories we tell one another are not what they appear to be. Beneath the visible surface of myth lies a truer, more primal and deeply human reality. For Harrison, all our mythological "sayings" are really "doings" in disguise. Myths are "really" attempts to explain religious rituals no longer recognized as such. Applying her views about religion to drama, not by any means her area of expertise, Harrison concluded that "for Greece at least, only in orgiastic religion did drama take its rise."[9]

Despite its fictionality, the idea that drama was originally the worship

---

immediate impression of the situation and story" (1930–34 5:221–22). But Hegel made textuality into an explicit theoretical problem in a way that most closely anticipates the anti-text trends of our time.

8. As Pavis describes the incommensurability of text and performance, "linguistic arbitrariness and stage iconicity cannot be reconciled or mutually canceled out by a common system" (1982:143).

9. Harrison 1991:568; orig. pub. 1903.

of a polyonymous "Year-Spirit" caught on. Certainly it was a much more exciting theory about the origins of drama than could be produced by such careful philologists as Oliver Taplin and Arthur W. Pickard-Cambridge. According to Robert Ackerman, Gilbert Murray's social connections may have had something to do with the theory's immunity to sound historical scholarship: because he knew the editor personally, Murray was able to get Harrison's ritual hypothesis into the *Encyclopaedia Britannica* before it could be subjected to unbiased scrutiny (1991:170). As a result, the ritual hypothesis received wider dissemination, and planted itself more deeply in the public imagination, than perhaps it deserved.

For Murray and followers such as Francis Fergusson (1949), characters like Oedipus, Orestes, and Hamlet were not realistic psychological portraits, but functioned rather as superficial masks for a single seasonal god of an ancient fertility rite. If theatre is "really" an ancient religious ritual disguised, then mythological characters are just decadent later additions, and the whole dramatic text is an irrelevant, concealing add-on. As Christopher Innes (1981) has shown, a similar belief in some primal disguised origin of theatre is at work throughout the century's avant-garde, anti-textual theories and theatrical experiments. As he notes, Artaud (1958), Grotowsky (1968), the Living Theatre, Barba (1990), Chaikin (1972), and Schechner (1971, 1973, 1976, 1977) all latched on in one way or another to the ritual hypothesis, and all concluded, in their disparate ways, that because theatre is an essentially irrational, preliterate phenomenon, writing can only pervert theatre's true calling. If theatre was originally a religious rite, a holy communion shared by initiates, then texts can only get in the way.[10]

Despite the shortage of evidence for the actual existence of such a religious ur-drama,[11] the hypothesis was welcomed as a panacea for all the theoretical uncertainties of the text-performance relation. The most tangible consequences of the theatre's enchantment with ritual were the many theatrical experiments, referred to earlier and discussed by Innes, in which practitioners ended up throwing the baby of theatre out with the bathwater of text.[12] Since Harrison and Murray's time, however, theorists of myth and ritual such as David Bynum and G. S. Kirk have argued that the early advocates of the ritual hypothesis were in any case demonstrably wrong in their

10. See Innes 1981 passim, esp. 257–58.

11. Pickard-Cambridge 1962:189; Else 1965b:7; Vickers 1973:33ff. Not surprisingly, Seaford's (1994) ritualistic study of ancient theatre must rely, to a disproportionate extent for such a long work, on Euripides' *Bacchai*.

12. See, for example, Kirby 1969; Benamou 1977; Schechner 1971, 1973, 1976, 1977; Artaud 1958.

claims that ritual always underlies myth. These are simply different types of phenomena, and their relationship to each other is much more complex than simply one of surface and depth or cause and effect (Kirk 1985:252). That myth and ritual, which tend to occur together at festivals and other social gatherings, are actually two different types of "social behaviour" is not, however, something that would be obvious to an anthropologist in the field; as Kirk suggests, "the ceremonial circumstances in which myths are most conspicuously recited naturally make the deepest impression on the direct observer" (1970:253). So we can understand why Western observers might have had a tendency to conflate the two and see the ritual as the crux of the event. Nevertheless, it can be shown that "the great majority of Greek myths were developed without any special attention to ritual" (Kirk 1985:253), and that "[Greek] rituals do not seem to generate myths except in rare and exceptional cases" (236). In fact, as Kirk has discovered through detailed cross-cultural analysis, most myths worldwide have no particular ritual connection whatever (1970:19). Sometimes existing myths are used to build up the etiology of a specific cult, and sometimes myths are invented to explain an ancient cult practice, but such direct connections between myth and ritual are rare.[13] And even where it does exist, "the relation between myth and ritual . . . is not a simple matter of cause and effect in either direction" (1985:252).

As Bynum (1981) explains, rituals are activities that communities use to symbolically mark their social customs, such as marriage; myths are the stories that people tell one another and do not necessarily have any particular ritual content at all. (Myths about sexual unions say nothing about *how* people celebrate marriage rites, or even *whether* they do.) Whereas rituals are by nature local, changeable, and in some cases superficial (Thomas 1996:191), it is rather in the telling of stories about experience that humans reveal something of their ultimate and often universalizable aspirations. According to Bynum, there are any number of different ritual methods of getting married, or being initiated into adulthood, or buried, or born into the community. These rituals, which vary from place to place and epoch to epoch, even within the same country (Thomas 1996:185), reveal almost nothing about the myths that coexist alongside them—myths about the creation of the world, relations between men and animals, between men and women, between people and nature or the supernatural, and so on. One community might ritually mark the birth of girls by a religiously sanctioned excision of their genitals; another might shower the mother in small pink

13. Kirk 1970:16, 18–19; also Kirk 1985:223–53.

gifts and force her to wear a hat made out of the ribbons from the wrapping paper. These rituals reflect local social conditions and values and do not usually produce myths, although they may well provide opportunities for enjoying those that already exist.[14] As Kirk points out, the natives of the Pacific Northwest practise the potlatch as one of their central rituals, yet have virtually no myths about potlatch situations (1985:248). This is because, in Kirk's words, "alongside the stream of religious imagination there runs a stream of purely narrative invention" which we call storytelling, or myth (1985:226).[15]

This complex relationship between myth and ritual was not grasped by the advocates of the ritual origins of theatre, and as a consequence they were unable to see theatre in its earliest days for what it was: a species of storytelling whose ritual associations were only circumstantial.[16] The theatre, of course, was not just any kind of storytelling: it was the first genre of storytelling to benefit from the preexistence of written stories, with all that that entailed. And it is precisely here that ritualism reveals its greatest weakness as a tool for theatrical theory. In addition to underestimating the autonomy and primacy of our narratological impulses, ritualism cannot grapple with a historical variable such as technology; indeed, many of ritualism's most influential ideas have depended on a willful discounting of technological differences between one culture and another. Instead, its insights were gathered from direct, ahistorical comparisons between anthropological data drawn from radically different cultures at various stages of technological advance. Concrete and culturally specific facts, such as whether the society in question learns from bards or from books, were not allowed to disturb the apparent symmetry. As Robert Weimann has argued in a discussion of the

14. One may perform a play in honor of a wedding, as the actors do in *Midsummer Night's Dream,* or attend a performance of *The Nutcracker* during the Christmas holidays, as we do today, or go to the theatre during the Festival of Dionysus, as was the practice in ancient Greece.

15. This distinction between myth and ritual is strongly confirmed by the circumstances surrounding the emergence of aboriginal theatre in Canada. Theatrical form did not emerge out of the potlatch or other Longhouse activities which continue to carry out such ritual functions as preserving social customs, affirming community solidarity, and celebrating local rites of passage. Such traditional ritual performances are "fully comprehensible only to the culturally initiated"; but dramas based on myths such as those of the Trickster can be enjoyed by any audience, not just the local one (Brask and Morgan 1992:x, xv). Brask and Morgan, who have studied the emergence of theatre in a number of aboriginal settings, conclude that native rituals are alien to the universalizing narrativity of theatrical performance (xiii).

16. For discussions of the circumstances that put theatre under the auspices of the Dionysian city festival, see Pickard-Cambridge 1962, 1968; Else 1965b; Gernet 1981; Segal 1986; Taplin 1978; Herington 1985; Vernant and Vidal-Naquet 1990.

so-called ritual sources of Shakespearean theatre, "anthropological models" taken from preliterate "canoe plays" and "jungle hunting games" are less pertinent than they might appear: "At this level of culture mimesis arises out of a community in which there is little division of labour[;] the 'spectators' take part in the game or join in the acting. The unity of player and audience is complete" (1978:2). In short, such models are not actually "theatrical" in the sense intended by members of a literate society such as ours. Nor are they theatrical in the sense assumed by the ancient Greeks, who observed in their artistic activities a separation between audience and performer that was absent from their religious activities. And yet, as Kirk has shown, the method of the early ritualists was precisely this: to accumulate catalogues full of items that looked vaguely similar, but in practice, in their actual social contexts, were unrelated (1970:4).[17]

As Bynum has argued, this downplaying of specific cultural and historical differences continues to compromise the work of anthropologists. For example, Victor Turner and Clifford Geertz, whose comparative anthropology is often applied to theatre research, betray a typical tendency to treat traditional religious rituals as if they were culturally equivalent to literate artworks such as *Macbeth* and *Moby Dick* (Bynum 1981:142–63). As laudable as it is in itself, this impulse, to find human similarities despite seeming cultural differences, can badly botch its evidence if the latter is simply ignored. The mimetic dances of the Bambuti pygmies *may* have something to teach us about theatrical performances in Elizabethan London, but only if it is remembered that the purpose and meaning of a given type of social behavior can change over time—and especially under the impact of such powerful social and technological factors as the division of labor and literacy. When comparing anthropological material from different cultures, in other words, theorists must take care to give historical and technological differences the weight they deserve.

For as we have seen throughout this study, literacy changes things. One of the effects of literacy that we noticed for ancient Greece was a generalized de-specialization of performance personnel, an inauguration of performative amateurism in poetic storytelling. That this amateurism is typical of a specifically *theatrical* mode of public performance only becomes visible, however, through a *historical* analysis of changing speech styles, and hence has not been recognized or adequately appreciated by modern, comparative-minded theorists. As a result, many have drawn specious parallels between

---

17. Kirk describes this method as, "even by the indulgent view . . . rather reprehensible—although no one reached the point of successfully reprehending it" (1970:4).

theatre and shamanistic performance. Theorists such as Richard Schechner (1976) and the early David Cole (1975), intrigued by superficial phenomenological similarities, have described theatre as essentially shamanistic, and shamanistic performance as essentially theatrical. The list of reasons why this comparison is misleading is actually rather long, and includes such pivotal divergences as the presence in the one and the absence in the other of religious and ritual elements, and the absence in theatre and the presence in shamanic performance of direct audience involvement. Tao-ching Hsu describes the main difference between the actor and the shaman as follows: "The shamanesses worked on the spirits, not on the spectators; they tried to invoke gods, not amuse men; in fact, in some cases there might not be any spectators at all" (1985:200). But aside from these obvious functional dissimilarities, there is the crucial difference which is all too easily overlooked by those not attuned to the historical realities of technological change. This is the fact that, like other preliterate speech genres, shamanistic performance is the exclusive preserve of specially initiated practitioners. Unlike the actor, the shaman is divinely "chosen" for his performative function; unlike the actor, the shaman must also undergo a physical "initiation" that marks him for life as a select practitioner of a sacred and secret "vocation" (Conquergood 1992:45–49). The actor, on the contrary, in antiquity no less than in modernity, is anyone with a script. For this reason, shamanic performance, if comparable to any mythological activity—which is itself by no means self-evident—would bear more meaningful comparison to epic than drama, for the shaman, like the oral bard, is the physical embodiment of a traditional style and is considered the divinely authorized repository of esoteric knowledge and a special technique not available to everyone.

There may be something in theatre practitioners that naturally draws them toward the oldest, most universally attested anthropological evidence in their search for the meaning and function of their art. Or perhaps, as Jack Goody has suggested, an enchantment with primitive, preliterate models is typical of all literates, not just those interested in drama: "A perpetual trend of complex, written cultures is the search for, and to some extent identification with, the simpler cultures of the past. One only has to recall the attraction of 'savage' cultures for the eighteenth-century Rousseau. . . . A modern version of the same theme lies behind the search for the natural, the untouched, the oral . . . and representing in some of its guises the apotheosis of the oral and the renunciation of the written as the real source of truth" (1987:293). The fact that the Western theatre has *always* consisted mainly of written plays should be enough to dissuade us from taking this "apotheosis of the oral" too far.[18] But the historical record, as we have seen, stands in the way of our even flirting with it. Writing had already been practised in Greece for almost two centuries by the time theatre made its first appearance, and there is little to be gained by pretending otherwise.

Cole's later work, of course, implicitly acknowledges that the premises of ritualism simply do not jibe with the historical facts. As Cole had to grant eventually, even adherents to ritualist doctrine are wedded to writing despite their wishes: "One can argue endlessly about whether the actor can or should or might function as a 'social critic' (Brecht) or 'skilled worker' (Meyerhold) or 'secular saint' (Grotowsky) or 'signal[er] through the flames' (Artaud); but meanwhile there is no question that he *is* functioning as a reader. Every actor—whether he works for Robert Wilson or the Shubert organization, the Royal Shakespeare Company or the high school dramatics club—*reads*" (1992:3). This is Cole's belated recognition of the role played by reading in the actor's work. Far from simply recognizing it, however, Cole goes on to overestimate it. Like so many theorists in recent years, Cole ultimately exaggerates the extent to which a textual activity such as reading can be used to explain everything that goes on in theatres. For, as we soon discover in *Acting as Reading,* all theatrical activities are subsumable under the aegis of textuality. Theatre is now no longer conceived by Cole as non-text; it is now *all* text.

Like the ritual hypothesis, which was borrowed, inappropriately, from Harrison's religious studies, so too were the textually based theories of reading on which Cole depends co-opted from sources inattentive to the historical and practical realities of theatre. In taking over the methods and terminology of contemporary literary theory, Cole and others have thus imported into theatrical theory all of literary theory's discomfort with the nontextual aspects of drama. The explosion of interest in literary theory throughout the last few decades may have had the effect of rehabilitating writing as an intellectually respectable subject; but the new text fetish has produced results for theatrical theory which have proven as absurd as those bequeathed us by the previous avant-garde. Theorists from the late 1970s into the 1990s, apparently intoxicated by the cachet of textuality, were moved to describe even the stage spectacle as a "performance text" "written" by a "stage-writer," the director, and "read" by an audience.[19] In sum, the

18. My concern is exclusively with the Western theatrical tradition. That the situation is quite different in the East is acknowledged and discussed in Chapter 1.

19. See esp. Lyotard 1977, Ubersfeld 1978, Elam 1980, Pavis 1982, Svenbro 1990, Cole 1992. Nor is there any sign of change at this writing: a theatre conference at the University of Toronto's Graduate Centre for Study of Drama in 1997 was titled "The Performance Text."

theoretical pendulum had swung so far in the opposite direction that even corporeal performance came to be seen, by theatre practitioners who should have known better, as if it too were a text.

According to my findings throughout the foregoing chapters, the impact of writing cannot be underestimated in any account of the rise of theatre nor in any description of its practice today. But neither can this historical evidence be taken as a licence to do away with the text-performance problem by pretending that even performances are texts. Having followed Kierkegaard's advice and having traced this problem back to its home, to its first appearance in ancient Greece, we find ourselves in an especially good position to evaluate the extent to which readerly theories can serve as a satisfactory replacement for the postulates of ritualism. In his remarks about the actor's dependence on reading, Cole refers to the textual activities of theatre practitioners *today;* but reading and writing have become occupational necessities for virtually everyone. Had we simply examined the theatre's use of writing *today,* we would have proved nothing more than that our culture is dependent on written modes. This we already know. What we needed to ascertain was not the extent of writing's influence on cultural life today, but the extent of its role in constituting the theatre as an art form; and the only way to do this was to return to the moment when theatrical form visibly emerged.

Sixth- and fifth-century Greece proved to be an ideal laboratory for evaluating the extent of theatre's dependence on writing. Writing at this time was being widely used, but it had not yet displaced oral habits altogether. Better still, the beginning of the classic age of drama in Greece is a period in which traces of mainly oral performance styles can still be found. Drama appeared on the performance scene at a time when the oral recitation of poetry was still the expected norm for most audiences; and yet, even in the earliest theatrical performances of the fifth century, the distinctive marks of literacy are evident. Having followed the progress of the hybridizing shift from exclusively oral performance to the performance of literary drama, we have been able to see what theatre does and does not owe to writing.

For example, in my discussion of Kallias' *ABC Show* in Chapter 1, I suggested that the art of the theatrical actor was at least partly constituted through a transference of the arbitrary semiotic principle from writing to poetic performance. As semioticians such as Veltrusky (1964) and Elam (1980) have noted, one of the first conventions of theatrical space is that it treats the things that fill it as unmotivated signs: a sack of potatoes can represent a dead body, a boy can represent a girl, a crooked index finger can represent a chink in a wall.

Nevertheless, an awareness of this "alphabetical" freedom of people and objects on stage can easily lead to incorrect theoretical conclusions. And it has, if we can judge from those theorists in our time who have declared that theatrical performance must *itself* be treated as a kind of writing. Jean-François Lyotard claims that staging a play involves the rewriting, or transcribing, of the text by the director, who is described as a kind of "writer" himself (1977:90). Kier Elam conceives performance as a "text" (1980:3, 7, 12, 213). Patrice Pavis similarly describes the director as a "writer," and performance as a "stage writing" or "text" which can be "read" by the audience; even the actor's body can be "read like a text" (1982: 31, 55, 73, 78, 124, 135, 174). Anne Ubersfeld does likewise (1978:24), as does Marco De Marinis.[20] Jesper Svenbro describes stage presentation as a "vocal rewriting of the text,"[21] and from that deduces that Athenian audiences actually improved their *reading* skills by watching plays (1990:371ff.). Cole begins by questioning the appropriateness of the stage-as-quick-book[22] trope, but ultimately makes the surprising decision to retain it on the grounds that, since we commonly speak of "reading" "photographs, drawings, films," we should be able to speak of reading a performance text, especially since so many reputable theorists and poets have already done so (1992:200).

In the first place, conformity with past theoretical precedent, no matter how illustrious, is *not* adequate justification for maintaining a descriptive trope, particularly one so fraught with generic significance. In the second place, Cole should have been alert to the fact that "photographs, drawings, films" have one thing in common which theatrical performance does not have: as artistic objects they are all inanimate, fixed, disembodied tissues of signs. A theatrical performance, however, is patently not a text in this sense, which really means that it is not a text at all. One of the effects of the popularity of semiotic models, especially those of Barthes and Derrida, has been to expand our notion of what a text is. In the main this has been a positive development, providing critics and theorists with a consistent vocabulary for speaking about all kinds of cultural phenomena (rather than just about books). But the theatre differs from many other products of culture in one key respect: its special character consists in the fact that it combines, explicitly, both textual and nontextual phenomena. The theatre's distinctive combination, and even contrast, of text and non-text, cannot be argued away; and recognition of this unerasable duality is therefore essential for an accu-

---

20. As cited by Carlson 1984:501.
21. But "vocal rewriting" is a contradiction in terms.
22. "Quick" in the medieval sense of "living;" see Cole 1992:199.

rate understanding of the genre. By calling both the textual, and the living, nontextual aspects of theatrical practice by the same name, theorists obscure the differences between them, and leave themselves no room to discuss the relation between texts and bodies, a relation that could be said to constitute the essence of the art. Certainly my discussion of the nature of the actor/ student in Chapter 2 suggests that a clearly delineated text-body relation is essential to any analysis of theatrical representation.

A wholesale adoption of textual models also causes problems when "readerly" hermeneutics are used to analyze the audience's experience of the-atrical performance. I am thinking in particular of Susan Bennett's disserta-tion, "The Role of the Theatre Audience" (1987), and again Cole's *Acting as Reading* (1992). Both of these works use varieties of "reader-response" criti-cism to describe theatrical processes. Relying on theorists of reading such as Wolfgang Iser (1978), Cole for example quotes, approvingly, such theoretical statements as the following: a text is "a sort of living organism" "formed out of living matter"; a text is "an organic web." [23] Or "the text is . . . a verbal body . . . that can be sounded, weighed"; the text is "a sort of human being." [24] Cole concludes that "to the extent that texts are experienced as others, reading tends to be experienced as interpersonal encounter" (13). Iser asserts that "a dialogue" exists between readers and their books, a "dyadic in-teraction" (80, 66). On the basis of such ideas, Cole theorizes that "texts are capable of standing in all the sorts of relations to their readers that one self may stand in to another": a book may serve the function of a "friend," "ther-apist," or "lover." Now, anyone who has had the pleasure of having a real friend, therapist, or lover is not likely to be convinced by this. But Cole is convinced, and goes on to say that "to be alone with a text . . . is already to be interacting with others." This is so because, thanks to reader-response criticism, "solitary reading is, at all moments, interaction with 'others' " (14). Reading is certainly *described* that way, but that does not make it true.

Their decision to equate corporeal performances with texts has led the-orists such as Bennett and Cole to some fairly preposterous conclusions. Cole ultimately asserts that "it is scarcely an exaggeration to say that acting begins and ends in reading" (1992:8) and that reading and acting are *equally* physical activities (29). In the process of his analysis, he cannot help but fal-sify the nature of *both* acting and reading. In the first place, books are not what Georges Poulet says they are: "living, feeling, resisting" *people.*[25] Con-

---

23. Yuri Lotman as cited in Iser 1978:66.
24. Georges Poulet as translated and cited by Cole 1992:65; Iser 1978:154.
25. As cited by Cole 1992:39–40.

sequently, encounters with them are not dialogues but complex mono-
logues. Books are mechanically reproducible, and often destructible without
serious consequences, which actors, for better or for worse, are not. And it is
of the nature of writing to have a deferred relation with its receiver, a relation strictly opposed to the simultaneity with which performances are produced and received. Furthermore, the word *audience,* when used of a text's
readership, has an abstract, almost imaginary quality to it, whereas audiences of stage plays are real, present "collectivit[ies], acting here and now on
one another and on the speaker" (Ong 1977:13). Theatre audiences, in short,
occupy the same spatiotemporal context as the performers. As Ong observes
further, texts are produced out of writers' *withdrawal* from direct immersion
in a social situation (1977:57), a feature of writing (and reading, for that
matter) which can hardly be predicated of acting. Writing can communicate
over time and distance in the absence of both the sender of the message and
any particular receiver, and again, this is something that theatrical actors do
not normally have an ability to do. Theatrical performance involves the spatial and temporal co-presence of sender and receiver, and surely this is
enough to guarantee that it cannot meaningfully be described as any kind of
writing.[26]

The ritualist approach may have been unnecessarily prejudiced toward
texts, but one cannot solve the problem of the relation of writing to the
stage in this way either. By any definition of text that is meaningful in the
context of theatre, the body of a live actor speaking in person to an equally
live audience is not a textual phenomenon. From whatever point of view
one wishes to adopt—structuralist, poststructuralist, semiotic, phenomenological—performances cannot be equated with texts. They make meaning
in different ways, produce different sorts of experiences, are composed of
radically different sensory material, are consumed by audiences according to
different principles, and communicate through different channels, different
media. To call them both texts is an abuse of the language.

The textual approach constitutes a slight advance over that of the ritualists,
for at least it acknowledges the everyday realities of theatre practice today
and throughout history. But the advance is not a great one, since reading is
not *all* that happens in theatres, nor is reading all that actors do. In response
to our theoretical quandary—what is the relation of writing to the stage?—
we have thus received two unsatisfactory answers in our time. The ritualists

26. In the case of broadcasts or films, this rule would seem to evaporate—which is
precisely why it *does* make sense to speak of films and recordings as texts.

banished the text as irrelevant and obscurantist; the textualists have made it all the world. Neither of these theoretical extremes can account for the peculiar, sometimes troubled, always fertile cooperation between texts and bodies that we see in the Western theatre from its very beginnings; neither can usefully locate dramatic art within literature as a whole.

For in the final analysis, it is theatre's knowledge of but stubborn non-absorption by writing which has guaranteed for it a special, even privileged position within the family of literary genres. Precisely because it is *not* textual itself, theatrical performance can "display" or represent writing in a way that a written medium itself cannot; in the theatre there is an "outside" of writing. In staging the Ionian alphabet for the Athenians, Kallias can both *use* a grammatological semiosis and *show* the difference between letters and bodies. The representing signs of a writing system cannot "get pregnant," as does Kallias' female writing student, who out of shame represents her baby with letters. This difference, between inanimate signs and real people, cannot be ignored theoretically. As Bert States observes, theatrical signs distinguish themselves from textual ones precisely in this way: "In the theatre [unlike in texts] there is always the possibility that an act of sexual congress between two so-called signs will produce a real pregnancy" (1985:20).

Writing is regularly *displayed* on stage, but theatre does not become writing by virtue of this. Methods of displaying writing range from Kallias' alphabet chorus, to the writing of "Thebes" on the scenery, to the pinning of Shakespearean love letters on trees, to Brechtian placards, to the multiplicity of avant-garde devices that have more recently been used for showing actors as readers.[27] For reasons similar to those already stated, directors can only be said, without sophistry, to be behaving as "writers" when they compose introductory notes for the playbill, or indicate therein that the performance will run without intermission.

As we see in *The ABC Show,* the theatre can represent writing, but it does this representing by means of a medium that is unambiguously *not* writing itself (i.e., actors' bodies and voices and real objects). Nevertheless, Kallias' letter/characters, who function on stage as signs for fictional personages or things that they themselves are not, do present us with a theoretical dilemma. If it is the nature of a sign *not* to be what it represents, what does this say about actors? If they represent passionate human beings, as they do in so many plays, does this mean that they must not be passionate human

27. See Cole's discussion of the readerly theatre of the Wooster Group, Daryll Chin, Robert Wilson, and La Mama's *Home Remedies* (1992:190–96). These productions actively explored, in performance, the phenomenology of reading by staging acts of reading, giant books, projected text, and so forth.

beings themselves? Diderot wrestled at length with this paradox, concluding at one point that actors must on some level be quite devoid of their own personality in order to represent other personalities (1957:16–20). The question goes further: Can men and women, who on stage represent men and women, albeit "other" ones,[28] even be said to function as signs at all, since at root they also *are* what they represent?

The answer involves the recognition that the actor remains a performer, even while she or he functions as a sign does. Like the epic rhapsode, and like the lyric performer, the actor is still *competing*—for the audience's love, for the prize, money, or fame. As a contestant in a festival agon, the actor is therefore still engaged in all the pragmatics of performance: exhibiting virtuosity, displaying bodily charms, flattering, seducing, shocking, moving the audience to tears and delighting in the effects. Plato's Ion provides us with a lovely description of the paradox of the actor, for whom the performative pragmatics of *pleasing* always underlie his semiotic activity of representing. The means of performance in drama may have become representational, but the end or goal remains "to please," and to do so through the agency of one's own present body.

To say that the actor preserves the performative function of the *aoidos* or rhapsode is therefore to say that he experiences the effects of his performance *as he performs*. Like other types of performer, the actor experiences the audience's enjoyment or disapproval simultaneously with his performance, which is to say that audience response will more or less directly affect the *way* he performs. And it is here that the difference between theatre and other literary arts makes itself most keenly felt. A text such as a novel is never a performance: the letters on the page do not get nervous before the reader's gaze or wither at the reader's restlessness, nor do they bloom before the reader's appreciative laughter, applause, cheers. This may seem obvious enough, but there have been many attempts among theorists of the disembodied literary arts to arrogate "performance" pragmatics to the novel. The most notorious of these is perhaps Bakhtin's insistence that novels are "plays . . . without footlights"—which in a Bakhtinian worldview makes them superior and more truly "dramatic" than plays (Wise 1989). Derrida also arrogates performance functions to texts in a number of discussions,[29] and Kristeva speaks of texts as theatrical performances as well (1989:185ff.). Cole has noticed that this affectation, by critics of texts, of a theatrical vocabulary

28. For an eloquent statement of this situation, see Handke 1969.
29. For example, the writer "put[s] things on stage . . . is on stage himself; writing is a theatrical "scene" (Derrida 1981:206, 290).

is rampant in critical camps from the New Critics to the phenomenologists of literary response: readers are said to "act out" the text, "impersonate" the characters, get "cast in roles," and so on (1992:23–29). Nevertheless, this use of performative metaphors to describe textual activities obscures the fact that written signs do not possess the same qualities as stage actors and objects: co-presence in a unique time-space context with a living audience, dialogic interaction with that audience, and an ever-changing corporeal, phenomenal reality. To call a textual artifact a performance is therefore no less mistaken than to call a performance a text.

Actors do indeed extend the arbitrary semiotic principle from page to stage, but they also preserve the performative function of the oral bard, who tries to delight the listener with his own present self. Although it is not easy to accept this, there would seem not to be any hard and fast rule that explains how these two functions interact in the actor's art. Some actors try to transcend their own personal oral-performative inclinations in pursuit of a perfectly transparent semiotic representation; others exploit their own deictic reality for use in the representation, as did the ancient actor who brought the ashes of a dead relative to the theatre with him in order to gain the audience's sympathy for his character by way of their sympathy for his real grief. For some performers, performative intentions and desires consist mainly of being beautiful and charming; others aim in performance above all to seduce their audiences, by various reality effects, into taking their representations for reality. In some cases the oral-performative and dramatic-semiotic functions enter into a conspicuous conflict. Sometimes this happens inadvertently—when an actor is poorly cast or does not understand the role— and sometimes to a purpose, as when she or he has decided to use the performative function to comment on or criticize the role as written. The exact nature of the balance struck between the two functions clearly varies greatly from performer to performer, play to play, even from one given moment in a given production to the next. As Brecht noted with his usual perspicacity, the actor, as performer, will always be taking up *some* attitude to his role (1964:37, 98, 137, 198). But between the Brechtian extremes of "naturalizing" the role (closing the gap as much as possible between semiosis and performance) and "alienating" it (deliberately widening the gap between the two), there are sure to be as many shades of gray as there are actors. Among North American "Method" actors, the assumption may exist that the performative function of the actor should merge with perfect equivalence into the representative function, but this is simply one style among many. In States's view, the nonrepresentational aspects of the stage presentation function by wounding the semiotic circuitry of the representation

(1985:12), but this view has no greater universality in the theatre than does its opposite. On the contrary, oral-performative phenomena are if anything more commonly used *in support* of semiotic functions: a comedian is cast in the role of a comedian; a pianist represents Mozart; real-life lovers are cast as lovers, or become lovers during rehearsal; memories of actual traumas are summoned up on stage; and so on.

One of the main reasons why the oral-performative and semiotic functions cannot be pitted against each other in any predictable, universally valid way is that the actor, in performing as his phenomenally real self, is even here involved in representations—not of the character but of himself. That is, he represents himself with an eye to gaining the audience's approval. How an actor, say, in Kallias' play chooses to represent the Ω of the script may be the product of his semiotic vision of the shape of the letter Ω, but it is also a function of how he wishes to show himself making an Ω, of what image of himself he wants the audience to have. In short, there is little that can be stated as axiomatic about the relation between an actor's own personal intercourse with his audience as a performer and his representation of absent signifieds. Only one thing can be said with certainty on the subject: that in representing the absent things that they are not, actors do so from the point of view of their own personal oral-performative present, which, as we saw in Chapter 3, they share with a judging audience, for better or for worse.

Cole's exploration of the role of reading in the actor's work usefully examines an area of theatre practice that has been too long neglected. Nevertheless, his approach is compromised by his use of a readerly hermeneutics which was developed for, and is better suited to, use in nonperformative genres such as the novel. And although Cole shrewdly observes that one of the central dialectics in theatre practice is between reading and "feeding the audience," he takes this "feeding," which is really but a convenient metaphor to describe the performer's need to "please," as a literal description of the atavistic pleasures lodged in reading. Thus, in effect, the root pleasure of performance for Cole can be traced back to the hidden psychological pleasures of reading—a very illogical and disappointing conclusion. It is certainly true that the actor, like the bard before him, aims to give pleasure; and we might add that bardic performance was originally intimately connected with actual feasting (Segal 1992:4–22).[30] But not all corporeal

30. It is interesting to reflect on the fact that of the surviving fragments of comedy, twenty-two are concerned with literate practices, while *hundreds* concern food. For this reason, the paradigmatic fragment from the lost fifth-century plays might well be that of the comic poet Plato: a Homeric parody in which a legendary hero stands on stage reading verbatim from a cookbook! (*Phaon* frag. 173 Edmonds 1957).

pleasures, on stage or off, are necessarily culinary. As we saw in Chapter 2, at least some of the pleasures of face-to-face discourse are connected with seduction and impregnation; others, as I suggested in Chapter 3, are connected with winning. Nor, in any case, can all of the pleasures of performance be seen as derivative of the pleasures lodged in reading. Western playwrights have undoubtedly all been readers, but actors and audience members may enjoy, and at various times probably have enjoyed, theatrical performance without having experienced the pleasures of reading themselves. Cole's theory is a perfectly illustrative case of the theoretical errors that must come of the uncritical use of (post-Romantic) literary theory in discussing theatrical phenomena. Modern literary theories tend to be characterized by a built-in bias in favor of print, a bias that strictly limits their use in dramatic theory.

As for the vexed question of theatre's place within literature, to conclude, with Ingarden, that drama is a "borderline" literary genre is at least not as inaccurate as to say that it is either preliterate or wholly textual; and yet it is not very helpful either. (The border of what?) In most modern dramatic theory, either theatre is categorized according to the prejudices of ritualism, and isolated from the rest of literature as an essentially nontextual art form, or theatre is absorbed so completely into the domain of textuality that its main generic features cease to be available for theoretical analysis at all.

Of contemporary theorists, Benjamin Bennett (1990) provides an analysis of drama's place within literature which is most in line with the evidence from ancient Greece. Bennett discusses theatre as an essentially literary event and drama as "the memory and the conscience of literature" (60). Drama for Bennett is "not merely one literary type among others, but rather is to literature as literature is to the whole of language, a focus of maximally intense self-reflection" (14). Bennett has regrettably chosen to retain a ritualist vocabulary, to conclude that "drama is the church of literature" (14), and to suggest that "the destiny of drama . . . is to become a ritual exercise in the ethics of reading" (54). But this is a quibble. For Bennett has ascertained, albeit through very different methods, what my own investigation into the historical genesis of theatre has discovered: that theatre "comes after" literature—not as an epigone but as an irritant. The special historical circumstances under which theatrical form was first constituted have determined that theatre must be located resolutely *within* literature, not as a "borderline case," but as the very genre that first inaugurated the practice we now take to be specifically "literary": a use of writing to tell a fictional story in which the text is demonstrably more than a record of an antecedent oral performance. But unlike the other literary arts that followed it, drama's peculiar *mode* of being-within-literature has determined that it always functions to some degree at the expense of literary dictates and models.

As we saw particularly in Chapter 2, whenever the technology of writing is put on stage, it is directly compared, and contrasted, with the real materiality of bodies and things. Plays and scenes that staged writing for the ancient Greeks nearly all suggest that writing has a built-in danger: that those who use it have a tendency to forget about the body, the organic body, which can never be reproduced in any text—or by any technology for that matter. Scenes of writing on the ancient stage show this forgetfulness of the body, and rebuke it—sometimes comically, sometimes with tragic seriousness. Because it conspicuously counters texts with bodies, writing with the corporeality of those who use it, the theatrical stage is unique in literate culture, able as it is to mount such a trenchant critique of the technology that produced it.

In fact, if this history of theatre's relationship with writing teaches us anything, it is that the theatre has a very special role to play in *all* technological revolutions. Unlike the art of the epic, for example, which was rendered culturally superfluous almost overnight by the advent of the alphabet, the theatre's function in a technological society cannot be exhausted, no matter what technologies we chance to invent. For unlike philosophical dialogues, novels, films, and all other representing media, the theatre puts real things, real bodies, real swollen feet beside and in opposition to all conceivable artificial representations of them.

As we move throughout theatre history, we find that no sooner does a new technology appear but the theatre puts it on stage. From Clytaemestra's smoke signals and Phaedra's letters, to Dr. Faustus's mechanical clock, to Prospero's books and star maps and astrolabes; from the locomotives of melodrama to the helicopters of *Miss Saigon;* from Cocteau's telephone to Beckett's tape recorder; from Svoboda's magic lantern projections to the live video rapiers of Robert Lepage—the theatrical stage has tested them all. Writing may have been the first technology to be subjected to critical scrutiny on the stage, but it was by no means the last. As new technological artifacts such as telephones and fax machines and computers continue to expand the range of our "natural" communication modes, the theatre continues not only to reflect their effects but also to provide a kind of corporeal analysis of them. Every time a character on stage picks up the phone or listens to his own voice on tape from an absent body, the theatre is carrying out its work of evaluating the changes wrought by technology upon our naturally occurring space-time categories, upon our bodily life. In the theatre, these space-time categories have never been entirely natural, since from the very beginning of the art form, Clytaemestra has received smoke signals from Troy, and men and women have communicated through writing from beyond the grave. But so long as the theatre remains *also* a genre in which real bodies communicate naturally in real time and space, such meditations on the impact of technology as the genre can mount will always retain the power to weigh, counteract, and even occasionally criticize new technologies without simply being absorbed by them. Of course, the dialectical nature of the natural-artifactual polarity guarantees that even our notion of theatrical "presence" may change—just as our notion of what constitutes a "unified" time, place, or action surely has been changed by the advent of satellite telephones and television and transcontinental flight. But the continued presence of real stuff on stage will also preserve for theatre, on behalf of literature generally, sufficient measures of naturalness to enact drama's ancient literary mandate: to provide an accurate aesthetic reflection of, as well as an effective bodily safeguard against, the use made by humans of all representing technologies—including writing.

Bibliography

Ackerman, Robert. 1991. *The Myth and Ritual School.* New York: Garland.

Allen, Thomas W. 1969 (1924). *Homer: The Origins and the Transmission.* Oxford: Clarendon.

Aristophanes. 1931. *The Comedies of Aristophanes.* The Athenian Society. Vol. 1. New York: Rarity Press,

———. 1982–85. *The Comedies of Aristophanes.* Vols. 3–5. Ed. Alan H. Sommerstein. Warminster, England: Aris Phillips.

Aristotle. 1927. *Poetics.* Loeb Classical Library. Cambridge: Harvard University Press.

———. 1941. *The Basic Works of Aristotle.* Ed. Richard McKeon. New York: Random House,

Arnott, Peter D. 1989. *Public and Performance in the Greek Theatre.* London: Routledge.

Artaud, Antonin. 1958. *The Theatre and Its Double.* Trans. M. C. Richards. New York: Grove Press.

Athenaeus. 1927. *The Deipnosophists.* 7 vols. Loeb Classical Library. Cambridge: William Heineman and Harvard University Press.

Auerbach, Erich. 1965. *Literary Language and Its Public in Late Antiquity and in the Middle Ages.* Trans. Ralph Manheim. New York: Bollingen Foundation.

Austin, J. L. 1975 (1962). *How to Do Things With Words.* Ed. J. O. Urmson and Marina Sbisa. Cambridge: Harvard University Press.

Ayrton, Michael. 1977. *Archilochus.* Trans. Michael Ayrton with essay by G. S. Kirk. London: Secker & Warburg.

Bakewell, Geoffrey. 1997a. "Metoikia in the *Supplices* of Aeschylus." *Classical Antiquity* 16, no. 2:205–24.

———. 1997b. " '*Eunous Kai polei soterios metoikos*': Metics, Tragedy, and Civic Ideology." Presented at "Crossing the Stages: The Production, Performance and Reception of Ancient Theatre," University of Saskatchewan, October 23.

Bakhtin, Mikhail. 1981. *The Dialogic Imagination.* Trans. Caryl Emerson and Michael Holquist. Austin: University of Texas Press.

——. 1984a. *Problems in Dostoevsky's Poetics.* Trans. Caryl Emerson. Minneapolis: University of Minnesota Press.

——. 1984b. *Rabelais and His World.* Trans. Helene Iswolsky. Bloomington: Indiana University Press.

——. 1986. *Speech Genres and Other Late Essays.* Trans. Vern W. McGee. Austin: University of Texas Press.

Barba, Eugenio. 1990. "Eurasian Theatre." Trans. Richard Fowler. In *The Dramatic Touch of Difference: Theatre Own and Foreign,* ed. Erika Fischer-Lichte et al. Tübingen: Gunter Narr Verlag.

Barish, Jonas. 1981. *The Antitheatrical Prejudice.* Berkeley: University of California Press.

Barnstone, Willis, and William E. McCulloch, trans. 1962. *Greek Lyric Poetry.* Bloomington: Indiana University Press.

Barthes, Roland. 1985. *The Grain of the Voice.* Trans. Linda Coverdale. New York: Hill and Wang.

Bauman, Richard. 1986. *Story, Performance, and Event: Contextual Studies of Oral Narrative.* Cambridge: Cambridge University Press.

Baumann, Gerd, ed. 1986. *The Written Word: Literacy in Transition.* New York: Oxford University Press.

Beck, Frederick A. G. 1964. *Greek Education.* London: Methuen.

——. 1975. *Album of Greek Education.* Sydney: Cheiron Press.

Beck, M. G. 1993. *Potlatch.* Seattle: Alaska Northwest Books.

Benamou, Michel, and Charles Caramello, eds. 1977. *Performance in Postmodern Culture.* Madison: University of Wisconsin–Milwaukee Press.

Bennett, Benjamin. 1990. *Theatre as Problem: Modern Drama and Its Place in Literature.* Ithaca: Cornell University Press.

Bennett, Susan. 1987. "The Role of the Theatre Audience." Ph.D. diss., MacMaster University.

Beye, Charles Rowan. 1987 (1975). *Ancient Greek Literature and Society.* Ithaca: Cornell University Press.

Bieber, Margarete. 1961 (1939). *The History of the Greek and Roman Theatre.* Princeton: Princeton University Press.

Blau, Herbert. 1992. *To All Appearances: Ideology and Performance.* New York: Routledge, Chapman and Hall.

Bowra, C. M. 1969 (1966). *Landmarks in Greek Literature.* Cleveland: Meridian.

Bowra, C. M., and T. F. Higham. 1950. *The Oxford Book of Greek Verse.* Oxford: Clarendon.

Brask, Per. 1992. "Recovering a Language." In *Aboriginal Voices: Amerindian, Inuit, and Sami Theatre,* ed. Per Brask and William Morgan. Baltimore: Johns Hopkins University Press.

Brask, Per, and William Morgan. 1992. *Aboriginal Voices: Amerindian, Inuit, and Sami Theatre.* Baltimore: Johns Hopkins University Press.

Brecht, Bertolt. 1964. *Brecht on Theatre.* Trans. J. Willet. New York: Hill and Wang.

Bristol, Michael D. 1985. *Carnival and Theatre: Plebeian Culture and the Structure of Authority in Renaissance England.* New York: Methuen.

Brockett, Oscar. 1982. *History of the Theatre.* Boston: Allyn and Bacon.

Burkert, Walter. 1966. "Greek Tragedy and Sacrificial Ritual." *Greek, Roman, and Byzantine Studies* 7:87–129.

Burn, A. R. 1960. *The Lyric Age of Greece.* London: Edward Arnold.

Burns, Alfred. 1981. "Athenian Literacy in the Fifth Century B.C." *Journal of the History of Ideas* 42:371–87.

Bynum, David E. 1981. "Myth and Ritual: Two Faces of Tradition." In *Oral Traditional Literature: A Festschrift for Alfred Bates Lord,* ed. John Miles Foley. Columbus, Ohio: Slavica Publishers.

Calder, William M. III, ed. 1991. *The Cambridge Ritualists Reconsidered.* Atlanta: Scholars Press.

Calhoun, George M. 1944. *Introduction to Greek Legal Science.* Oxford: Clarendon.

Carlson, Marvin. 1984. *Theories of the Theatre.* Ithaca: Cornell University Press.

——. 1990. *Theatre Semiotics: Signs of Life.* Bloomington: Indiana University Press.

Cartledge, Paul. 1978. "Literacy in the Spartan Oligarchy." *Journal of Hellenic Studies* 98:25–37.

Chadwick, John. 1990 (1958). *The Decipherment of Linear B.* Cambridge: Cambridge University Press.

Chafe, Wallace L. 1985. "Linguistic Differences Produced by Differences between Speaking and Writing." In *Literacy, Language, and Learning: The Nature and Consequences of Reading and Writing,* ed. D. R. Olson, N. Torrence, and Angela Hilyard. Cambridge: Cambridge University Press.

Chaikin, Joseph. 1972. *The Presence of the Actor.* New York: Atheneum.

Changeux, Jean-Pierre. 1988. "Learning and Selection in the Nervous System." In *The Alphabet and the Brain,* ed. Derrick de Kerckhove and Charles Lumsden. Berlin: Springer Verlag.

Christy, T. Craig. 1989. "Humboldt on the Semiotics of Writing." In *The Semiotic Bridge: Trends from California,* ed. Irmengard Rauch and Gerald F. Carr. Berlin: Mouton de Gruyter, 1989.

Clanchy, M. T. 1979. *From Memory to Written Record: England, 1066–1307.* Cambridge: Harvard University Press.

Cole, David. 1975. *The Theatrical Event.* Middletown: Wesleyan University Press.

——. 1992. *Acting as Reading: The Place of the Reading Process in the Actor's Work.* Ann Arbor: University of Michigan Press.

Cole, Douglas, and Bradley Lockner, eds. 1993. *To the Charlottes: George Dawson's 1878 Survey of the Queen Charlotte Islands.* Vancouver: University of British Columbia Press.

Cole, Susan Guettel. 1981. "Could Greek Women Read and Write?" *Women's Studies* 8:129–55.

Conacher, D. J. 1967. *Euripidean Drama.* Toronto: University of Toronto Press.

Conquergood, Dwight. 1992. "Performance Theory, Hmong Shamans, and Cultural Politics." In *Critical Theory and Performance,* ed. J. Reinelt and J. Roach. Ann Arbor: University of Michigan Press.

Coulmas, Florian. 1989. *The Writing Systems of the World.* Oxford: Basil Blackwell.

Craig, Edward Gordon. 1956. *On the Art of the Theatre.* New York: Theatre Books.

Cross, Frank Moore. 1989. "The Invention and Development of the Alphabet." In *The Origins of Writing,* ed. W. M. Senner. Lincoln: University of Nebraska Press.

Csapo, Eric, and William J. Slater. 1995. *The Context of Ancient Drama.* Ann Arbor: University of Michigan Press.

Cuddon, J. A. 1991. *A Dictionary of Literary Terms.* Oxford: Blackwell Reference.

Davison, J. A. 1962. "Literature and Literacy in Ancient Greece." *Phoenix* 16, no. 3:141–56

De Francis, John. 1989 (1984). *The Chinese Language.* Honolulu: University of Hawaii Press.

de Kerckhove, Derrick. 1979. "Sur la fonction du théâtre comme agent d'intériorisation des effets de l'alphabet phonétique à Athènes au V^{c}siècle." *Les Imaginaires II,* no. 10/18:345–68.

———. 1981. "A Theory of Greek Tragedy." *Sub-Stance* 29:23–35.

———. 1982. "Écriture, théâtre, et neurologie" *Études Françaises* 18:109–28.

———. 1983. "Synthèse sensorielle et tragédie: l'éspace dans *Les Perses* d'Eschyle." In *Tragique et tragédie dans la tradition occidentale,* ed. P. Gravel and T. J. Reiss. Montreal:

———. 1988. "Critical Brain Processes Involved in Deciphering the Greek Alphabet." In *The Alphabet and the Brain,* ed. Derrick de Kerckhove and Charles Lumsden. Berlin: Springer Verlag.

de Kerckhove, Derrick, and Charles Lumsden, eds. 1988. *The Alphabet and the Brain.* Berlin: Springer-Verlag.

Delza, Sophia. 1969. "The Classic Chinese Theatre." In *Total Theatre,* ed. E. T. Kirby. New York: E. P. Dutton.

De Marinis, Marco. 1993. *The Semiotics of Performance.* Trans. Aine O'Healy. Bloomington: Indiana University Press.

Derrida, Jacques. 1973. *Speech and Phenomena.* Trans. David B. Allison. Evanston: Northwestern University Press.

———. 1976 (1974). *Of Grammatology.* Trans. Gayatri Chakravorty Spivak. Baltimore: Johns Hopkins University Press.

Diamond, Elin. 1992. "The Violence of the 'We': Politicizing Identification." In *Critical Theory and Performance,* ed. J. Reinelt and J. Roach. Ann Arbor: University of Michigan Press.

Diderot, Denis. 1957. *The Paradox of Acting.* New York: Hill and Wang.

Dillon, Matthew, and Lynda Garland. 1994. *Ancient Greece: Social and Historical Documents from Archaic Times to the Death of Socrates.* London: Routledge.

Diogenes Laertius. 1925. *Lives of Eminent Philosophers.* Trans. R. D. Hicks. London: Heinemann.

Dolan, Jill. 1992. "Practicing Cultural Disruptions." In *Critical Theory and Performance,* ed. J. Reinelt and J. Roach. Ann Arbor: University of Michigan Press.

Dolby, William. 1976. *A History of Chinese Drama.* London: Paul Elek.

Donkin, Ellen. 1992. "Mrs. Siddons Looks Back in Anger: Feminist Historiography for 18th-Century British Theatre." In *Critical Theory and Performance,* ed. J. Reinelt and J. Roach. Ann Arbor: University of Michigan Press.

Donlan, Walter. 1981. "Scale, Value, and Function in the Homeric Economy." *American Journal of Ancient History* 6:101–17.

Dover, K. J. 1972. *Aristophanic Comedy.* Berkeley: University of California Press.

Duggan, Joseph J. 1990. "Formulaic Language and Mode of Creation." In *Oral-Formulaic Theory: A Folklore Casebook,* ed. J. M. Foley. New York: Garland.

Eco, Umberto. 1977. "Semiotics of Theatrical Performance." *TDR* 21:

———. 1984 (1979). *The Role of the Reader.* Bloomington: Indiana University Press.

Edmonds, John Maxwell, ed. and trans. 1957. *The Fragments of Attic Comedy.* Vol 1. Leiden: E. J. Brill.

———. 1964. *Lyra Graeca.* Cambridge: Harvard University Press.

Ehrenberg, Victor. 1975. *From Solon to Socrates.* London: Methuen.

Eisenstein, Elizabeth. 1985. "On the Printing Press as an Agent of Change." In *Literacy, Language, and Learning: The Nature and Consequences of Reading and Writing,* ed. D. R. Olson, N. Torrence, and A. Hildyard. Cambridge: Cambridge University Press.

Elam, Kier. 1980. *The Semiotics of Theatre and Drama.* London: Methuen.

Ellen, William Henri. 1918. *Ibsen in Germany.* Boston: Gorham Press.

Else, G. F. 1965a. *Homer and the Homeric Problem.* Cincinnati: University of Cincinnati Press.

———. 1965b. *The Origin and Early Form of Greek Tragedy.* Cambridge: Harvard University Press.

Elsky, Martin. 1989. *Authorizing Words: Speech, Writing, and Print in the English Renaissance.* Ithaca: Cornell University Press.

Enders, Jody. 1992. *Rhetoric and the Origins of Medieval Drama.* Ithaca: Cornell University Press.

Erp Taalman Kip, A. Maria van. 1990. *Reader and Spectator: Problems in the Interpretation of Greek Tragedy.* Amsterdam: J. C. Gieben.

Felman, Shoshana. 1983. *The Literary Speech Act: Don Juan and J. L. Austin.* Trans. Catherine Porter. Ithaca: Cornell University Press.

Felperin, Howard. 1985. " 'Tongue-tied our queen?' The Deconstruction of Presence in *The Winter's Tale.*" In *Shakespeare and the Question of Theory,* ed. Patricia Parker and Geoffrey Hartman. New York: Methuen.

Fergusson, Francis. 1949. *Idea of a Theater.* Princeton: Princeton University Press.

Filewod, Alan. 1992. "Averting the Colonial Gaze: Notes on Watching Native Theatre." In *Aboriginal Voices: Amerindian, Inuit, and Sami Theatre,* ed. Per Brask and William Morgan. Baltimore: Johns Hopkins University Press.

Finkel, Leif H. 1988. "Neuronal Group Selection: A Basis for Categorization by the Nervous System." In *The Alphabet and the Brain,* ed. Derrick de Kerckhove and Charles Lumsden. Berlin: Springer-Verlag.

Finley, M. I. 1968 (1960). *Aspects of Antiquity.* New York: Viking.

——. 1983. *Politics in the Ancient World.* Cambridge: Cambridge University Press.

Finnegan, Ruth. 1977. *Oral Poetry.* Cambridge: Cambridge University Press.

——. 1990. "What Is Oral Literature Anyway? Comments in Light of Some African and Other Comparative Material." In *Oral-Formulaic Theory: A Folklore Casebook,* ed. J. M. Foley. New York: Garland.

——. 1992. *Oral Traditions and the Verbal Arts.* London: Routledge.

Fischer-Lichte, Erika, et al., eds. 1990. *The Dramatic Touch of Difference. Theatre Own and Foreign.* Tübingen: Gunter Narr Verlag.

Flickinger, R. C. 1973 (1918). *The Greek Theatre and Its Drama.* Chicago: University of Chicago Press.

Foley, John Miles. 1991. *Immanent Art: From Structure to Meaning in Traditional Oral Epic.* Bloomington: Indiana University Press.

Foley, John Miles, ed. 1981. *Oral Traditional Literature: A Festschrift for Albert Bates Lord.* Columbus, Ohio: Slavica Publishers.

——. 1986. *Oral Tradition in Literature.* Columbia: University of Missouri Press.

——. 1990. *Oral-Formulaic Theory: A Folklore Casebook.* New York: Garland.

Forte, Jeanie. 1992. "Focus on the Body." In *Critical Theory and Performance,* ed. J. Reinelt and J. Roach. Ann Arbor: University of Michigan Press.

Fowler, Robert L. 1987. *The Nature of Early Greek Lyric.* Toronto: University of Toronto Press.

——. 1991. "Gilbert Murray: Four (Five) Stages of Greek Religion." In *The Cambridge Ritualists Reconsidered,* ed. William M. Calder III. Atlanta: Scholars Press.

Frazer, Sir James George. 1951 (1922). *The Golden Bough.* New York: Macmillan.

Gagarin, Michael. 1986. *Early Greek Law.* Berkeley: University of California Press.

Garland, Robert. 1990. *The Greek Way of Life.* Ithaca: Cornell University Press.

Garner, Richard. 1990. *From Homer to Tragedy.* London: Routledge.

Garvie, A. F. 1969. *Aeschylus' Supplices: Play and Trilogy.* Cambridge University Press.

Gelb, I. J. 1952. *A Study of Writing: The Foundations of Grammatology.* Chicago: University of Chicago Press.

Gentili, Bruno. 1988. *Poetry and Its Public in Ancient Greece.* Baltimore: Johns Hopkins University Press.

Gernet, Louis. 1981. *The Anthropology of Ancient Greece.* Trans. John Hamilton, S.J., and Blaise Nagy. Baltimore: Johns Hopkins University Press.

Gjerset, Knut. 1924. *History of Iceland.* New York: Macmillan.

Godzich, Wlad, and Jeffrey Kittay. 1987. *The Emergence of Prose.* Minneapolis: University of Minnesota Press.

Goethe, Johann Wolfgang von. 1986. *Essays on Art and Literature.* Trans. Ellen von Nardroff and Ernest von Nardroff. New York: Suhrkamp.

Goldhill, Simon. 1986. *Reading Greek Tragedy.* Cambridge: Cambridge University Press.

———. 1989. "Reading Performance Criticism." *Greece and Rome* 36, no. 2 (October):172–82.

———. 1990. "The Great Dionysia and Civic Ideology." In *Nothing to Do with Dionysus? Athenian Drama in Its Social Context,* ed. John J. Winkler and Froma Zeitlin. Princeton: Princeton University Press.

Goody, Jack. 1986. *The Logic of Writing and the Organization of Society.* Cambridge: Cambridge University Press.

———. 1987. *The Interface between the Written and the Oral.* Cambridge: Cambridge University Press.

Goody, Jack, ed. 1968. *Literacy in Traditional Societies.* Cambridge: Cambridge University Press.

Gredley, Bernard. 1984. "Greek Tragedy and the 'Discovery' of the Actor." In *Drama and the Actor,* ed. James Redmond. Cambridge: Cambridge University Press.

Green, Richard, and Eric Handley. 1995. *Images of the Greek Theatre.* Austin: University of Texas Press.

Grene, David. 1950. *Greek Political Theory.* Chicago: University of Chicago Press.

Grene, David, and Richmond Lattimore, eds. 1991–92. *The Complete Greek Tragedies.* Chicago: University of Chicago Press.

Grotowsky, Jerzy. 1968. *Towards a Poor Theatre.* New York: Simon and Schuster.

Hadas, Moses. 1954. *Ancilla to Classical Reading.* New York: Columbia University Press.

Hagège, Claude. 1988. "Writing: The Invention and the Dream." In *The Alphabet and the Brain,* ed. Derrick de Kerckhove and Charles Lumsden. Berlin: Springer Verlag.

Halpern, Barbara Kerewsky. 1990. "Genealogy as Oral Genre in a Serbian Village." In *Oral-Formulaic Theory: A Folklore Casebook,* ed. J. M. Foley. New York: Garland.

Handke, Peter. 1969. *Kaspar and Other Plays.* Trans. Michael Roloff. New York: Farrar, Straus and Giroux.

Harris, Roy. 1986. *The Origin of Writing.* London: Gerald Duckworth and Co.

———. 1989. "How Does Writing Restructure Thought?" *Language and Communication* 9, no. 2/3:99–106.

Harris, William V. 1989. *Ancient Literacy.* Cambridge: Harvard University Press.

Harrison, Jane Ellen. 1991 (1903). *Prolegomena to the Study of Greek Religion.* Princeton: Princeton University Press.

Harvey, F. D. 1966. "Literacy in the Athenian Democracy." *Revue des Études Grècques* 79, 2, no. 376/378:585–635.

Hatto, A. T., ed. 1980. *Traditions of Heroic and Epic Poetry.* 2 vols. London: Modern Humanities Research Association.

Havelock, Eric A. 1963. *Preface to Plato.* Cambridge: Belknap Press of Harvard University Press.

———. 1977. "The Preliteracy of the Greeks." *New Literary History* 8:369–91.

———. 1986. *The Muse Learns to Write.* New Haven: Yale University Press.

Havelock, E. A., and J. P. Hershbell, eds. 1978. *Communication Arts in the Ancient World.* New York: Hastings House.

Hazlitt, William. 1930–34. *The Complete Works.* Ed. P. P. Howe. 21 vols. London: J. M. Dent.

Hegel, G. W. F. 1975. *Aesthetics.* Trans. T. M. Knox. Oxford: Clarendon Press.

Heidegger, Martin. 1962. *Being and Time.* Trans. John Macquarrie and Edward Robinson. New York: Harper and Row.

Henderson, Jeffrey. 1990. "The Demos and Comic Competition." In *Nothing to Do with Dionysus? Athenian Drama in Its Social Context,* ed. John J. Winkler and Froma Zeitlin. Princeton: Princeton University Press.

Herington, John. 1985. *Poetry into Drama.* Berkeley: University of California Press.

Hermans, Hubert J. M., et al. 1992. "The Dialogical Self: Beyond Individualism and Rationalism." *American Psychologist* 47, no. 1 (January):23–33.

Herodotus. 1987. *The History.* Trans. David Grene. Chicago: University of Chicago Press.

Herondas. 1981. *The Mimes of Herondas.* Trans. Guy Davenport. San Francisco: Grey Fox Press.

Hesiod. 1967. *Fragmenta Hesiodea,* ed. R. Merkelbach and M. L. West. London: Oxford University Press.

———. 1973. *Theogony.* Trans. Dorothea Wender. London: Penguin.

Highway, Tomson. 1988. *The Rez Sisters.* Saskatoon: Fifth House.

Hsu Tao-Ching. 1985. *The Chinese Conception of the Theatre.* Seattle: University of Washington Press.

Hsun Lu. 1959. *A Brief History of Chinese Fiction.* Trans. Yang Hsien-Yi and Gladys Yang. Peking: Foreign Languages Press.

Humboldt, Wilhelm von. 1988 (1836). *On Language: The Diversity of Human Language Structure and Its Influence on the Mental Development of Mankind.* Trans. Peter Heath. Cambridge: Cambridge University Press.

Humphreys, S. C. 1978. *Anthropologies and the Greeks.* London: Routledge and Kegan Paul.

———. 1985. "Social Relations on Stage: Witnesses in Classical Athens." *History and Anthropology* 1:313–69.

Hunter, I. M. L. 1964 (1957). *Memory.* London: Penguin.

Ihde, Don. 1993. *Philosophy of Technology.* New York: Paragon House Publishers.

Immerwahr, Henry R. 1964. "Book Rolls on Attic Vases." In *Classical, Mediaeval, and Renaissance Studies in Honour of Berthold Louis Ullman.* Rome: Edizioni di Storia e Litteratura.

Ingarden, Roman. 1973. *The Literary Work of Art.* Trans. George G. Grabowicz. Evanston: Northwestern University Press.

Innes, Christopher. 1981. *Holy Theatre: Ritual and the Avant Garde.* Cambridge: Cambridge University Press.

Iser, Wolfgang. 1978. *The Act of Reading.* Baltimore: Johns Hopkins University Press.

Jaeger, Werner. 1960 (1939). *Paideia: The Ideals of Greek Culture.* Trans. Gilbert Highet. 3 vols. New York: Oxford University Press.

Jeffrey, L. H. 1990 (1961). *The Local Scripts of Archaic Greece.* Oxford: Oxford University Press.

Jones, John R. Melville. 1993. *Testimonia Numeria: Greek and Latin Texts Concerning Ancient Greek Coinage.* Vol. 1. London: Spink.

Jousse, Marcel. 1990. *The Oral Style.* Trans. Edgard Sienaert and Richard Whitaker. New York: Garland.

Kalmár, Ivan. 1985. "Are There Really No Primitive Languages?" In *Literacy, Language, and Learning: The Nature and Consequences of Reading and Writing,* ed. D. R. Olson, N. Torrence, and A. Hildyard. Cambridge: Cambridge University Press.

Kassel, Rudolf. 1965. *Aristotelis De Arte Poetica Liber.* Oxford: Oxford University Press.

Kirby, E. T. 1969. *Total Theatre.* New York: E. P. Dutton.

Kirby, Michael. 1982. "Nonsemiotic Performance." *Modern Drama* 25 (March):105.

Kirk, G. S. 1970. *Myth: Its Meaning and Functions in Ancient and Other Cultures.* Cambridge: Cambridge University Press.

———. 1985 (1974). *The Nature of Greek Myths.* Harmondsworth: Penguin.

Kirk, G. S., J. E. Raven, and M. Schofield. 1987. *The Presocratic Philosophers.* Cambridge: Cambridge University Press.

Knox, Bernard. 1968. "Silent Reading in Antiquity." *Greek, Roman, and Byzantine Studies* 9:421–35.

———. 1983. "Greece à la Française." *New York Review of Books* 30, no. 3:26–30.

Kobialka, Michael. 1988. "The Quem Quaeritis: Theatre History Displacement." *Theatre History Studies* 8:35–51.

Kraay, Colin M. 1976. *Archaic and Classical Greek Coins.* Berkeley: University of California Press.

Kristeva, Julia. 1989. *Language: The Unknown.* Trans. Anne M. Menke. New York: Columbia University Press.

Kurzon, Dennis. 1986. *It Is Hereby Performed: Explorations in Legal Speech Acts.* Amsterdam: John Benjamins.

Lafont, Robert. 1988. "Relationships between Speech and Writing Systems in Ancient Alphabets and Syllabaries." In *The Alphabet and the Brain,* ed. Derrick de Kerckhove and Charles Lumsden. Berlin: Springer-Verlag.

Lakoff, Robin. 1972. "Language in Context." *Language* 48, no. 4:907–27.

Lamberton, Robert, and John J. Keaney, eds. 1992. *Homer's Ancient Readers.* Princeton: Princeton University Press.

Lattimore, Richmond. 1964. *Story Patterns in Greek Tragedy.* Ann Arbor: University of Michigan Press.

——, trans. 1951. *The Iliad of Homer.* Chicago: University of Chicago Press.

——. 1977 (1965). *The Odyssey of Homer.* New York: Harper and Row.

——. 1992. "Introduction to *Iphigenia in Tauris.*" In *The Complete Greek Tragedies* ed. David Grene and Richmond Lattimore. Chicago: University of Chicago Press.

Lentz, Tony M. 1989. *Orality and Literacy in Hellenic Greece.* Carbondale: Southern Illinois University Press.

Lesher, J. H. 1992. *Xenophanes of Colophon: Fragments.* Toronto: University of Toronto Press.

Lévi-Strauss, Claude. 1982. *The Way of Masks.* Trans. Sylvia Modelski. Seattle: University of Washington Press.

Liddell, Henry George, and Robert Scott. 1983 (1859). *A Lexicon Abridged from Liddell and Scott's Greek-English Lexicon.* Oxford: Clarendon.

Linell, Per. 1988. "The Impact of Literacy on the Conception of Language: The Case of Linguistics." In *The Written Word: Studies in Literate Thought and Action,* ed. Roger Saljo. Berlin: Springer-Verlag.

Lloyd, G. E. R. 1990. *Demystifying Mentalities.* Cambridge: Cambridge University Press.

Lock, Andrew, ed. 1978. *Action, Gesture, and Symbol: The Emergence of Language.* London: Academic Press.

Loftus, Elizabeth F. 1979. *Eyewitness Testimony.* Cambridge: Harvard University Press.

——. 1980. *Memory.* Reading, Mass.: Addison-Wesley.

Logan, Robert. 1986. *The Alphabet Effect: The Impact of the Phonetic Alphabet on the Development of Western Civilization.* New York: St. Martin's.

Lord, Albert Bates. 1960. *The Singer of Tales.* Cambridge: Harvard University Press.

——. 1981. "Memory, Fixity, and Genre in Oral Traditional Poetries." In *Oral Traditional Literature: A Festschrift for Albert Bates Lord,* ed. John Miles Foley. Columbus, Ohio: Slavica Publishers.

——. 1986. "The Merging of Two Worlds: Oral and Written Poetry as Carriers of Ancient Values." In *Oral Tradition in Literature,* ed. John Miles Foley. Columbia: University of Missouri Press.

——. 1990. "Perspectives on Recent Work on the Oral Traditional Formula." In *Oral-Formulaic Theory: A Folklore Casebook,* ed. J. M. Foley. New York: Garland.

——. 1991. *Epic Singers and Oral Tradition.* Ithaca: Cornell University Press.

Lorimer, H. L. 1948. "Homer and the Art of Writing." *American Journal of Archaeology.* 52:11–23.

Luria, A. R. 1981. *Language and Cognition*. Ed. James V. Wertsch. Washington, D.C.: V. H. Winston.

Lyotard, Jean-François. 1977. "The Unconscious as *Mise-en-scène*." Trans. Joseph Maier. In *Performance in Postmodern Culture*, ed. Michel Benamou and Charles Caramello. Madison: University of Wisconsin–Milwaukee Press.

Maitland, Frederic William, ed. 1891. *The Court Baron*. London: B. Quaritch.

Matejka, Ladislav, and Irwin Titunik. 1976. *Semiotics of Art: Prague School Contributions*. Cambridge: MIT Press.

May, Keith M. 1990. *Nietzsche and the Spirit of Tragedy*. London: Macmillan.

McLuhan, Marshall. 1964. *Understanding Media*. New York: McGraw Hill.

Meier, Christian. 1990. *The Greek Discovery of Politics*. Trans. David McLintock. Cambridge: Harvard University Press.

Miller, Paul Allen. 1994. *Lyric Texts and Lyric Consciousness*. London: Routledge.

Morgan, William. 1992. "The Trickster and Native Theatre: An Interview with Tomson Highway." In *Aboriginal Voices: Amerindian, Inuit, and Sami Theatre*, ed. Per Brask and William Morgan. Baltimore: Johns Hopkins University Press.

Moses, D. D. and Terry Goldie, eds. 1992. *An Anthology of Canadian Native Literature in English*. Toronto: Oxford University Press.

Mukarovsky, Jan. 1978 (1977). *Structure, Sign, Function*. Trans. John Burbank and Peter Steiner. New Haven: Yale University Press.

Müller, F. Max. 1976 (1881). *Selected Essays on Language, Mythology, and Religion*. 2 vols. New York: AMS Press.

Murko, Matija. 1990. "The Singers and Their Epic Songs." In *Oral-Formulaic Theory: A Folklore Casebook*, ed. J. M. Foley. New York: Garland.

Murray, Gilbert. 1907 (1897). *A History of Ancient Greek Literature*. London: Heinemann.

Myres, John L. 1958. *Homer and His Critics*. London: Routledge and Kegan Paul.

Nagler, A. M. 1952. *A Source Book in Theatrical History*. New York: Dover.

Nagler, Michael N. 1990. "The Traditional Phrase: Theory of Production." In *Oral-Formulaic Theory: A Folklore Casebook*, ed. J. M. Foley. New York: Garland.

Nagy, Gregory. 1981. "An Evolutionary Model for the Text Fixation of Homeric Epos." In *Oral Traditional Literature: A Festschrift for Albert Bates Lord*, ed. John Miles Foley. Columbus: Slavica Publishers.

——. 1986. "Ancient Greek Epic and Praise Poetry: Some Typological Considerations." In *Oral Tradition in Literature*, ed. John Miles Foley. Columbia: University of Missouri Press.

Natoli, Joseph, ed. 1989. *Literary Theory's Future(s)*. Urbana: University of Illinois Press.

Nauck, August. 1964. *Tragicorum Graecorum Fragmenta*. With supplement by Bruno Snell. Hildesheim: Georg Olms Verlag.

Naveh, Joseph. 1988. "The Origin of the Greek Alphabet." In *The Alphabet and the Brain,* ed. Derrick de Kerckhove and Charles Lumsden. Berlin: Springer-Verlag.

Nietzsche, Friedrich. 1956. *The Birth of Tragedy.* Trans. Francis Golffing. New York: Doubleday.

Nilsson, Martin P. 1968 (1933). *Homer and Mycenae.* New York: Cooper Square.

O'Barr, William M. 1982. *Linguistic Evidence: Language, Power, and Strategy in the Courtroom.* New York: Academic Press.

Ober, Josiah, and Barry Strauss. 1990. "Drama, Political Rhetoric, and the Discourse of the Athenian Democracy." In *Nothing to Do with Dionysus? Athenian Drama in Its Social Context,* ed. John J. Winkler and Froma Zeitlin. Princeton: Princeton University Press.

Olson, David R. 1985. "Introduction." In *Literacy, Language, and Learning: The Nature and Consequences of Reading and Writing,* ed. David Olson, Nancy Torrence, and Angela Hildyard. Cambridge: Cambridge University Press.

———. 1988. "Mind, Media, and Memory: The Archival and Epistemic Functions of the Written Text." In *The Alphabet and the Brain,* ed. Derrick de Kerckhove and Charles Lumsden. Berlin: Springer-Verlag.

Olson, D. R., Nancy Torrence, and Angela Hildyard, eds. 1985. *Literacy, Language, and Learning: The Nature and Consequences of Reading and Writing.* Cambridge: Cambridge University Press.

O'Neill, John. 1985. *Five Bodies: The Human Shape of Modern Society.* Ithaca: Cornell University Press.

Ong, Walter J. 1977. *Interfaces of the Word.* Ithaca: Cornell University Press.

———. 1982. *Orality and Literacy: The Technologizing of the Word.* London: Methuen.

Orgel, Stephen. 1988. "The Authentic Shakespeare" *Representations* 21 (Winter):1.

Ostwald, Martin. 1986. *From Popular Sovereignty to the Sovereignty of Law: Law, Society, and Politics in Fifth-Century Athens.* Berkeley: University of California Press.

O'Sullivan, Neil. 1996. "Written and Spoken in the First Sophistic." In *Voice into Text: Orality and Literacy in Ancient Greece,* ed. Ian Worthington. Leiden: E. J. Brill.

Padel, Ruth. 1990. "Making Space Speak." In *Nothing to Do with Dionysus?,* ed. John J. Winkler and Froma I. Zeitlin. Princeton: Princeton University Press.

Page, Denys L. 1962. *Select Papyri.* Vol. 3. Cambridge and London: Harvard University Press and William Heinemann.

———. 1987 (1934). *Actors' Interpolations in Greek Tragedy.* New York: Garland.

Palmer, Richard. 1977. "Postmodern Hermeneutics of Performance." In *Performance in Postmodern Culture,* ed. Michel Benamou and Charles Caramello. Madison: University of Wisconsin–Milwaukee Press.

Parke, Herbert William. 1967. *Greek Oracles*. London: Hutchinson.

Parker, Patricia, and Geoffrey Hartman, eds. 1985. *Shakespeare and the Question of Theory*. New York: Methuen.

Parry, Adam, ed. 1971. *The Making of Homeric Verse: The Collected Papers of Milman Parry*. Oxford: Clarendon.

———. 1989. *The Language of Achilles and Other Papers*. Oxford: Clarendon.

Pausanias. 1965. *Description of Greece*. Trans. J. G. Frazer. New York: Biblo and Tannen.

Pavis, Patrice. 1982. *Languages of the Stage*. New York: Performing Arts Journal Publications.

Peacock, Sandra J. 1991. "An Awful Warmth about Her Heart: The Personal in Jane Harrison's Ideas about Religion." In *The Cambridge Ritualists Reconsidered*, ed. William M. Calder III. Atlanta: Scholars Press.

Petrone, Penny. 1990. *Native Literature in Canada: From the Oral Tradition to the Present*. Toronto: Oxford University Press.

Pfeiffer, Rudolf. 1968. *History of Classical Scholarship*. Oxford: Clarendon.

Pfister, Manfred. 1988. *The Theory and Analysis of Drama*. Trans. John Halliday. New York: Cambridge University Press.

Pickard-Cambridge, Arthur W. 1962 (1927). *Dithyramb, Tragedy, and Comedy*. Oxford: Oxford University Press.

———. 1968. *The Dramatic Festivals of Athens*. Oxford University Press.

Plato. 1955. *Hipparchus*. Loeb Classical Library. Cambridge: Harvard University Press.

———. 1962. *Ion*. Loeb Classical Library. Cambridge: Harvard University Press.

———. 1968. *The Republic of Plato*. Trans. Allan Bloom. New York: Basic Books.

———. 1986a. *Phaedrus*. Trans. C. J. Rowe. Warminster, England: Aris and Phillips.

———. 1986b. *Theaetetus*. Trans. Seth Benardete. Chicago: University of Chicago Press.

———. 1996. *Protagoras, Philebus, and Gorgias*. Trans. Benjamin Jowett. New York: Prometheus Books.

Podlecki, Anthony J. 1966. *The Political Background of Aeschylean Tragedy*. Ann Arbor: University of Michigan Press.

———. 1984. *The Early Greek Poets and Their Times*. Vancouver: University of British Columbia Press.

Pomeroy, Susan B. 1975. *Goddesses, Whores, Wives, and Slaves: Women in Classical Antiquity*. New York: Dorset Press.

Powell, Barry B. 1991. *Homer and the Origin of the Greek Alphabet*. Cambridge: Cambridge University Press.

Pratt, Mary Louise. 1977. *Toward a Speech Act Theory of Literary Discourse*. Bloomington: Indiana University Press.

Purdy, Anthony, ed. 1992. *Literature and the Body*. Amsterdam and Atlanta: Editions Rodopi B.U.

Raschke, Wendy J., ed. 1988. *The Archaeology of the Olympics: The Olympics and Other Festivals in Antiquity.* Madison: University of Wisconsin Press.

Redmond, James. 1984. *Drama and the Actor.* Cambridge: Cambridge University Press.

Reinelt, Janelle G., and Joseph R. Roach, eds. 1992. *Critical Theory and Performance.* Ann Arbor: University of Michigan Press.

Reynolds, L. D., and N. G. Wilson. 1968. *Scribes and Scholars.* Oxford: Clarendon.

Rhodes, P. J. 1986. *The Greek City States: A Sourcebook.* Norman: University of Oklahoma Press.

Richardson, N. J. 1992. "Aristotle's Reading of Homer and Its Background." In *Homer's Ancient Readers,* ed. R. Lamberton and J. J. Keaney. Princeton: Princeton University Press.

Ricoeur, Paul. 1981. *Hermeneutics and The Human Sciences.* Trans. John B. Thompson. Cambridge: Cambridge University Press.

Robb, Kevin. 1994. *Literacy and Paideia in Ancient Greece.* New York: Oxford University Press.

Rothenberg, Jerome. 1977. "New Models, New Visions: Some Notes toward a Poetics of Performance." In *Performance in Postmodern Culture,* ed. Michel Benamou and Charles Caramello. Madison: University of Wisconsin–Milwaukee Press.

Rowe, C. J. 1986. *Phaedrus: Translation and Commentary.* Warminster, England: Aris and Phillips.

Safire, William. 1992. *Lend Me Your Ears: Great Speeches in History.* New York: W. W. Norton.

Saljo, Roger, ed. 1988. *The Written Word: Studies in Literate Thought and Action.* Berlin: Springer-Verlag.

Sallis, John. 1991. *Crossings: Nietzsche and the Space of Tragedy.* Chicago: University of Chicago Press.

Sandys, Sir John Edwin. 1958. *A History of Classical Scholarship.* Vol. 1. New York: Hafner.

Sapir, Edward. 1949 (1921). *Language.* New York: Harcourt Brace.

Saussure, Ferdinand de. 1974 (1959). *Course in General Linguistics.* Trans. Wade Baskin. London: Fontana.

Schechner, Richard. 1971. "Actuals." *Theatre Quarterly* 1, no. 2 (Spring):49–66.

———. 1973. *Environmental Theatre.* New York: Hawthorne Books.

———. 1977. *Essays on Performance Theory.* New York: Drama Book Specialists.

Schechner, Richard, and Mady Schuman, eds. 1976. *Ritual, Play, and Performance.* New York: Seabury Press.

Schlegel, A. W. 1914. *Lectures on Dramatic Art and Literature.* Trans. John Black. London: Bohn Library.

Schlegel, Friedrich. 1880. *Lectures on the History of Literature.* London: George Bell and Sons.

——. 1957. *Literary Notebooks, 1797–1801*. Ed. Hans Eichner. London: Athlone Press.

——. 1968. *Dialogue on Poetry and Literary Aphorisms*. Trans. Ernst Behler and Roman Struc. University Park: Penn State University Press.

Schlesier, Renate. 1991. "Prolegomena to Jane Harrison's Interpretation of Ancient Greek Religion." Trans. Michael Armstrong. In *The Cambridge Ritualists Reconsidered,* ed. William M. Calder III. Atlanta: Scholars Press.

Schmandt-Besserat, Denise. 1989. "Two Precursors of Writing: Plain and Complex Tokens." In *The Origins of Writing,* ed. W. M. Senner. Lincoln: University of Nebraska Press.

Scinto, Leonard F. M. 1986. *Written Language and Psychological Development*. London: Academic Press.

Scribner, Sylvia, and Michael Cole. 1981. *The Psychology of Literacy.* Cambridge: Harvard University Press.

Seaford, Richard. 1994. *Reciprocity and Ritual: Homer and Tragedy in the Developing City-State*. Oxford: Clarendon.

Seale, David. 1982. *Vision and Stagecraft in Sophocles*. Chicago: University of Chicago Press.

Searle, J. R. 1975. "The Logical Status of Fictional Discourse." *New Literary History* 5:328.

——. 1992 (1969). *Speech Acts*. Cambridge: Cambridge University Press.

Segal, Charles. 1986. *Interpreting Greek Tragedy.* Ithaca: Cornell University Press.

——. 1992. "Bard and Audience in Homer." In *Homer's Ancient Readers,* ed. R. Lamberton and J. J. Keaney. Princeton: Princeton University Press.

Senner, Wayne M. 1989. *The Origins of Writing*. Lincoln: University of Nebraska Press.

Shakespeare, William. 1965. *The Complete Works*. Ed. W. J. Craig. Oxford: Oxford University Press.

Shrimpton, Gordon. 1997. *History and Memory in Ancient Greece*. Montreal: McGill–Queen's University Press.

Silk, M. S., and J. P. Stern. 1981. *Nietzsche on Tragedy.* Cambridge: Cambridge University Press.

Simon, John. 1975. *Singularities*. New York: Random House.

Slater, Niall. 1990. "The Idea of the Actor." In *Nothing to Do with Dionysus? Athenian Drama in Its Social Context,* ed. John J. Winkler and Froma Zeitlin. Princeton: Princeton University Press.

——. 1996. "Literacy and Old Comedy." In *Voice into Text: Orality and Literacy in Ancient Greece,* ed. Ian Worthington. Leiden: E. J. Brill.

Sommerstein, Alan H. 1982–85. *The Comedies of Aristophanes*. Vols. 3–5. Warminster, England: Aris and Phillips.

Sörbom, Göran. 1966. *Mimesis and Art*. Stockholm: Bonniers.

Stallybrass, Peter, and Allon White. 1986. *The Politics and Poetics of Transgression*. Ithaca: Cornell University Press.

States, Bert O. 1985. *Great Reckonings in Little Rooms: On the Phenomenology of Theatre.* Berkeley: University of California Press.

Steiner, Deborah Tarn. 1994. *The Tyrant's Writ: Myths and Images of Writing in Ancient Greece.* Princeton: Princeton University Press.

Steiner, George. 1977. *Language and Silence.* New York: Atheneum.

Stock, Brian. 1983. *The Implications of Literacy: Written Language and Models of Interpretation in the Eleventh and Twelfth Centuries.* Princeton: Princeton University Press.

Stockton, David. 1990. *The Classical Athenian Democracy.* Oxford: Oxford University Press.

Stone, George Winchester, Jr., and George M. Kahrl. 1979. *David Garrick.* Carbondale: Southern Illinois University Press.

Stott, John C., et al. 1993. *The HBJ Anthology of Literature.* Toronto: Harcourt Brace Jovanovich.

Street, Brian V. 1988. "Literacy Practices and Literacy Myths." In *The Written Word: Studies in Literate Thought and Action,* ed. Roger Saljo. Berlin: Springer-Verlag.

Stroud, Ronald S. 1989. "The Art of Writing in Ancient Greece." In *The Origins of Writing,* ed. W. M. Senner. Lincoln: University of Nebraska Press.

Svenbro, Jesper. 1990. "The 'Interior' Voice: On the Invention of Silent Reading." In *Nothing to Do with Dionysus? Athenian Drama in Its Social Context,* ed. John J. Winkler and Froma Zeitlin. Princeton: Princeton University Press.

Szondi, Peter. 1986. *On Textual Understanding and Other Essays.* Trans. Harvey Mendelsohn. Minneapolis: University of Minnesota Press.

———. 1987. *Theory of the Modern Drama.* Trans. Michael Hays. Minneapolis: University of Minnesota Press.

Taplin, Oliver, 1977. *The Stagecraft of Aeschylus.* Oxford: Oxford University Press.

———. 1978. *Greek Tragedy in Action.* London: Methuen.

Taylor, Insup. 1988. "Psychology of Literacy: East and West." In *The Alphabet and the Brain,* ed. Derrick de Kerckhove and Charles Lumsden. Berlin: Springer-Verlag.

Thomas, Carol G. 1977. "Literacy and the Codification of Law." *Studia et Documenta Historiae et Juris* 43:455-58.

———. 1996. "Wingy Mysteries in Divinity." In *Voice into Text: Orality and Literacy in Ancient Greece,* ed. Ian Worthington. Leiden: E. J. Brill.

Thomas, Rosalind. 1989. *Oral Tradition and Written Record in Classical Athens.* Cambridge: Cambridge University Press.

———. 1992. *Literacy and Orality in Ancient Greece.* Cambridge: Cambridge University Press.

Thomson, Peter. 1994. *Shakespeare's Professional Career.* Cambridge: Cambridge University Press.

Thucydides. 1954. *History of the Peloponnesian War.* Trans. Rex Warner. London: Penguin.

Todorov, Tzvetan. 1982a. *Theories of the Symbol.* Trans. Catherine Porter. Ithaca: Cornell University Press.

———. 1982b. "French Poetics Today." In *French Literary Theory Today,* ed. Tzvetan Todorov. Trans. R. Carter. Cambridge: Cambridge University Press.

Turner, E. G. 1951. *Athenian Books in the Fifth and Fourth Centuries B.C.* London: H. K. Lewis.

———. 1965. "Athenians Learn to Write: Plato *Protagoras* 326d." *Bulletin of the University of London Institute of Classical Studies* 12:65–67.

———. 1971. *Greek Manuscripts of the Ancient World.* Oxford: Clarendon.

Turner, Victor. 1974. *Dramas, Fields, and Metaphors.* Ithaca: Cornell University Press.

Ubersfeld, Anne. 1978. *Lire le théâtre.* Paris: Editions Sociales.

Udall, Nicholas. 1912. *Ralph Roister Doister.* Ed. C. G. Child. Boston: Houghton Mifflin.

Underhill, Ruth Murray. 1938. *Singing for Power.* Berkeley: University of California Press.

Vanderpool, Eugene. 1970. *Ostracism at Athens.* Cincinnati: University of Cincinnati Press.

Vansina, Jan. 1985. *Oral Tradition as History.* Madison: University of Wisconsin Press.

Veltrusky, Jiri. 1964. "Man and Object in the Theatre." In *A Prague School Reader on Esthetics, Literary Structure, and Style,* trans. Paul L. Garvin. Washington, D.C.: Georgetown University Press.

———. 1977. *Drama as Literature.* Lisse: Peter de Ridder Press.

Vernant, Jean-Pierre. 1978. "Ambiguity and Reversal: On the Enigmatic Structure of *Oedipus Rex.*" *New Literary History* 9 (Spring):475–501.

Vernant, Jean-Pierre, and Pierre Vidal-Naquet. 1990. *Myth and Tragedy in Ancient Greece.* Trans. Janet Lloyd. New York: Zone Books.

Vickers, Brian. 1973. *Towards Greek Tragedy.* London: Longman.

Vygotsky, Lev. 1978. *Mind in Society: The Development of Higher Psychological Processes.* Ed. Michael Cole et al. Cambridge: Harvard University Press.

———. 1992. *Thought and Language.* Trans. Alex Kozulin. Cambridge: MIT Press.

Wade-Gery, H. T. 1952. *The Poet of the Iliad.* Cambridge: Cambridge University Press.

Walter, Bettyruth. 1988. *The Jury Summation as Speech Genre.* Amsterdam: John Benjamins.

Webster, T. B. L. 1959. *Greek Art and Literature, 700–530 B.C.* Westport, Conn.: Greenwood Press.

Weijie, Yu. 1990. "Topicality and Typicality: The Acceptance of Shakespeare in

China." In *The Dramatic Touch of Difference: Theatre Own and Foreign,* ed. Erika Fischer-Lichte et al. Tübingen: Gunter Narr Verlag.

Weimann, Robert. 1978. *Shakespeare and the Popular Tradition in the Theatre.* Ed. Robert Schwartz. Baltimore: Johns Hopkins University Press.

Weiser, Joshua. 1992. "Indigenous Theatre." In *Aboriginal Voices: Amerindian, Inuit, and Sami Theatre,* ed. Per Brask and William Morgan. Baltimore: Johns Hopkins University Press.

Wellbery, David E. 1984. *Lessing's Laocoon: Semiotics and Aesthetics in the Age of Reason.* Cambridge: Cambridge University Press.

Wellek, René. 1981. *A History of Modern Criticism,* 1750–1950. Cambridge: Cambridge University Press.

Wheeler, Jordan. 1992. "Voice." In *Aboriginal Voices: Amerindian, Inuit, and Sami Theatre,* ed. Per Brask and William Morgan. Baltimore: Johns Hopkins University Press.

Whitaker, Richard. 1996. "Orality and Literacy in the Poetic Traditions of Archaic Greece and Southern Africa." In *Voice into Text: Orality and Literacy in Ancient Greece,* ed. Ian Worthington. Leiden: E. J. Brill.

White, Allon. 1993. *Carnival, Hysteria, and Writing.* Oxford: Clarendon.

Whiteman, Marcia Farr, ed. 1981. *Writing: The Nature, Development, and Teaching of Written Communication.* Lawrence Erlbaum.

Whitman, Cedric. 1951. *Sophocles.* Cambridge: Harvard University Press.

Wiles, Timothy J. 1980. *The Theatre Event: Modern Theories of Performance.* Chicago: University of Chicago Press.

Willcock, M. M. 1990. "The Search for the Poet Homer." *Greece and Rome* 37, no. 1 (April):1–13.

Winchester, Ian. 1985. "Atlantans, Centaurians, and the Litron Bomb." In *Literacy, Language, and Learning: The Nature and Consequences of Reading and Writing,* ed. D. R. Olson, N. Torrence, and A. Hildyard. Cambridge: Cambridge University Press.

Winkler, John J. 1990. "The Ephebes' Song: Tragoidia and Polis." In *Nothing to Do with Dionysus? Athenian Drama in Its Social Context,* ed. John J. Winkler and Froma Zeitlin. Princeton: Princeton University Press.

Winkler, John J., and Froma Zeitlin, eds. 1990. *Nothing to Do with Dionysus? Athenian Drama in Its Social Context.* Princeton: Princeton University Press.

Wise, Jennifer. 1989. "Marginalizing Drama: Bakhtin's Theory of Genre." *Essays in Theatre* 8, no. 1 (November):15–22.

Wood, Robert. 1976 (1769). *An Essay on the Original Genius of Homer.* Hildesheim: Georg Olms Verlag.

Woodbury, Leonard. 1976. "Aristophanes' *Frogs* and Athenian Literacy: *Ran.* 52–53, 1114." *Transactions of the American Philological Association* 106:349–57.

Worthington, Ian, ed. 1996. *Voice into Text: Orality and Literacy in Ancient Greece.* Leiden: E. J. Brill.

Yangzhong, Ding. 1990. "On the Insatiable Appetite and Longevity of Theatre." In *The Dramatic Touch of Difference: Theatre Own and Foreign,* ed. Erika Fischer-Lichte et al. Tübingen: Gunter Narr Verlag.
Yates, Frances A. 1966. *The Art of Memory.* Chicago: University of Chicago Press.

Zeitlin, Froma I. 1990. "Playing the Other: Theater, Theatricality, and the Feminine in Greek Drama." In *Nothing to Do with Dionysus? Athenian Drama in Its Social Context,* ed. John J. Winkler and Froma Zeitlin. Princeton: Princeton University Press.

Index